John Buchan Telfer, Johannes Schiltberger, Filip Jakob Bruun

The Bondage And Travels of Johann Schiltberger, a Native of Bavaria

In Europe, Asia, and Africa, 1396-1427

John Buchan Telfer, Johannes Schiltberger, Filip Jakob Bruun

The Bondage And Travels of Johann Schiltberger, a Native of Bavaria
In Europe, Asia, and Africa, 1396-1427

ISBN/EAN: 9783744754293

Printed in Europe, USA, Canada, Australia, Japan

Cover: Foto ©ninafisch / pixelio.de

More available books at **www.hansebooks.com**

WORKS ISSUED BY

The Hakluyt Society.

THE BONDAGE AND TRAVELS OF
JOHANN SCHILTBERGER.

THE
BONDAGE AND TRAVELS

OF

JOHANN SCHILTBERGER,

A NATIVE OF BAVARIA,

IN EUROPE, ASIA, AND AFRICA,

1396-1427.

TRANSLATED FROM THE

HEIDELBERG MS. EDITED IN 1859 BY PROFESSOR KARL FRIEDRICH NEUMANN,

BY

COMMANDER J. BUCHAN TELFER, R.N.,
F.S.A., F.R.G.S.

With Notes by

PROFESSOR P. BRUUN,
OF THE IMPERIAL UNIVERSITY OF SOUTH RUSSIA, AT ODESSA;

AND A PREFACE, INTRODUCTION, AND NOTES BY THE

TRANSLATOR AND EDITOR.

No respice ad cum qui dixit, sed respice ad id quod dixit.—SCALIGER, *Proverb. Arab.*

WITH A MAP.

LONDON:
PRINTED FOR THE HAKLUYT SOCIETY.

MDCCCLXXIX.

FRIDERICO GVLIELMO

HEREDITARIO GERMANIAE PRINCIPI

HAEC NARRATIO ANGLO IDIOMATA CONSCRIPTA

DE CASIBVS MISERRIMIS CVIVSDAM BAVARI MILITIS

IPSIVS PRINCIPIS GRATIA ET ASSENSV

REVERENTER ET IN OBSEQVI TESTIMONIAM

INSCRIPSIT

IOANNES BVCHAN TELFER.

COUNCIL

OF

THE HAKLUYT SOCIETY.

COLONEL H. YULE, C.B., PRESIDENT.
ADMIRAL C. R. DRINKWATER BETHUNE, C.B. } VICE-PRESIDENTS.
MAJOR-GENERAL SIR HENRY RAWLINSON, K.C.B. }
W. A. TYSSEN AMHERST, ESQ.
REV. DR. G. P. BADGER, D.C.L., F.R.G.S.
J. BARROW, ESQ., F.R.S.
WALTER DE GREY BIRCH, ESQ.
E. A. BOND, ESQ.
E. H. BUNBURY, ESQ.
ADMIRAL SIR RICHARD COLLINSON, K.C.B.
THE EARL OF DUCIE.
AUGUSTUS W. FRANKS, ESQ., F.R.S.
LIEUT.-GENERAL SIR J. HENRY LEFROY, C.B., K.C.M.G.
R. H. MAJOR, ESQ., F.S.A.
COLONEL SIR WM. L. MEREWETHER, C.B., K.C.S.I.
ADMIRAL SIR ERASMUS OMMANNEY, C.B., F.R.S.
LORD ARTHUR RUSSELL, M.P.
THE LORD STANLEY OF ALDERLEY.
EDWARD THOMAS, ESQ., F.R.S.
MAJOR-GENERAL SIR HENRY THUILLIER, C.S.I., F.R.S.

CLEMENTS R. MARKHAM, ESQ., C.B., F.R.S., SEC. R.G.S., HONORARY SECRETARY.

PREFACE.

"An editor, or a translator, collects the merits of different writers, and, forming all into a wreath, bestows it on his author's tomb."—SHENSTONE.

THE world is indebted to the late Professor Karl Friedrich Neumann, for having rendered the perusal of Johann Schiltberger's travels generally accessible. Until his edition of the Heidelberg MS. appeared, in 1859, there had been no publication of the interesting work, in its integrity, since the year 1700, the supposed date of an edition, *sine anno, sine loco;* so that, as a fact, the work had become scarce, and could be consulted in a few libraries only, or in private collections of rare books. In 1813, and again in 1814, was published Abraham Jacob Penzel's edition of what was known as the Nuremberg MS.; but its sole merit consisted in the insertion of Proper and Geographical names in their original orthography, the work being otherwise vitiated by its modern and paraphrased style, and by the introduction of passages, of

b

which Schiltberger never could have been the author.

Scheiger* condemns this book as being written in a very extraordinary and uncommonly empty style, in which the narrative of the honest old Bavarian drags itself along very uncouthly. Tobler† stigmatises it as being an unhappy translation into modern German, with no Introduction; and Neumann,‡ a still severer critic, says:—" This edition, in its modern garb, does honour to nobody. The additions to the original text are absurd, and testify to the editor's ignorance of Schiltberger's character, and of the times in which he lived. Take, for instance, the following sentence, with which Penzel concludes the author's address to the reader:—'Just as the doctor smears with honey the glass of physic prepared for a sick child, so have I also, as an agreeable pastime, introduced here and there some wonderful stories which, I flatter myself, will prove agreeable and instructive reading.'" Neumann might have added, that Penzel was not even the originator of the idea conveyed in this passage, evidently borrowed from Tasso!

* *Taschenbuch für die vaterländische Geschichte. Herausgegeben durch die Freyherren von Hormayr und von Mednyansky.* Wien, 1827, p. 161.

† *Bibliographia Geographica Palæstinæ*, etc. Leipzig, 1867.

‡ In the Introduction to his edition of Schiltberger's Travels, 1859.

"Sai, che là corre il mondo, ove più versi
Di sue dolcezze il lusinghier Parnaso,
E che 'l vero condito in molli versi
I più schivi allettando ha persuaso.
Così all' egro fanciul porgiamo aspersi
Di soave licor gli orli del vaso:
Succhi amari ingannato intanto ei beve,
E dall' inganno suo vita riceve."

La Gerusalemme Liberata, Can. I, iii.

In 1823 these travels were again published, in 8vo., at Munich; but this is a copy of which it would seem that very little is known.

Judging by the numerous editions of the fifteenth and sixteenth centuries, each issue being an almost exact transcript of the copy that preceded it, Schiltberger must have been a popular author during that period. One long blank occurs from 1557 to 1606, after which the book of travels was not again reprinted until 1700.

The version now offered is a literal translation of Neumann's edition in mittelhoch Deutsch, an exact transcript of the Heidelberg MS., with the exception of a few errors that have been rectified, and slight alterations in the headings of some chapters. Neumann believes his book to be the first printed edition that faithfully represents what Schiltberger wrote, the wording in all previous editions having been changed to suit the language of the times. He has added an

Introduction and Notes by himself, and Notes by Fallmerayer and Hammer-Purgstall; such of those Notes as are referred to in the new Notes at the end of this volume, appear in their proper places at foot in the text, each bearing the initial of the writer.

Koehler* finds fault very unsparingly with Neumann, whom he reproaches with neglect in not correcting and elucidating the wording of the text. Tobler, on the contrary, considers Neumann's work more acceptable than Penzel's unfortunate translation into modern German, because there is an Introduction, and the Oriental names employed by the author are explained.

The travels of Johann Schiltberger had never been translated into any tongue until Professor Bruun's edition, in Russian, appeared at Odessa in 1866; although a somewhat free interpretation of the original, it has been of no small assistance to me where passages in the old German seemed obscure, as also in the identification of names. I am under a deep sense of gratitude to that learned gentleman, for having enriched my translation with a large number of most valuable and interesting Notes. They were supplied to me in French, and to ensure their faithful repro-

---

* *Germania*, etc., *herausgegeben von F. Pfeifer*, viii. Wien, 1862, p. 371-380.

duction, my MS. in the first instance, and the proofs afterwards, were sent to Odessa, for the Professor's corrections or alterations, and approval.

I have to express my thanks to Aly Bey Riza, Cadri Bey, and Rassek Bey of Alexandria, for their kind aid in simplifying the Turkish and Arabic sentences that occur in various chapters; to Mr. Mnatzakan Hakhoumoff, of Shousha, for making clear to me the several phrases in Armenian; and to Dr. Niccolo Quartano de Calogheras, of Corfu, for his explanation of customs and rites as they are now observed in the Greek Church. I am also desirous of acknowledging the courtesy of those gentlemen who have been good enough to reply to my enquiries, for information that would assist me in compiling a Bibliography of existing editions of Schiltberger's travels; and it gives me much pleasure to name the Rev. Leo Alishan, Venice; Dr. K. A. Barack, Strasburg; the Rev. A. Baumgarten, at the Kremsmünster near Wels; Mr. A. Bytschkoff, St. Petersburg; Mr. E. Förstemann, Dresden; Mr. A. Gutenæker, Munich; M. Edouard Hesse, Paris; Professor Heyd, Stuttgard; Dr. M. Isler, Hamburg; Mr. J. Kraenzler, Augsburg; Professor Lepsius, Berlin; Dr. J. E. A. Martin, Jena; Dr. Noack, Giessen; Dr. Joh. Priem, Nuremberg; Dr. E. Ritter von Birk, Vienna; Dr. G. T. Thomas,

Munich; and Professor Karl Zangemeister, Heidelberg; also the Principal Librarian of the public library at Frankfort, and of the Bibliotheca Medicea-Laurentiana at Florence. I have likewise to express my obligations to Colonel Yule, for some useful and timely hints, so readily given.

Many of the Proper and Geographical names that occur in the Notes, and they are very numerous, are spelled as they ordinarily appear in English works, the orthography of the rest being in accordance with their pronunciation by a Persian and an Armenian gentleman, who did me the favour to settle my doubts. It being impossible to produce certain sounds with vowels that are so variously pronounced in the English language, I have had recourse to giving a phonetic value to various letters, in some instances accentuating the word for the sake of stress, with the acute or grave accent as in the Greek. The apostrophe ' denotes an independent but rather soft breathing of a letter.

    a, as in hart.
    e, as in met.
    g, usually hard.
    o, as in ozone.
    ou, as in routine.
    u, as in sum.
    y, like *e* in English, and sometimes *y*.
    tch, like *ch* in church.

LONDON,
 July 18th, 1879.

BIBLIOGRAPHY.

MANUSCRIPTS.

1. A MS. of Schiltberger's travels, undoubtedly of the fifteenth century, preserved in the University Library at Heidelberg and known as the Heidelberg MS., consists of ninety-six carefully and neatly written sheets of paper, in good style, and evidently the work of a professional scribe. It is about eight inches long by six inches broad, bound in leather, with bronze corner plates and clasps, and bears on the upper board a portrait in gold of the Elector, with the initials O. H.—P. C., Otto Heinrich—Palatinus Comes, and the date 1558. Another date, 1443, probably the year in which the MS. was written, appears inside the binding, which is beautifully ornamented with illustrations from the Old and New Testaments. This volume was included in the Palatine Library that was carried off by Tilly in 1621, and presented by Maximilian, duke of Bavaria, to Gregory XV. as a trophy of the Catholic cause. After the general peace of 1815, Pius VII. restored the collection to Heidelberg, at the instance of the King of Prussia.

2. The ducal library at Donaueschingen possesses a MS. on paper, of the fifteenth century, consisting of 134 leaves in sheepskin boards, with brass corner plates and clasps. The work is contemporary with the Heidelberg MS., or at all events not of a later period.

   First page.—ICh Johanns schiltperger zoch vsz von miner haymat mit namen vs der Statt München gelegen in Bayern in der czit als kúnig Sygmund zu vngern in die haydenschafft zoch Das was als man zalt von Crists gebúrt drwczehenhundert vnd in dem vier vnd nünczigisten Järe mit ainem herrn genant lienhart Richartinger vnd kam vs der haydenschafft wider zu land Als man zalt von Cristi gepúrt vierczehenhundert vnd in dem Súben vnd zwainczigosten Jär, etc.

At the last page is the Pater Noster in the Armenian and Tatar tongues.*

3. Another MS. of Schiltberger's travels, of the end of the fifteenth or of the early part of the sixteenth century, in the public library at Nuremberg, is entitled:

> Hanns Schiltperger von München ist auszgezogen da man zalt 1394—wiedergekommen 1427.
>
> *First page.*—Ich Hanns Schiltperger pin von meine Heymatt auszgezogen von der statt genaudt Munchen die da leyt zu päyren da man zalt von cristgepüret MCCCLXXXXIIII und das ist gescheen da konig Sigmundt zu ungern in die Haydenschafft zocht† und da zoch ich auss der obgenannten stat gerennes weyss mit und bin wider zu land chomen da ma zalt von crist gepurt M.CCCC.XXVII auss der Haydenschafft und das ich In der zeitt erfaren han In der Haydenschafft dat stet hernach geschreibenn Ich mag es aber nicht alles vorschreyben das ich erfaren han Wann ich es alles nicht Indechtig bin u. s. w.‡

Concluding paragraph at the end.

> Gott dem sey gedanckt das mir der macht und Krafft gegeben hat und mich behüett vnd beschirmet hatt zwai vnd dreyssig Jare die ich Hansz Schiltperger jnn der Haidenschafft gewesen pin vnd alles das vorgeschreiben stet erfaren vnd geschen han.§

This MS. was formerly the property of Adamnanus Rudolph Solger, protestant pastor of the church of St. Laurence in Nuremberg, whose library was sold in 1766, for the sum of 15,000 florins, to the municipality of the free

---

* *Die Handschriften der Fürstlich-Fürstenbergischen Hofbibliothek zu Donaueschingen. Geordnet und beschreiben von* Dr. K. A. Barack, Vorstand der Hofbibliothek. Tubingen, 1865, p. 326.

† Communicated by Dr. Joh. Priem of Nuremberg.

‡ Completed from Panzer, *Annalen der ältern deutschen Litteratur* etc., 1788-1805, i, 41.

‖ Communicated by Dr. Joh. Priem of Nuremberg.

town of Nuremberg, and now forms part of the public library in that city. The MS. is bound in the same volume with others, and is thus described in Solger's Catalogue.*

> 66. Ein starker Foliant von unterschiedlichen Reissbeschreibungen: 1) Marcho Polo von Venedig ein Edler Wandrer und Ritter ist ausgezogen A. 1230.† 2) Der Heil. Vatter und Abt S. Brandon und mit seinen Brüdern und mehr fahrt. 3) Der Edle Ritter und allervornehmste Landfahrer Johannis de Monttafilla ist von Engelland ausgezogen 1322, und wiederkommen 1330. 4) Der Heil. Bruder Ulrich Friaul der minder Brüder Baarfüsser Orden ein Mönch, ist ausgezogen und wiederkommen 1330. 5) Hanss Schildberger ein wahrhaftig frommer Edelmann der ein Diener ist gewesen des Durchlauchtigen Fürsten Albrecht Pfalzgraf bey Rhein, ist von München ausgezogen 1394.

4. In 1488, a MS. of Schiltberger's travels was in the possession of a Receiver of Revenue, named Matthias Bratzl, who caused it to be bound in one volume, with MSS. of Marco Polo, St. Brandon, Sir John Mandevile, and Ulrich of Frioul, and then wrote on the fly-leaf a note to the following effect:—" Having acquired the herein-named books, I have had them bound together, and have added a valuable and accurate map. Should the reader of these writings not know where the countries are, whose customs and habits are described, they are to look into the map. The map will also serve to complete what may be wanting in the books, and indicate the roads by which the travellers went. The map and the books quite agree. Whoever inherits this volume after my death, is to leave the different books together, and the map with them." When Gottlieb von Murr, the distinguished bibliographer and antiquary (1733—1811), saw the volume, the map was missing.

This MS. was originally at Munich, but being sent to

---

* *Bibliotheca sive supellex Librorum impressorum in omni genere scientiarum maximam partem rarissimorum et Codicum Manuscriptorum* etc. Nuremberg.

† Printed by Anton Sorg, Augsburg, 1481.

Nuremberg for the purpose of being published, was there kept in the city library. Schlichtegroll, the biographer, sanctioned the loan of it to Penzel, who turned its contents into modern German, producing the editions of 1813 and 1814. Penzel died at Jena in 1819, leaving his body to the anatomical theatre, his books to the public library, and all his debts to the grand-duke of Weimar. He had not returned the MS., and it was never afterwards recovered. Neumann thinks that it may have been in the author's own handwriting.

Printed Books.

(1.) *s. a.* *s. l.* fol. with woodcuts; 37 lines (?) in each page.

Printed, probably, by Günther Zainer, Ulm. 1473?

> *Title.*—Hie vahet an d Schildberger der vil wunders erfaren hatt in der heydenschafft und in d türckey.

A copy of this edition is in the public library at Augsburg; another is at Munich, but in a very defective state.

This edition, believed to be the earliest, is mentioned by Panzer, Ebert, Kobolt, Brunet, Hain, Ternaux-Compans, and Grässe.

(2.) *s. a.* *s. l.* fol. with 15 woodcuts.

Forty-six leaves without pagination, register or catchwords; 33, 34, 35, or 36 lines in each page.

Printed, probably, by A. Sorg, Augsburg. 1475?

> Ich Schildtberger zoche auss von meiner heimet mit Namen auss der stat münchen gelegen in bayern in der zeyt als künig Sigmund zu vngern in die heydenschafft zoch das was als man zalt von christi geburt dreizechenhundert und an dem vier und neüntzigesten Jar etc.

A copy at the British Museum is bound in one volume with duke Ernest of Bavaria; S. Brandon, abbot; and Ludolphus de Suchem. Another copy is in the public library, Munich.

(3.) *s. a. s. l.* Fifty-seven leaves.

> Hyē vahet an der Schildtberger der vil wunders erfaren hat in der heydenschafft vnd in d Türckey.

A copy at the public library, Munich, is bound in one volume with duke Ernest, and S. Brandon. A duplicate is defective. The imperial and royal library at Vienna also possesses a copy.

(4.) 1494. Frankfort. 4°.

Mentioned by Tobler who quotes Grässe.

(5.) 1513.

Tobler mentions an edition of this date, being a reprint of Zainer's edition, 1473?

(6.) *s. a.* J. v. Berg and U. Newber, Nuremberg. 4°. with woodcuts. No pagination, but with catchwords.

> *Title.*—Ein wunderbarliche vnnd kürtzweylige Histori wie Schildtberger einer auss der Stat München in Bayern von den Türcken gefangen in die Heydenschafft gefüret vnnd wider heymkommen Item was sich für krieg vnnd wunderbarlicher thaten diervyl er inn der Heydenschafft gewesen zugetragen gantz kürtzweylig zu lesen Nürmberg durch Johann vom Berg Vnd Ulrich Newber.

Copies of this edition are in the royal library, Dresden, and the public library, Munich.

Mentioned by Ebert and Tobler.

(7.) 1549. Herman Gülfferich, Frankfort. 4°. with 37 woodcuts. Seventy leaves; 32 lines in each page. No pagination, but with catchwords. Has a preface.

Title.—Ein wunderbarliche vnd kurtzweilige History wie Schildtberger einer auss der Stad München inn Beyern von den Türcken gefangen inn die Heydenschafft gefüret vnnd widder heimkommen ist sehr lüstig zu lesen. M.D.XLIX.

Colophon.—Gedruckt zu Franckfurdt am Mayn durch Herman Gülfferichen inn der Schnurgassen zu dem Krug.

Copies of this edition are in the British Museum, in the public library, Munich, and imperial public library, St. Petersburg.

Mentioned by Panzer, Ebert, Kobolt, Ternaux-Compans, Grässe, and Tobler.

(8.) 1549? Nuremberg. $4^?$.

Title.—Similar to that printed at Frankfort in 1549.

Mentioned by Panzer who quotes Meusel.

(9.) *s. a. s. l.* small $4°$.

Scheiger saw at Wels, in Austria, a copy which was supposed to be of the year 1551, and published at Munich. It was stated in a MS. marginal note, that Schiltberger was born at mid-day, on the 8th day of May.

(10.) *s. a.* Weygandt Han, Frankfort. $4°$. with 37 woodcuts, similar to those in the edition of 1549. Seventy leaves; 32 lines in each page. No pagination, but with catchwords. Has a preface.

Title.—Ein wunderbarliche unnd kurtzweilige History Wie Schildtberger einer auss der Stadt München in Beyern von den Türcken gefangen in die Heydenschafft gefüret vnd wider heimkommen ist sehr lüstig zu lesen.

Colophon.—Gedruckt zu Franckfurdt am Mayn durch Weygandt Han in der Schnurgassen zum Krug.

Copies of this edition are in the British Museum, where it is catalogued, 1554? In the royal library, Dresden; public library, Frankfort; public library, Hamburg; imperial public library, St. Petersburg.

Mentioned by Panzer, Ebert, and Tobler who says that the above Title, and the Title of the edition printed at Nuremberg by J. v. Berg and U. Newber (see 6), are identical!

(11.) 1557. Frankfort. 4°.

> *Title.*—Gefangenschaft in der Türckey. (According to Ternaux-Compans.)

(12.) 1606. J. Francke, Magdeburg. 4°., with woodcuts.

> *Title.*—Eine wunderbarliche vnnd kurtzweilige History, Wie Schildtberger, einer aus der Stadt München in Bayern, von den Türcken gefangen, in die Heydenschafft geführet, vnd wider heymkommen ist, sehr lustig zu lesen.

A copy of this edition is in the library of the imperial university, Strasburg.

Mentioned by Freytag, Ebert, Kobolt, Tobler who quotes Grässe, and Ternaux-Compans from whom we learn of another edition—

(13.) 1606. Frankfort. 8vo.

> *Title.*—Reise in die Heydenschaft.

(14.) *s. a. s. l.*

Supposed by Tobler to be of the year 1700.

(15.) 1813. Edited by A. J. Penzel. Munich. small 8vo.

> *Title.*—Schiltberger's aus München von den Türken in der Schlacht von Nicopolis 1395 gefangen, in das Heidenthum geführt, und 1427 wieder heimgekommen. Reise in den Orient und wunderbare Begebenheiten von ihm selbst geschrieben. Aus einer alten Handschrift übersetzt und herausgegeben von A. J. Penzel.

(16.) 1814. Edited by A. J. Penzel. Munich. small 8vo.

A copy of the last edition, with similar title-page.

(17.) 1823. Munich. 8vo.

> *Title.*—Sch. a. München v. d. Türken in d. Schlacht v. Nico-

polis 1395 in d. Heidenthum geführet u. 1417 (*sic*) wieder heimgekommen, Reise in den Orient u. wunderb. Beg. v. ihm. s. geschr.

Thus quoted by Grässe.

(18.) 1859. Edited by Prof. K. F. Neumann. Munich. small 8vo.

With Introduction and Notes by the editor, and Notes by Fallmerayer and Hammer-Purgstall.

> *Title.*—Reisen des Johannes Schiltberger aus München, in Europa, Asia, und Afrika, von 1394 bis 1427. Zum ersten Mal nach der gleichzeitigen Heidelberger Handschrift herausgegeben und erläutert von Karl Friedrich Neumann.

In the copy of this edition at the Institut, Paris, are several loose sheets containing a resumé of the Travels, in MS., by D'Avezac.

(19.) 1866. Edited by Professor Philip Bruun. Odessa. 8vo.

> *Title.*—Pouteshestvy'ye Ivana Schiltbergera pa Yevrope, Asii y Afrike, s. 1394 po 1427 god.

Published in the Records of the Imperial University of New Russia, vol. i.

This attempt at a Bibliography of the Travels of Johann Schiltberger is no doubt far from being complete; but I believe it to be the first of its sort. The details given by Bibliographers are not, in many cases, very explicit, and no little difficulty has been experienced in collecting desirable information, replies to enquiries not being always readily obtained.

According to Tobler, for instance, the university at Berlin possesses copies of six different editions; but my requests for particulars have not been successful—and so in other quarters.

Feci quod potui, faciant meliora potentes.

INTRODUCTION.

> " was ich die zit in dem land der haidenschafft
> strites und wunders herfaren Und och was ich
> hoptstett und wassers gesehen und gemercken
> mügen hab Davon vindent ir hienach geschriben
> villicht nicht gar volkomenlich Dorumb das ich
> ein gefangener man vnd nicht min selbs was Aber
> sovil ich des hon begriffen vnd mercken mocht
> So hon ich die land vnd die stett genant nach den
> sprachen der land"—SCHILTBERGER.

IF any reliance is to be placed in a MS. marginal note that appears on a page of an old edition of the Travels of Schiltberger, presumed to be of the year 1551, and preserved at Wels in Austria,* then the author of the work before us was born at mid-day on the 9th day of May—in the year 1381, according to his own showing, because he states in the opening of his narrative, that he had not yet attained his sixteenth year when at the battle of Nicopolis (Sept. 28, 1396). So completely does Schiltberger eschew all reference to himself, that he leaves us quite in the dark even with regard to the place of his birth; for, in addressing the Reader, he states that his home was near the city of Munich; but upon his return to Bavaria, he

* I regret that two applications to the library at Wels for the fullest particulars with reference to this marginal note, have been unsuccessful.

proceeds to Frisingen, near which town he was born. Nothing whatever is known of his parentage or childhood; and that he has not remained entirely neglected and forgotten is owed to Thurnmaier, better known as Aventinus, who states, that upon his return from bondage, Schiltberger was taken in hand by the duke Albrecht III., and nominated his Chamberlain, an appointment that was probably made, in Neumann's opinion, before the duke's reign began, in 1438. This is all the Bavarian annalist has to say of his interesting countryman.

In the Introduction to his edition, Neumann offers a few particulars on the Schiltberge family, as they were communicated to him by Cölestin von Schiltberg, Manager of the Royal Salt Mines at Reichenhall.

The origin of the ancient name of Schiltberger, or Schiltberge, is not known, but it is, in all probability, composite, from Schild—a coat of arms—and Berg, the mount on which the arms were raised. A certain Berchtholdus Marescalcus de Schiltberg is mentioned in a document of the year 1190, and others of the name appear at later dates as burghers, and marshals to the dukes of Bavaria.*

The Schiltberges of to-day trace their pedigree to our author, who is styled Chamberlain and Commander of the Body-guard to Albrecht III. Several of their

---

* For notices on the Schiltberger family, see *Monumenta Boica*, iii, 170; vi, 532, 538; vii, 137; viii, 150, 504; ix, 93, 577; and many other records in this collection. Also Hund's *Bayrischen Stammbuche*, i, 332, ii, 108, 478; Meichelbeck's *Historia Fris.*, ii, 43, etc.

ancestors, during the 18th century, were Counsellors in the Bavarian Electorate, and two Schiltberges, Johann Peter and Franz Joseph, were Professors of Law at the University of Ingolstadt. An Imperial decree, dated March 27, 1786, raising three brothers of the "ancient and noble lineage of Schiltberg" to the dignity of nobles of the State, having been confirmed by the Bavarian Electorate, the Schiltberges have ever since been included in the peerage of Bavaria.

Neumann's complaint that our author has never been fully appreciated by his countrymen, appears to be only too true; but the same cannot be said of aliens. Leunclavius has availed himself largely, in his *Pandects*,* of the information supplied by an eye-witness, for the purpose of illustrating the history of the Turks; and in later times, such men as J. R. Forster, M. C. Sprengel, J. Chr. von Engel, Hugh Murray, Hammer, Scheiger, Aschbach, Vivien de Saint-Martin, Fallmerayer, D'Avezac, Bruun, and Yule, have borne witness to the worth of what Schiltberger has left behind. If he is charged by Karamsin with making confused and senseless statements, the historian at least believes him to be truthful, and to have really been at all the places he claims to have visited.

Johann Schiltberger left his home in the year 1394, as he himself informs us, with his master, Leonard Richartinger. That was two years before the battle of Nicopolis was fought, ten months of which time he

* *Neuwe Chronica Türckischer nation von Türcken selbs beschreiben* etc., Franckfurt am Mayn, 1590. iii, 207.

spent in Hungary, where his lord was in all probability serving in the auxiliary forces under Sigismund, king of that country. He must therefore have been launched into the world when in his fourteenth year only, and whatever the state of his education at that early age, certainly no opportunities could have been afforded him for improving it, during his long term of servitude. The composition of his work, throughout, and the diversified and undetermined mode of spelling Proper and Geographical names, show that the scribe was not a careful one, and tends to prove Schiltberger's inability to read what was written, and correct the mistakes that were made; it is thus fairly conclusive, I venture to say, that his book, like so many other narratives of the Middle Ages, was written under dictation, a fact exhibiting marvellous retention of memory, when it is considered that the incidents extend over the space of about thirty-three years. That no journal was kept, is apparent from errors in computation of time. Of this there are two striking instances; the first, in the estimate of length of service under Bajazet, from September 1396 to July 1402, which is calculated at twelve years; and the author's statement that he was six years with Timour, when, as a matter of fact, the actual period extended from July 1402 to February 1405.

Schiltberger no doubt dictated his adventures soon after his return to his native country, because in the concluding chapter he explains "how and through what countries I have come away". The various incidents of his career in the East are recorded without method, and were evidently related just as the recollection of them occurred to him, so that the attempt to follow in his footsteps, with any precision, becomes a hopeless task ; and irregularly interspersed with his narrative, are descriptions of places and events, that he learnt from hearsay only, not having been either a spectator or participator. This inconsistent and incongruous style, again, betokens the man wanting in instruction ; but every page affords evidence of the intelligence, veracity, modesty, and high principles of the honest-minded Bavarian ; indeed the whole, so straightforward, truthful, and certainly useful, will compare favourably with the most trustworthy of mediæval writers, not excepting even Marco Polo. "Notwithstanding a few historical and geographical errors," says Hammer, "this book of Travels remains a precious monument of the history and topography of the middle ages, of which Bavarians may be as justly proud as Venice is of her Marco Polo."* There is nothing to show that Schiltberger was a reading man, or that he availed himself of the writings of others, except in one instance, in which it can scarcely be doubted that he had recourse to some authority when giving the dimensions of the walls of Babylon, which coincide so exactly with what is found recorded in Herodotus. How otherwise could the poor slave have traced and verified such measurements ?

* *Berichtigung der orientalischen Namen Schiltberger's*, in *Denkschriften der Königlichen Akademie der Wissenschaften zu München, für Jahre* 1823 *und* 1824. Band ix.

Schiltberger has wisely distinguished what he heard from what he himself saw, and therefore does not hesitate to indulge in the recital of the marvellous and ridiculous, without, however, the least touch of humour or criticism. A battle was fought between serpents and vipers, near Samsoun on the Black Sea coast; not whilst he was in the city, but "during the time I was with Bajazet". Entering with childlike pleasure into the fullest particulars on the Castle of the Sparrow-hawk, he takes care to say, that when one of his companions wanted to visit it and see the virgin who resided there, nobody could be found to show the way, because the castle was hidden by trees, and the Greek priests also forbade approach to it. Then there is the story of the destruction of the mirror at Alexandria, related in the most perfect simplicity, and, as is his custom, without a word of comment; but that the Pope's conduct was iniquitous in the sight of good Schiltberger is very certain, for he seeks to excuse his lesson of dissimulation to the priest, on the plea that all was done "for the sake of the Christian faith". *Vera sunt vera et falsa sunt falsa; sed si ecclesia dicit vera esse falsa et falsa esse vera, falsa sunt vera et vera sunt falsa.* If Bellarmine was really the first to pen these lines, verily it was no new precept that he was promulgating. Another instance of Schiltberger's appreciation of the truth is to be found in his relation of the tale of the saintly man in Khorasan, who had attained his three hundred and fiftieth year. "So the Infidels said," are the words added. Such is the manner in which Schiltberger treats these and all the other absurd inventions to which he listened in his leisure hours.

When the text is largely illustrated with Notes—in the present work they form the greater part of the volume—little room is left for introductory remarks; nor is it necessary to recapitulate the substance of the text. It will therefore suffice to give a rapid outline of the author's movements during his lengthened captivity.

The battle of Nicopolis is the most important episode in the busy and eventful career of Schiltberger, whose circumstantial account of the action fully agrees with what we learn from other sources. He escaped the general massacre of prisoners, upon the defeat and flight of Sigismund, through the timely intervention of Soulciman, the eldest son of Bajazet. Thurnmaier says that Schiltberger was spared on account of his good looks, and at once appointed page to the Sultan;* but this is probably a fancy of the Bavarian annalist, because it is very distinctly asserted in the text that none under twenty were executed, and the youthful captive was barely sixteen years of age. He suffered considerably from the effects of three wounds, a circumstance to which he casually and most modestly refers in a subsequent chapter. Whilst in the service of

---

* "Joannes Schildtperger tum puer, Monachi oppido Bojariæ ortus, captus, ob elegantiam formæ a filio Basaitis servatus, in aula Turcarum educatus et victo Basaite a Tamerlano rege Persarum, arma victoris secutus est, et tandem mortuo Tamerlane in patriam postliminio reversus a Cubiculo Alberto avo Principum nostrorum fuit. etc."—*Annalib. p. m.*, 805.

Bajazet, he was employed as one of his personal attendants in the quality of runner; he possibly took part in the siege of Constantinople; was in an expedition sent to Egypt for the relief of the sultan Faradj, when he probably embarked at some port in Cilicia; and in various expeditions in Asia Minor.

Upon the fall of Bajazet at the battle of Angora, July 20th, 1402, our runner became the prisoner of Timour, with whom he remained in Asia Minor; the Sultan himself being a captive in the camp. The fable of the iron cage is scarcely worth recalling to mind; but had there been a shadow of truth in it, Schiltberger would not have failed to notice the circumstance of the powerful monarch he had served so long being thus ignominiously treated.

Schiltberger's first acquaintance with Armenia and Georgia was made upon the occasion of Timour's invasion of those countries after his conquests in Asia Minor. Then followed the expedition to Abhase, the period of rest in the plain of Karabagh, and the return to Samarkand across the Araxes and through the kingdoms of Persia.

As the victories of the invincible Timour in India, Azerbaijan, and Syria, were related to him by his new comrades, so has Schiltberger recorded them, with some fresh details on the horrible atrocities committed.

Upon the death of Timour, at Otrar, in 1405, our author passed into the hands of his son, Shah Rokh, probably taking part in the expeditions of that monarch into Mazanderan and the Armenian provinces, Samarkand, and the territories about the Oxus, spending his winters in the plain of Karabagh, where good pasturage was to be found; but after the defeat of Kara Youssouf, Chief of the Turkomans of the Black Sheep, he remained in the contingent left by Shah Rokh, at the disposal of his brother, Miran Shah. This amir was afterwards himself overthrown by Kara Youssouf, and Schiltberger became subject to Aboubekr, a son of Shah Rokh, under whom he served for some time, first at Kars* and then at Erivan, where he had frequent opportunities for again enjoying the society of his friends and co-religionists, the Armeno-Catholics, and perfecting himself in their language.

From Erivan, Schiltberger was dispatched with four other Christians as part escort to the Tatar prince, Tchekre, recalled to assume the supreme power in the Golden Horde. Traversing the provinces on the western shore of the Caspian Sea, and passing through Derbent into Great Tatary, they reached a place that we find named "Origens", and which Professor Bruun is at some pains to prove was no other than Anjak, at one time a port on the Caspian, near Astrahan. Some curious details are given on the succession to the Khanate of the Golden Horde, which serve to authenticate historical accounts, as will be found on reference to the Notes thereon; and we also read of the warlike qualities of the Tatars of the Horde, of their hardy mode of living, eating meat raw and drinking the blood of their horses, a custom of war mentioned by Marco Polo.

We now come to what may be considered to be

* Gouria, according to Professor Bruun.

about the most interesting portion of the travels before us, viz. : the expedition to Siberia for the purpose of conquest. The customs, religion, food, mode of travelling, and clothing of its inhabitants, are so circumstantially laid before the reader, that it cannot be doubted Schiltberger saw with his own eyes all he recounts ; he would never otherwise have observed that there were many wild beasts in the country, the names of which he could not tell, because they did not exist in Germany; nor would he have concluded the chapter in which he speaks of these things, by saying : "All this I have seen, and was there with the above-named king's son, Zeggra."

In alluding to the sledge-dogs of Great Tatary and Siberia, Rubruquis, Marco Polo, and Ibn Batouta, dwell upon their large size. It is not a little remarkable that Marco Polo, who never saw those animals, should have heard that they were as big as donkeys ; the very simile employed by Schiltberger. They now are certainly much inferior in size.

The conquest of Siberia by Ydegou, was followed by that of Great Bolgara ; after which, Tchekre returned into Great Tatary, and in due course became ruler of the Horde. Upon his death, the author fell into the hands of one of his counsellors, named "Manstzusch", who, being forced to flee, traversed the kingdom of Kiptchak, and arrived at Kaffa in the Crimea. It was when upon this journey that Schiltberger saw the river Don ; the city of Tana, Solkhat the capital of Kiptchak, and the cities of Kyrkyer and Sary Kerman.

In Chapter 37, the author says that he was present at the marriage festivities of a daughter of the sultan, Boursbaï, a monarch who ascended the throne in 1422; and as he did not lose his lord, Tchekre, until about the year 1424 or 1425, it follows that he must have gone to Egypt, at least for the second time, subsequently to the latter date, but by what route and for what purpose there are no means of determining ; although this was probably the occasion of his passing the island of Imbros, and touching at the port of Salonica. During his sojourn in Egypt, the author was afforded the opportunity of witnessing the reception of foreign ambassadors at the Court of the Mamelouk monarch, some portion of the ceremonial observed upon those occasions reminding us of the brilliant doings in the palace of the Greek Emperors, amongst whose earliest predecessors those magnificent state formalities were introduced by the Romans, who had themselves adopted them from the Kings of Persia, after their conquests in the far East.

From Egypt, Schiltberger was sent into Palestine, when he visited several of the holy places, and to Arabia, where it may be taken for granted that he assisted at one of the customary Mahomedan pilgrimages. Being too devotedly attached to his own Church to entertain the least sympathy for Islamism, our traveller is careful to avoid saying anything that might be construed into a semblance of his having renounced his religion, under whatsoever circumstances ; but that he must have done so, inevitably, may be accepted as an unquestionable fact, for where is the page in the history of Bajazet, of Timour, and of his successors, that tells of a Christian having been spared persecution, followed by torture and death? Nor is it credible that the presence of a slave, professing Christianity, would have been at all tolerated in the camps of those barbarous and fanatic rulers. Schiltberger has taken delight in supplying all the information he was able to obtain on the forms and solemnities of the Armenian and Greek Churches, showing at the same time the respect in which he held Saints in general, by never failing to relate the miracles attributed to them, for

"Our superstitions with our life begin ;"

but he has equally proved his proficiency in Mahomedanism, in devoting no less than eleven chapters to an exposition of its history, doctrines, and legends.

Whether or not Schiltberger traversed the Hyjaz of Arabia, will possibly remain a controverted point; the probability is that he did do so, not from the shores of the Red Sea, but from Syria and Palestine. We find him describing from personal observation, first, the pelican, a bird which, according to Buffon, frequents the borders of Palestine and Arabia, and even the arid wastes of Arabia and Persia; then the "giant's shinbone", that spanned a ravine between two mountains and served as a bridge; an indication that leads Professor Bruun to the neighbourhood of Kerak and Shaubek, on the beaten track to the Hyjaz. More than this, mention is made of the tomb of the prophet at a place called "Madina", its situation and ornamentations being clearly explained; accuracy that is quite exceptional, as nearly all mediæval notices of the tomb of Mahomet place it at Mecca. If our author did indeed travel into Arabia from Palestine, he would have been the predecessor of Varthema (1503) by that route, and he is also the first European known to have visited the holy places of Islam.

Quitting Egypt, Schiltberger returned to the Crimea, afterwards accompanying his lord, "Manstzusch", to the Caucasus, where he found the slave trade in full swing, a traffic he vigorously condemns by saying of the people, who sold even their own children, that they were " bös lüt". Whilst in Circassia, at that time tributary to the Golden Horde, the Great Khan required of its ruler that "Manstzusch" should be expelled his territory. That prince being thus forced to change his residence, proceeded to Mingrelia, through Abhase and Soukhoum its chief town. An unhealthy country, says our author, when describing the peculiar customs, dress, and religion of the people.

It is singular that, although Schiltberger notices the existence of Christians at Samsoun, Joulad, in Georgia, the Crimea, and other places, he makes no mention of the large European community at Savastopoli, as Soukhoum was called by the Genoese, who, especially, were very numerous, and had had a consul at that port from the year 1354. That there were many Roman Catholics at Savastopoli is very certain, for the place was constituted a bishop's see, a condition not at all gratifying to the native population which belonged to the Greek Church, as would appear from the following circumstance :—

In 1330, Peter, bishop of Senascopoli (sic) or Savastopoli, addressed a letter to the Archbishop of Canterbury and the bishops of England, collectively, in which he complains of the oppression practised on Christians in the East, who were carried off into slavery; an infamous traffic he was unable to suppress because the local authorities, who belonged to the schismatic Greek religion, were inimical to him. He entreats the bishops of England to present the bearer of the letter, one Joachim of Cremona, to the warriors of England, who fight for God and aspire to power! That letter is preserved in the public library at Ratisbon, and can scarcely be supposed to have reached its destination at any time.

Being in Mingrelia, Schiltberger was in a Christian country temptingly situated on the borders of the Black Sea. It is most likely that he received sufficient encouragement from the people to induce him to attempt to regain his liberty, and, at a favourable moment, he and four of his Christian comrades made their escape and succeeded in reaching the coast at Poti,* where they had hoped to find some friendly vessel that would receive them. Failing in this, they rode along the shore to the hills in Lazistan, and one evening, after dark, had the good fortune to communicate, by means of signal fires, with a European ship off the land. Our traveller and his companions were obliged to prove their identity by repeating the Pater Noster, Ave Maria, and Credo, before the boat's crew could be prevailed upon to take them off to the ship; and after a

* Batoum, according to Professor Bruun.

tedious voyage of many weeks, during which the vessel was chased by pirates and detained by contrary gales, and the crew had suffered from want of provisions, Constantinople was reached. There the runaways were kindly received and cared for by the emperor (John VIII. Palæologos), who placed them in charge of the patriarch, in whose house they lived. Schiltberger is full of admiration for the great palaces, the church of St. Sophia, and the magnificent walls of the imperial city; but not being free to move about as he pleased, during his long stay in it, the account of Constantinople and of its marvels is exceedingly meagre, when compared with the descriptions left by other visitors. Indeed, what little Schiltberger was able to do in the way of sight-seeing was effected surreptitiously, with the connivance of the patriarch's servants, whom he accompanied on their errands as opportunities offered.

At the expiration of three months, our author and his comrades were sent to Kilia at the estuary of the Danube. Hence Johann Schiltberger easily found his way to his native country, where he arrived some time in the year 1427, offering thanks to Almighty God for his escape "from the Infidel people and their wicked religion", and for having preserved him from "the risk of perdition of body and soul".

INDEX TO THE CHAPTERS.

	PAGE
SCHILTBERGER TO THE READER	1
1. Of the first combat between King Sigmund and the Turks	1
2. How the Turkish king treated the prisoners	4
3. How Wyasit subjugated an entire country	6
4. How Wyasit made war on his brother-in-law, and killed him	7
5. How Weyasit drives away the king of Sebast	10
6. What sixty of us Christians had agreed upon	10
7. How Wyasit took the city of Samson	12
8. Of serpents and vipers	12
9. How the Infidels remain in the fields with their cattle, in winter and summer	14
10. How Weyasit took a country that belonged to the Sultan	18
11. Of the King-Sultan	19
12. How Temerlin conquered the kingdom of Sebast	20
13. Weyasit conquers Lesser Armenia	20
14. How Tämerlin goes to war with the King-Sultan	22
15. How Tämerlin conquered Babiloni	24
16. How Tämerlin conquered Lesser India	24
17. How a vassal carried off riches that belonged to Tämerlin	26
18. How Tämerlin caused MMM children to be killed	27
19. Tämerlin wants to go to war with the Great Chan	28
20. Of Tämerlin's death	29
21. Of the sons of Tämerlin	30
22. How Joseph caused Mirenschach to be beheaded, and took possession of all his territory	31
23. How Joseph vanquished a king and beheaded him	32
24. How Schiltberger came to Aububachir	33
25. Of a king's son	33
26. How one lord succeeds another lord	36
27. Of an Infidel woman, who had four thousand maidens	37
28. In what countries I have been	38
29. In which countries I have been, that lay between the Tonow and the sea	39
30. Of the castle of the sparrow-hawk, and how it is guarded	41
31. How a poor fellow watched the sparrow-hawk	42

32. More about the castle of the sparrow-hawk . . 42
33. In which countries silk is grown, and of Persia and of other kingdoms 44
34. Of the tower of Babilony that is of such great height . 46
35. Of great Tartaria 48
36. The countries in which I have been, that belong to Tartary . 49
37. How many kings-sultan there were, whilst I was amongst the Infidels 51
38. Of the mountain of St. Catherine . . . 54
39. Of the withered tree 56
40. Of Jherusalem and of the Holy Sepulchre . . 57
41. Of the spring in Paradise, with IIII rivers . . 61
42. How pepper grows in India 61
43. Of Allexandria 62
44. Of a great giant 64
45. Of the many religions the Infidels have . . . 65
46. How Machmet and his religion appeared . . . 65
47. Of the Infidels' Easter-day . . . 70
48. Of the other Easter-day . . . 71
49. Of the law of the Infidels . . 71
50. Why Machmet has forbidden wine to Infidels . 72
51. Of a fellowship the Infidels have among themselves 73
52. How a Christian becomes an Infidel . . 74
53. What the Infidels believe of Christ . . 75
54. What the Infidels say of Christians . . 76
55. How Christians are said not to hold to their religion 77
56. How long ago it is, since Machmet lived . . 78
57. Of Constantinoppel 79
58. Of the Greeks 80
59. Of the Greek religion 81
60. How the city of Constantinoppel was built 83
61. How the Jassen have their marriages . 85
62. Of Armenia 86
63. Of the religion of the Armenians . . 87
64. Of a Saint Gregory . . . 89
65. Of a dragon and a unicorn . . 90
66. Why the Greeks and Armani are enemies . 96
67. Through which countries I have come away . 99
The Armenian Pater Noster . . . 102
The Tartar Pater Noster 102

SCHILTBERGER TO THE READER.

I, JOHANNS SCHILTBERGER, left my home near the city of Munich, situated in Payren, at the time that King Sigmund of Hungary left for the land of the Infidels. This was, counting from Christ's birth, in the thirteen hundred and ninety-fourth year,* with a lord named Leinhart Richartinger And I came back again from the land of the Infidels, counting from Christ's birth, fourteen hundred and twenty seven. All that I saw in the land of the Infidels, of wars, and that was wonderful, also what chief towns and seas I have seen and visited, you will find described hereafter, perhaps not quite completely, but I was a prisoner and not independent. But so far as I was able to understand and to note, so have I [noted] the countries and cities as they are called in those countries, and I here make known and publish many interesting and strange adventures, which are worth listening to.

1.—Of the first combat between King Sigmund and the Turks.

From the first, King Sigmund appealed in the above-named year, thirteen hundred and ninety-four, to Christendom for assistance, at the time that the Infidels were

* Neumann states in a note that this date, through the transcriber's error, appears as 1344 in the Heidelberg MS.

doing great injury to Hungern. There came many people from all countries to help him; (¹) then he took the people and led them to the Iron Gate, which separates Ungern from Pulgery and Walachy, and he crossed the Tunow into Pulgary, and made for a city called Pudem.(²) It is the capital of Pulgery. Then came the ruler of the country and of the city, and gave himself up to the king; then the king took possession of the city with three hundred men, good horse and foot soldiers, and then went to another city where were many Turks. There he remained five days, but the Turks would not give up the city; but the fighting men expelled them by force, and delivered the city to the king. Many Turks were killed and others made prisoners. The king took possession of this city also, with two hundred men, and continued his march towards another city called Schiltaw, but called in the Infidel tongue, Nicopoly.(³) He besieged it by water and by land for XVI days, then came the Turkish king, called Wyasit, with two hundred thousand men, to the relief of the city. When the king, Sigmund, heard this, he went one mile to meet him with his people, the number of whom were reckoned at sixteen thousand men. Then came the Duke of Walachy, called Werterwaywod,*(⁴) who asked the king to allow him to look at the winds.† This the king allowed, and he took with him one thousand men for the purpose of looking at the winds, and returned to the king and told him that he had looked at the winds, and had seen twenty banners, and that there were ten thousand men under each banner, and each banner was separate from the other. When the king heard this, he wanted to arrange the order of battle. The Duke of Walachy asked that he might be the first to attack, to which the king would willingly have consented. When the

* This name appears as Martin in edition of 1814; Merter Waywod in edition of 1475; and Merte Weydwod in that of 1549.

† To reconnoitre. In the edition of 1814 the term employed is "zu recognosciren".

Duke of Burguny heard this, he refused to cede this honour to any other person, for the just reason that he had come a great distance with six thousand men,(⁵) and had expended much money in the expedition, and he begged the king that he should be the first to attack. The king asked him to allow the Ungern to begin, as they had already fought with the Turks, and knew better than others how they were armed. This he would not allow to the Ungern, and assembled his men, attacked the enemy, and fought his way through two corps; and when he came to the third, he turned and would have retreated, but found himself surrounded, and more than half his horsemen were unhorsed, for the Turks aimed at the horses only, so that he could not get away, and was taken prisoner. When the king heard that the Duke of Burgony was forced to surrender, he took the rest of the people and defeated a body of twelve thousand foot soldiers that had been sent to oppose him. They were all trampled upon and destroyed, and in this engagement a shot killed the horse of my lord Lienhart Richartinger; and I, Hanns Schiltberger his runner, when I saw this, rode up to him in the crowd and assisted him to mount my own horse, and then I mounted another which belonged to the Turks, and rode back to the other runners. And when all the [Turkish] foot-soldiers were killed, the king advanced upon another corps which was of horse. When the Turkish king saw the king advancing, he was about to fly, but the Duke of Irisch, known as the despot,(⁶) seeing this, went to the assistance of the Turkish king with fifteen thousand chosen men and many other bannerets, and the despot threw himself with his people on the king's banner and overturned it; and when the king saw that the banner was overturned and that he could not remain, he took to flight.*
Then came he of Cily,† and Hanns,‡ Burgrave of Nurem-

---

* The battle of Nicopolis was fought September 28th, 1396.
† Herman of Cily. *N*.

berg, who took the king and conducted him to a galley on board of which he went to Constantinoppel. When the horse and foot soldiers saw that the king had fled, many escaped to the Tünow and went on board the shipping; but the vessels were so full that they could not all remain, and when they tried to get on board they struck them on the hands, so that they were drowned in the river; many were killed on the mountain as they were going to the Tunow. My lord Lienhart Richartinger, Wernher Pentznawer, Ulrich Kuchler, and little Stainer, all bannerets, were killed in the fight, also many other brave knights and soldiers. Of those who could not cross the water and reach the vessels, a portion were killed; but the larger number were made prisoners. Among the prisoners were the Duke of Burgony ([7]) and Hanns Putzokardo,* and a lord named Centumaranto.† These were two lords of France, and the Great Count of Hungern. And other mighty lords, horsemen, and foot-soldiers, were made prisoners, and I also was made a prisoner.

2.—How the Turkish king treated the prisoners.

And now when the King Weyasat had had the battle, he went near the city where King Sigmund had encamped with his army, and then went to the battle-field and looked upon his people that were killed; and when he saw that so many of his people were killed, he was torn by great grief, and swore he would not leave their blood unavenged, and ordered his people to bring every prisoner before him the next day, by fair means or foul. So they came the next day, each with as many prisoners as he had made, bound with a cord. I was one of three bound with the same cord, and was taken

* Boucicault, who has described the battle in his *Memoirs*. *H.*
† Saint Omer. *F.*

by him who had captured us. When the prisoners were brought before the king, he took the Duke of Burgony that he might see his vengeance because of his people that had been killed. When the Duke of Burgony saw his anger, he asked him to spare the lives of several he would name; this was granted by the king. Then he selected twelve lords, his own countrymen, also Stephen Synüher and the lord Hannsen of Bodem.([1]) Then each was ordered to kill his own prisoners, and for those who did not wish to do so the king appointed others in their place. Then they took my companions and cut off their heads, and when it came to my turn, the king's son saw me and ordered that I should be left alive, and I was taken to the other boys, because none under xx years of age were killed, and I was scarcely sixteen years old. Then I saw the lord Hannsen Greiff, who was a noble of Payern, and four others, bound with the same cord. When he saw the great revenge that was taking place, he cried with a loud voice and consoled the horse- and foot-soldiers who were standing there to die. "Stand firm", he said, "when our blood this day is spilt for the Christian faith, and we by God's help shall become the children of heaven." When he said this he knelt, and was beheaded together with his companions. Blood was spilled from morning until vespers, and when the king's counsellors saw that so much blood was spilled and that still it did not stop, they rose and fell upon their knees before the king, and entreated him for the sake of God that he would forget his rage, that he might not draw down upon himself the vengeance of God, as enough blood was already spilled. He consented, and ordered that they should stop, and that the rest of the people should be brought together, and from them he took his share and left the rest to his people who had made them prisoners. I was amongst those the king took for his share, and the people that were killed on that day were reckoned at ten thousand men. The prisoners of the king were then sent to Greece to a chief city called Andranopoli, where we remained prisoners for fifteen days. Then we were taken by sea to a city called Kalipoli;(²) it is the city where the Turks cross the sea, and there three hundred of us remained for two months confined in a tower. The Duke of Burgony also was there in the upper part of the tower with those prisoners he had saved; and whilst we were there, the King Sigmund passed us on his way to Windischy land.(³) When the Turks heard this, they took us out of the tower and led us to the sea, and one after the other they abused the king and mocked him, and called to him to come out of the boat and deliver his people; and this they did to make fun of him, and skirmished a long time with each other on the sea. But they did not do him any harm, and so he went away.

3.—How Wyasit subjugated an entire country.

On the third day after the Turkish king had killed the people and sent us prisoners to the above named city, he marched upon Ungern and crossed the river called the Saw, at a city called Mittrotz, and took it and all the country around; and then he went into the Duchy of Petaw, and took with him from the said country sixteen thousand men with their wives and children and all their property, and took the city of the above name and burnt it; and the people he took away and some he left in Greece.*(¹) And after he passed the river called the Saw, he sent orders to Karipoli that we were to be taken across the sea; and when we were taken across the sea, we were taken to the king's capital called Wursa, where we remained until he himself came. And when he arrived in the city he took the Duke of

* Styrian historians have overlooked this statement of Schiltberger. *H*.

Burgony and those the duke had saved, and lodged them in a house near to his palace. The king then sent a lord named Hoder of Ungern, with sixty boys, as a mark of honour to the king-sultan; (²) and he would have sent me to the king-sultan, but I was severely wounded, having three wounds, so for fear I might die on the way I was left with the Turkish king. Other prisoners were sent as an offering to the king of Babilony(³) and the king of Persia,(⁴) also into White Tartary,*(⁵) into Greater Armenia,(⁶) and also into other countries. I was taken to the palace of the Turkish king; there for six years I was obliged to run on my feet with the others, wherever he went, it being the custom that the lords have people to run before them. After six years I deserved to be allowed to ride, and I rode six years with him, so that I was twelve years with him; and it is to be noted what the said Turkish king did during these twelve years, all of which is written down piece by piece.

4.—How Wyasit made war on his brother-in-law, and killed him.

From the first he was at war with his brother-in-law, who was called Caraman, and this name he had because of his country. The capital of the country is called Karanda,(¹) and because he would not be subject to him, he marched upon him with one hundred and fifty thousand men. When he knew that King Weyasit had advanced, he went to meet him with seventy thousand men, the best he had in the land, and with whom he intended to resist the king. They met each other on the plain in front of the city called Konia, which belonged to the said lord, Caraman. Here they attacked each other and began to fight, and had on the same day two

* White Tartars, *i.e.*, Free Tartars. White signifies free in the Tartar and Russian tongues; black, on the contrary, signifies subject-races or those that are tributary. *N.*

encounters by which one tried to overcome the other, and both sides had rest at night, that one might not do harm to the other. That same night Karaman made merry with trumpets, with drums, and with his guards, with the object of causing alarm to Weyasit; but Weyasit arranged with his people that they should not make a fire except for cooking, and should immediately again put it out. At night he sent thirty thousand men to the rear of the enemy, and said to them that when he should attack in the morning they should also attack. When the day broke, Weyasit went against the enemy, and the thirty thousand men attacked in the rear as they were ordered, and when Karaman saw that the enemy was attacking him in front and behind, he fled into his city of Konia, and remained in it to defend himself. Weyasit lay siege to the city for XI days without being able to take it; then the citizens sent word to Weysat that they would surrender the city if he would secure to them their lives and property. To this he agreed. Then they sent word to say that they would retire from the walls when he came to storm, and thus he might take the city. And this occurred. And when Karaman saw that Weyasit was entering the city, he attacked him with his warriors, and fought with him in the town, and if he had received the least assistance from the inhabitants he would have forced Weyasit out of the city; but when he saw that he had no assistance, he fled, but was taken before Weyasit, who said to him: "Why wilt thou not be subject to me?" Karaman answered, "Because I am as great a lord as thyself." Weyasit became angry, and asked three times if there was anybody who would rid him of Karaman. At the third time came one who took him aside and cut off his head and went back with it to Weyasit, who asked what he had done with him? He answered, "I have beheaded him." Then he shed tears and ordered that another man should do to him what he did to Karaman, and he was taken to the place where he beheaded Karaman and he was also beheaded. This was done because Weyasit thought that nobody should have killed so mighty a lord, but should have waited until his lord's anger had passed away. He then ordered that the head of Karaman should be fixed on a lance and carried about the country, so that other cities might submit to him on hearing that their lord was killed. After this he occupied the city of Konia with his people and marched upon the city of Karanda, and called upon them to surrender as he was their lord, and if they would not do so he would compel them with the sword. Then the citizens sent out to him four of their most eminent [fellow citizens], to beg that he would ensure to them their lives and their property, and begged, as their lord Karaman was dead, and they had two of his sons in the city, that he would appoint one of them to be their lord; and should he do so, they would surrender to him the city. He replied that he should spare their lives and property, but when he would have possession of the city, he should know what lord to appoint, whether the son of Karaman or one of his own sons. And so they parted. When the citizens heard Weyasit's answer they would not give up the city, and said that although their lord was dead he had left two sons, under whom they will recover or die. And so they defended themselves against the king until the fifth day. And as Weyasit saw that they continued to resist, he sent for more people and ordered arquebuses to be brought, and platforms to be constructed. When Karaman's sons and their mother saw this, they sent for the chief citizens and said to them: "You see plainly that we cannot resist Weyasit, who is too powerful for us; we should be sorry if you died for our sakes, and we have agreed with our mother that we will trust to his mercy." The citizens were pleased at this, and the sons of Karaman and their mother, and the chief citizens of the city, opened the gates and went out. And as they were advancing, the mother took a son in each hand and went up to Weyasit, who, when he saw his sister with her sons, went out of his tent towards her, and when they were near him they threw themselves at his feet, kissed them, and begged for mercy, and they gave the keys of the gates and of the city. When the king saw this, he ordered his lords who were near him to raise them. When this was done he took possession of the city, and appointed one of his lords to be governor, and he sent his sister and her two sons to his capital called Wurssa.

5.—How Weyasit drives away the king of Sebast.(¹)

There was a vassal named Mirachamat who resided in a city called Marsüany; it was on the border of Karaman's country. When Mirachamad heard that King Weyasit had conquered Karaman's country, he sent to him to ask him to drive away also the king of Sebast, who was called Wurthanadin, who had seized upon his territory because he could not himself expel him, and he should give him the territory in exchange for one in his own country. Weyasit sent to his assistance his son Machamet with thirty thousand men, and they forcibly expelled the king called Wurthanadin out of the country.* Then Mirachamad bestowed upon Machamet† the capital and all the territory, because his first engagement had been in its behalf. Then Weyasit took Mirachamad with him to his own country, and gave him another territory for his own.

6.—What sixty of us Christians had agreed upon.

And when Weyasit came to his capital, there were sixty of us Christians agreed that we should escape, and made a

* 1394.   † Mouhammed, a younger son of Bajazet.

bond between ourselves and swore to each other that we should die or succeed together; and each of us took time to get ready, and at the time we met together, and chose two leaders from amongst ourselves by lot, and whatever they ordered we were to obey. Then we rose after midnight and rode to a mountain and came to it by daybreak. And when we came to the mountain we dismounted, and let our horses rest until sunrise, when we remounted and rode the same day and night. And when Weyasit heard that we had taken to flight, he sent five hundred horse with orders that we were to be found, that we were to be caught, and brought to him. They overtook us near a defile, and called to us to give ourselves up. This we would not do, and we dismounted from our horses and defended ourselves against them as well as we could. When their commander saw that we defended ourselves, he came forward and asked for peace for one hour. We consented. He came to us and asked us to give ourselves up as prisoners; he would answer for the safety of our lives. We said we would consult, and did consult, and gave him this answer: We knew that so soon as we were made prisoners, we should die so soon as we came before the king, and it would be better that we should die here, with arms in our hands, for the Christian faith. When the commander saw that we were determined, he again asked that we should give ourselves as prisoners, and promised on his oath that he would ensure our lives, and if the king was so angry as to want to kill us, he would let them kill him first. He promised this on his oath, and therefore we gave ourselves up as prisoners. He took us before the king, who ordered that we should be killed immediately; the commander went and knelt before the king, and said that he had trusted in his mercy and had promised us our lives, and asked him also that he should spare us because he had even sworn that such would be the case. The king then asked him if we had done any harm? He said: No.

Then he ordered that we should be put into prison; there we remained for nine months as prisoners, during which time twelve of us died. And when it was the Easter-day of the Infidels, his eldest son Wirmirsiana,*(¹) begged for us, then he set us free, and ordered that we should be brought to him; then we were obliged to promise him that we should never try to escape again, and he gave us back our horses and increased our pay.

7.—How Wyasit took the city of Samson. (¹)

Afterwards, in the summer, Wyasit took eighty thousand men into a country called Genyck, and lay siege to a capital called Samson. This city was built by the strong man Samson, from whom it has its name. The lord of the country was of the same name as the country, Zymayd, and the king expelled the lord out of the land; and when it was heard in the city that their lord was driven away, the people gave themselves up to Weyasit, who occupied the city and all the country with his people.

8.—Of serpents and vipers.

A great miracle is to be noted which took place near the said city of Samson, during the time that I was with Weyasit. There came around the city such a lot of vipers and serpents, that they took up the space of a mile all round. There is a country called Teyenick which belongs to Sampson; it is a wooded country in which are many forests. One part of the vipers came from the said forests, and one part came out of

* The Amir Souleiman. The other sons of Bajazet were Mouhammed and Mousa.

the sea. The vipers remained for XI days, and then they fought with each other, and nobody dared to leave the city on account of the vipers, although they did no harm either to men or to cattle. Then the lord of the city and of the country gave orders that likewise no harm should be done to these reptiles, and said it was a sign and a manifestation from Almighty God. And now on the tenth day, the serpents and vipers fought with each other from morning until the going down of the sun, and when the lord and the people of the city saw what was done, the lord caused the gate to be opened, and rode out with a few people out of the city, and looked where the vipers were fighting, and saw that the vipers from the sea had to succumb to those of the forests. And the next morning early, the lord again rode out of the city to see if the reptiles were still there; he found none but dead vipers, which he ordered to be collected and counted. There were eight thousand. He then ordered a pit to be made, and ordered all to be thrown in and covered with earth, and he sent to Weyasit, who at that time was lord in Turkey, to tell him of the marvel. He took it for a piece of luck, as he had only just taken the city and country of Samson, and almost rejoiced that the forest adders had succumbed to the sea adders, and said it was a manifestation from Almighty God, and he hoped that as he was a powerful lord and king of the sea-board, so he would also, by the help of God the Almighty, become the powerful lord and king of the sea. Samson consists of two cities opposite to each other, and their walls are distant, one from the other, an arrow's flight. In one of these cities there are Christians, and at that time the Italians of Genoa (¹) possessed it. In the other are Infidels to whom the country belongs. At that time the lord of the city and country was a duke called Schuffmanes, son of [the duke of] Middle Pulgrey, the chief city of which country is Ternowa,(²) and who at that time had three hundred fortified towns, cities, and castles. This country was conquered by Weyasit who took the duke and his son. The father died in prison, and the son became converted to the faith of the Infidels, so that his life might be spared. Weyasit conquered Samson and the country, and conquered Zyenick; and the city and the country he gave to him for his lifetime, in place of his fatherland.

9.—How the Infidels remain in the fields with their cattle, in winter and summer.

It is the custom among the Infidels for some lords to lead a wandering life with their cattle, and when they come to a country that has good pasturage, they rent it of the lord of the country for a time. There was a Turkish lord called Otman, who wandered about with his cattle, and in the summer came to a country called Tamast, and the capital of the country is also so called. He asked the king of Tamast, who was called Wurchanadin,(1) that he would lend him a pasturage where he and his cattle might feed during the summer. The king lent him such a pasturage, to which he went with his dependants and cattle, and remained there the summer; and in autumn he broke up and returned to his country, without the king's permission and knowledge; and when the king heard of this he became very angry, and took one thousand men with him and went to the pasturage that Otman had occupied, and encamped there, and sent four thousand horsemen after Otman, and ordered that they should bring back Otman alive, with all his belongings. And when Otman heard that the king had sent after him, he hid himself in a mountain, so that those who rode after him could not find him; and they encamped on a meadow in front of the mountain where Otman was with his people, and remained there that night without troubling themselves about him. And when the day dawned, Otman took one thousand of his best horsemen to look at the winds, and when he saw that they were not on their guard, and were without care, he rode towards them and suddenly took them by surprise, so that they could not defend themselves, and many of them were killed; the others took to flight. The king was told how Otman had annihilated his expedition, but he would not believe it, and thought that fun was being made of him, until some of them came running to him. Even then he would not believe it, and sent one hundred horsemen to see if such was the case; and when the hundred horsemen went to see about it, Otman was on his way with his people to attack the king; and when he saw the hundred horsemen he overtook them, and came with them into the camp. And when the king and his people saw that they were overtaken, and that they could not defend themselves any more, they took to flight. The king himself had scarcely time to mount his horse, and took to flight to a mountain; but one of Otman's servants saw him, and hastened after him on the mountain; then the king could fly no farther, and the soldier called upon him to surrender; but he would not give himself up. Then he took his bow and would have shot him, when the king made himself known and asked him to let him go, promising to give him a fine castle, and he wanted to give him the ring he had on his hand as a pledge. The soldier would not do so, and made him a prisoner and brought him to his lord. And Otman pursued the people all day until the evening, and killed many of them, and encamped where the king had stayed, and sent for the people and cattle that he had left to run about the mountains. And when the people came with the cattle, he took the king, and went to the capital called Tamastk, where he encamped with all his people, and sent word into the city that he had captured the king, and that if they would deliver to him the city, he would give peace and security. The city made this answer: If he had their king, they had his son, and they had lords enough, as he was too weak to be a lord. He then said to the king, that if he wanted his life to be spared, he should speak to the citizens that they give up the city. So they took him before the city, and he asked the citizens that they should deliver him from death, and give up the city to Otman. They replied: We will not give up the city to Otman, because he is too feeble a lord for us; and if thou shouldst no longer care to be our lord, we have thy son, whom we will have for our lord. When Otman heard this, he was angry, and seeing his anger, the king begged him to spare his life, promising to give him the city of Gaissaria, with all its dependancies. This Otman would not do, and he ordered the king to be beheaded in sight of the people of the city, and ordered that afterwards he should be quartered, each part being fixed on a stake stuck in the ground in sight of the city, and the head on the point of a lance, together with the four quarters. And whilst the king lay before the city, the king's son sent to his father-in-law, the powerful ruler of White Tartary, that he should come to his assistance, because Otman had killed his father and many others, and that he was before the city. And so soon as his father-in-law heard this, he took with him all his people, with their wives, children, and all their cattle, as is the custom of the country, because he intended going to Tamast to deliver the country from Otman, and his people were numbered at forty thousand men, without including women and children. When Otman heard that the Tartar king was approaching, he went with his people to the mountains, where he encamped. The Tartar king encamped before the city, and so soon as Otman heard of it, he took fifteen hundred men and divided them into two parts, and when night came he marched upon them on both sides with loud cries. When the Tartar king heard of this, he thought they wanted to betray him, and fled into the city, which, when his people heard, they also took to flight. Otman pursued them and killed a great many, and captured much booty. They returned to their country, and Otman took with him to the mountain where he had left his cattle, the cattle and the booty that he had taken from them. Before it was day, the Tartar king rode after his people to make them turn back; this they would not do, so he turned back again. Then Otman again lay siege to the city, and invited them to give him the city, and he would do as he had promised. This they would not do, and sent to beg Weyasit to come and drive Otman out of the country, and they would surrender the city to him. Weyasit sent his eldest son, with twenty thousand horsemen and four thousand foot-soldiers, to the help of the town; and I also was in this expedition. And when he heard that the son of Weyasit was coming, he sent his property and cattle to the mountain where he had been, and he himself remained in the plain with one thousand horsemen. Then the king's son sent two thousand horsemen to see if they could find Otman; and when they saw Otman, they attacked each other. And when they saw that they could not overcome him, they sent for assistance. Then came Weyasit's son, with all his people. But when Otman saw him, he rode against him, and would quickly have put him to flight, for the people were not close together. The king's son cried to his people, and they began to fight, and they fought for three hours consecutively. And when they were fighting with each other, four thousand foot-soldiers attacked the tent of Otman, and when he heard this, he sent four hundred horsemen, who, with the assistance of those who kept the goods and cattle, expelled the foot-soldiers out of the tent. Otman went with a force into the mountain, where his property was, and sent it away, and remained during that time before the mountain. Then the king's son appeared before the city, and the citizens opened the gates of Damastchk,

c *

and rode out and asked him to take the city. This he would not do, and sent to his father, that he should come and take the city and territory. He came with one hundred and fifty thousand men, took the city and country, and gave them to his son Machmet, and not to him who had expelled Otman from being king of the city and country.(²)

10.—How Weyasit took a country that belonged to the Sultan.

After Weyasit had installed his son in the kingdom, he sent to the king-sultan in respect to a city called Malathea, (¹) and the country that belonged to the city, because the city and the country belonged to the above-named kingdom which was in the possession of the king-sultan, and therefore required that he should surrender the city of Malathea and the territory, because he had conquered the kingdom. The king-sultan sent word to him that he had won the kingdom by the sword, and he who wished to have it must also win it by the sword. When Weyasit received this answer, he went into the country with two hundred thousand men, and lay siege to the city for two months; and when he found that it would not surrender, he filled up the ditches and surrounded the city with his people, and began to storm. When they saw this they asked for mercy, and gave themselves up. Then he took the city and the country, and occupied it.

At about the same time, the White Tartars besieged the city called Angarus, which belonged to Weyasit; and when he heard of this, he sent to its assistance his eldest son with thirty-two thousand men. He fought a battle, but he was obliged to return to Wyasit, who ordered more men, and sent him back again. But he fought with him, and took the Tartar lord and two vassals, and brought them as prisoners to Weyasit, and thus the White Tartars gave themselves up to Weyasit. He put another lord over them, took the three lords to his capital, and then marched against another city called Adalia,* which belonged to the sultan, and the city is not far from Zypern; and in the country to which the city belongs, there are no other cattle but camels. After Weyasit took the city and the country, the country made him a present of ten thousand camels; and after he occupied the city and the country, he took the camels into his own country.

11.—Of the King-Sultan.

About this time died the king-sultan, named Warchhoch, and his son named Joseph became king; but one of his father's dependants went to war with him for the kingdom. Then Joseph sent to Weyasit, and became reconciled with him, and asked him that he should come to help him. So he sent twenty thousand men to help him, in which expedition I was also. Thus Joseph expelled his rival, and became a powerful king.([1]) After this it was told him, that five hundred of his dependants were against him, and were in favour of his rival. He ordered that they should be taken to a plain, where they were all cut into two parts. Afterwards, we again returned to our lord, Weyasit.

* Adalia or Satalia, on the sea-shore. William of Tyre so called the chief city of Pamphylia. The town lies, as correctly stated, opposite to Cyprus. *N.*

12.—How Temerlin conquered the kingdom of Sebast.

When Weyasit had expelled Otman from Tamast, as has already been stated, he went to his lord named Tämerlin, to whom he was subject, and complained of Weyasit, how he had driven him away from the kingdom of Tamask, which he had conquered, and at the same time asked him to help him to reconquer his kingdom. Tämerlin said that he would send to Weyasit, to restore the country. This he did, but Weyasit sent word that he would not give it up, for as he had won it by the sword, it might as well be his as another's. So soon as Tämerlin heard this, he assembled ten hundred thousand men, and conducted them into the kingdom of Sebast, and lay siege to the capital, before which he remained XXI days, and he undermined the walls of the city in several places, and took the city by force, although there were in it five thousand horsemen sent by Weyasit.([1]) They were all buried alive in this way. When Tämerlin took the city, the governor begged that he would not shed their blood. To this he consented, and so they were buried alive. Then he levelled the city, and carried away the inhabitants into captivity in his own country. There were also nine thousand virgins taken into captivity by Tämerlin to his own country.([2]) Before he took the city, he had at least three thousand men killed. Then he returned to his own country.

13.—Weyasit conquers Lesser Armenia.

Scarcely had Tämerlin returned to his own country, ([1]) than Weyasit assembled three hundred thousand men, and went into Lesser Ermenia and took it from Tämerlin, and took the capital called Ersingen, together with its lord who was named Tarathan, (²) and then went back to his own country. So soon as Tämerlin heard that Weyasit had conquered the said country, he went to meet him with sixteen hundred thousand men; and when Weyasit heard this, he went to meet him with fourteen hundred thousand men. They met near a city called Augury, where they fought desperately. Weyasit had quite thirty thousand men of White Tartary, whom he placed in the van at the battle. They went over to Temerlin; then they had two encounters, but neither could overcome the other. Now Tämerlin had thirty-two trained elephants at the battle, and ordered, after mid-day, that they should be brought into the battle. This was done, and they attacked each other; but Weyasit took to flight, and went with at least one thousand horsemen to a mountain. Tämerlin surrounded the mountain so that he could not move, and took him.* Then he remained eight months in the country, conquered more territory and occupied it, and then went to Weyasit's capital and took him with him, and took his treasure, and silver and gold, as much as one thousand camels could carry; and he would have taken him into his own country, but he died† on the way‡ (³). And so I became Tämerlin's prisoner, and was taken by him to his country. After this I rode after him. What I have described took place during the time that I was with Weyasit.

* July 20th, 1402.
† March 8th, 1403, at Aksheher.
‡ Schiltberger's accounts agree perfectly with the statements made by Byzantine and Eastern historians. We are forced to conclude, after Hammer's searching enquiries, that there is no truth whatever in the story of Bajasid having been confined by Timur in an iron cage. *N.*

14.—How Tämerlin goes to war with the King-Sultan.

After Tämerlin had overcome Weyasit and returned to his own country, he went to war with the king-sultan, who is the chief king among Infidels. He took with him XII hundred thousand men, went into his territory, and lay siege to a city called Hallapp, which contains four hundred thousand houses. Then the lord and governor of the city took with him eighty thousand men, and went out and fought with Tämerlin, but he could not overcome him, and fled again into the city, and many people were killed in his flight. He continued to defend himself, but Tämerlin took a suburb on the fourth day, and the people he found in it he threw into the moat of the city, put timber and mire upon them, and filled the moat in four places. The moat was twelve fathom deep, and [cut] in the solid rock. Then he stormed the city, and took it by assault and captured the governor, and fully occupied the city, and then went to another city called Hrumkula, which surrendered. Then he went to another city called Anthap. There he lay siege for VIIII days, and took it on the tenth day by assault, and pillaged it, and went to another city called Wehessum. There he lay siege for XV days. After that they gave themselves up and he occupied it. The cities I have named are chief cities in Syria.([1]) Then he went to another city called Damaschk; it is the principal capital in the country. When the king-sultan heard that he was laying siege to Tamasch, he sent and begged that he would not injure the city, and spare the temple. To this he consented, and went further on. The temple in the city of Tamasch is so large, that it has externally forty gates. Inside the temple hang twelve thousand lamps, of which number IX thousand are lit daily. But every week, on Friday, all of them are lit. Amongst these lamps are many in gold and silver, made by the order of kings and great lords. So soon as Tämerlin had gone out from the city, the king-sultan left his capital Alchei Terchei, with thirty thousand men, hoping to arrive before Tämerlin took it, and he sent twelve thousand men to Tamaschen. When Tämerlin heard this, he marched towards him, and the king-sultan returned again to his capital. Tämerlin pursued him, and where the king-sultan passed the night, there in the morning he caused the water and the grass to be poisoned; and wherever Tämerlin came, he suffered great losses amongst his people and cattle, and could not overtake him. Then he turned again against Tamaschen and besieged it for III months, but could not take it. During those three months they fought every day, and when the twelve M men saw that they had no assistance from their lord, they asked Tämerlin to be allowed to pass. He consented, and they left the city at night and returned to their lord. Then Tämerlin stormed the city and took it by assault. And now, soon after he had taken the city, came to him the Geit, that is as much as to say a bishop, and fell at his feet, and begged mercy for himself and his priests. Tämerlin ordered that he should go with his priests into the temple; so the priests took their wives, their children and many others, into the temple for protection, until there were thirty thousand young and old. Now Tämerlin gave orders that when the temple was full, the people inside should be shut up in it. This was done. Then wood was placed around the temple, and he ordered it to be ignited, and they all perished in the temple. Then he ordered that each one of his [soldiers] should bring to him the head of a man. This was done, and it took three days; then with these heads were constructed three towers, and the city was pillaged.([2]) After this he went into another country called Scherch,([3]) a country where no cattle are bred, and this country gave itself up. He ordered them to bring food for his people who were famished, although they had been before a city so rich in spices. Then he returned to his country, having left that country and occupied the cities.

15.—How Tämerlin conquered Babiloni.

Now when he returned from the land of the king-sultan, he took ten hundred thousand men with him and marched upon Babilonie. When the king* heard this, he left a garrison in the city and went out of it. Tämerlin besieged it for a whole month, during which time he undermined the walls, took the city and burnt it. Then he had the earth ploughed and barley planted there, because he had sworn that he would destroy the city, so that nobody should know whether there had been houses or no. Then he went to a fortress; it stood in a river, and the king kept his treasure there.([1]) He could not take this fortress, across the water, so he turned away the water, and found under the water three leaden chests full of gold and silver; each chest was two fathoms long, and one fathom broad. The king sank them here, so that if the fortress was taken, the gold would remain. The chests he removed, and he took the fortress and found fifteen men in it. They were hanged. They also found in the fortress four chests full of silver and gold, which he also took away, and then conquered three cities. Then summer began, so that on account of the heat he could not remain in the country.

16.—How Tämerlin conquered Lesser India.([1])

When Tämerlin returned home from Babiloni, he sent word to all in his land that they were to be ready in four

* Sultan Achmed, of the last Ilchans.—See Deguignes, Germ. Trans., iii, 313. *N*.

months, as he wanted to go into Lesser India, distant from his capital a four months' journey. When the time came, he went into Lesser India with four hundred thousand men, and crossed a desert of twenty days' journey; there, is a great want of water, and then he got to a mountain which it took him eight days, before he came out of it. On this mountain there is a path, where camels and horses must be bound to planks and lowered. Then he came to a valley where it is so dark, that people cannot see each other by the light of day, and it is of half a day's journey.(²) Then he came to a high mountainous country, in which he travelled for three days and three nights, and then got to a beautiful plain, where lies the capital of the country. He stopped with his people in the plain, near the wooded mountain, and sent word to the king of the country: Mirttemirgilden, that is as much as to say, Give up thyself, the lord Tämerlin is come.(³) When the king received the message, he sent word to tell him that he would settle with him with the sword. Then he marched against Tämerlin with four hundred thousand men, and with four hundred elephants trained for war; upon each elephant was a turret, in each of which were at least ten armed men. When Tämerlin heard of this, he advanced with his people to meet him; in the mean time the king placed the elephants in the front, and when they engaged, Tämerlin might easily have conquered; but he could not overcome the king, because his horses were afraid of the elephants and would not advance. This went on from morning until mid-day, so that Tämerlin retired and had his counsellors to consult, how the king and his elephants were to be overcome? One named Suleymanschach advised, that camels should be taken and wood fastened on them, and when the elephants advanced, the wood should be ignited, and the camels driven up against the elephants; thus would they be subdued by the fire and the cries of the camels, because the elephants are afraid of fire. Then

Tämerlin took twenty thousand camels and prepared them as above described, and the king came with his elephants in front. Tämerlin went to meet him, and drove the camels up against the elephants, the wood on them being on fire. The camels cried out, and when the elephants saw the fire and heard the great cries, they took to flight, so that none could hold them. When Tämerlin saw this, he pursued them with all his force, and of the elephants many were killed.(⁴) When the king saw this, he went back into his capital. Tämerlin followed him up and besieged the city for ten days. In the mean time the king agreed with him, to give him two zentner of gold of India, which is better than the gold of Arabia, and he also gave him many precious stones, and promised to lend him thirty thousand men whenever he might want them; and so they were reconciled with each other. The king remained in his kingdom, and Tämerlin returned to his country, and took with him one hundred elephants and the riches the king had given him.

17.—How a vassal carried off riches that belonged to Tämerlin.

When Tämerlin returned from Lesser India, he sent one of his vassals named Chebakh, with ten thousand men, to the city of Soltania,*(¹) to bring to him the five-yearly tribute of Perssia and Ermenia which was kept in that city. He came, and took the tribute, and loaded one thousand waggons, and then he wrote to a lord in the country of Massan-

* Sultania, to the north of Kaswin. The construction of this city was begun by Ilchan, or by Argun the Persian viceroy, and completed by Chasan. These powerful despots of Persia wanted to acquire, as is not rarely the case with other despots, immortal fame for themselves, by extorting from their subjects for the purpose of constructing magnificent buildings. Their wishes have not been realised. *N.*

der, who was his friend. He came with fifty thousand men, they made an alliance with each other, and the treasure was taken to Massenderam. When Tämerlin heard of this, he sent a great many people to conquer the above-named country, and bring to him the two lords as prisoners. When the people got to the country, they could not do any harm because of the large forests which surround it, and they sent to Tämerlin for more people. He sent other seventy thousand men to clear the woods and make a road. They did so for ten miles, but could not conquer the territory. They sent to tell Tämerlin, and he ordered them to go home, which they did, without having done anything.

18.—How Tämerlin caused MMM children to be killed.

Then he went into a kingdom called Hisspahan and made for the capital, Hisspahan, and required it to surrender. They gave themselves up, and went to him with their wives and children. He received them graciously, occupied the city with six thousand of his people, and took away with him the lord of the city, whose name was Schachister. And so soon as the city heard that Tämerlin was gone out of the country, they closed all the gates and killed the six thousand men. When Tämerlin knew this, he returned to the city and besieged it for xv days, but he could not take it, and made peace with them on condition that they should lend him the archers that were in the city, for an expedition; after that, he should send them back. They sent to him twelve thousand archers; he cut off all their thumbs, and forced them back into the city and himself entered it. He assembled all the citizens, and ordered all those over fourteen years to be beheaded, and the boys under XIII years he ordered to be spared, and with the heads was constructed a tower in the centre of the city; then he ordered the women and children to be taken to a plain outside the city, and ordered the children under seven years of age to be placed apart, and ordered his people to ride over these same children. When his counsellors and the mothers of the children saw this, they fell at his feet, and begged that he would not kill them. He would not listen, and ordered that they should be ridden over; but none would be the first to do so. He got angry, and rode himself [amongst them] and said: "Now I should like to see who will not ride after me?" Then they were all obliged to ride over the children, and they were all trampled upon.(¹) There were seven thousand. Then he set fire to the city, and took the other women and children into his own city; and then went to his capital called Semerchant, where he had not been for twelve years.

19.—Tämerlin wants to go to war with the Great Chan.

At about this time, the great Chan, king of Chetey, sent an ambassador with four hundred horsemen, to demand of him the tribute which he had forgotten, and kept for five years. Tämerlin took the ambassador with him, until he came to his above-named capital, and sent him from there to tell his lord, that he would neither pay tribute nor be subject to him, and that he should himself pay him a visit. Then he sent messengers all over his country that they should prepare, as he wished to advance on Cetey, and taking eighteen hundred thousand men, he marched for a whole month. He then came to a desert that was seventy days journey across; there he travelled ten days, and lost many people there for want of water. Great harm also befel his horses and other cattle, because it was very cold in that country;(¹) and when he perceived his great losses amongst his people and cattle, he turned and went back to his capital and fell ill.

20.—Of Tämerlin's death.

It is to be noted, that three causes made Tämerlin fret, so that he became ill, and died of that same illness. The first cause was grief that his vassal had escaped with the tribute; the other it is to be noted was, that Thämerlin had three wives, and that the youngest, whom he loved very much, had been intimate with one of his vassals whilst he was away. When Tämerlin came home, his eldest wife told him that his youngest wife had cared for one of his vassals, and had broken her vow. He would not believe it. She came to him and said: "Come to her and order her to open her trunk: you will find a ring with a precious stone, and a letter which he has sent to her." Thämerlin sent to tell her that he would pass the night with her, and when he came into her room, he told her to open her trunk. This was done, and he found the ring and the letter. He sat down near her, and asked whence the ring and letter had come to her? She fell at his feet, and begged he would not be angry, because one of his vassals had sent them to her without any right.* After this he went out of the room, and ordered that she should be immediately beheaded. This was done. He then sent five thousand horsemen after this same vassal, that they might bring him as a prisoner; but he was warned by the commander who was sent after him, and the vassal took with him five hundred men, his wife and children, and fled to the country of Wassandaran. There Tämerlin could not get at him. It fretted him so much that he had killed his wife, and that the vassal had escaped, that he died, and was

* " One alle Geüard."—See chap. 65, note 3.

buried in the country with great magnificence. Be it also known that, after he was buried, the priests that belong to the temple, heard him howl every night during a whole year. His friends gave large alms, that he should cease his howlings. But this was of no use. They asked advice of their priests, and went to his son and begged that he would set free the prisoners taken by his father in other countries, and especially those that were in his capital, who were all craftsmen he had brought to his capital, where they had to work. He let them go, and so soon as they were free, Tämerlin did not howl any more. All that is written above, happened during the six years that I was with Tämerlin,* and I also was present.

21.—Of the sons of Tämerlin.

You should know that Tämerlin left two sons. The eldest was named Scharoch, who had a son to whom Tämerlin gave his capital and the country that belonged to it, and to each of his two sons, Scharoch and Miraschach, he gave a kingdom in Persia, and other large territories that belonged to them. After the death of Tämerlin, I came to his son named Scharoch, who had the kingdom of Horossen, the capital of which is called Herren. Here Schiltberger remained with Miraschach, the son of Tämerlin.

The younger son of Tämerlin had in Persia a kingdom called Thaures, and after his father's death came a vassal named Joseph, who expelled Miraschach from his kingdom. He sent to his brother Scharoch, and asked him to help him to recover his kingdom. His brother came with eighty thousand men, and sent thirty thousand men to his brother,

* This is an error in dates, as regards his period of service under Bajasid. Schiltberger was with Timur from July 20th, 1402, only. *N.*

that he might expel the vassal, and kept to himself forty-two thousand men. With these he marched against Joseph, who, on learning this, went to meet him with sixty thousand men, and they fought a whole day, without either the one or the other being overcome. Then Mirenschach asked his brother, Scharoch, to come with the rest of his people. He came. Then he fought with Joseph and drove him away, and Mirenschach returned to his kingdom. There were also two countries that were subdued by Joseph; the one was called Churten,* the other was Lesser Armeny. Scharoch went into these countries and conquered them, and bestowed them on his brother, and then returned into his own country, leaving, for the assistance of his brother, twenty thousand men from amongst his people, with whom I also remained. (^{1})

22.—How Joseph caused Mirenschach to be beheaded, and took possession of all his territory.

After Mirenschach had remained in peace for one year, Joseph entered his country with a large number of people, which, when he perceived, he went to meet him with fully four hundred thousand men. They met each other at a plain called Scharabach,†(^{1}) and fought together for two days. Mirenschach was overcome and made a prisoner.

* Kourdistan.
† Karabagh, to the West of the Caspian Sea. Karabagh, " Black Garden", is the name given by the Persians and Turks to the entire district extending from Shirwan, on the west, to that point where the Kur and Araxes unite. In ancient times the Armenians called this region Arzach. The city of Karabagh is the birth-place of the Armenian historian, Thomas Medzopezi. Indschidschean is unable to state on good grounds, why this district and place are so called. He holds, on the contrary, that Karabagh is the same as that called Chachchach by Agathangelos and older Armenian chroniclers. N.

Soon afterwards, Joseph ordered he should be beheaded. It is to be noted why Joseph killed Mirenschach. Joseph had a brother named Miseri, who killed a brother of Mirenschach, called Zychanger. When they met in a battle, Mirenschach took Miseri and killed him in prison, so that Mirenschach also was put to death; (²) and Joseph had Mirenschach's head stuck on a spear, and taken to the city called Thaures after the kingdom, and showed it there, that they might give themselves up the sooner. When they saw that their lord was dead, they gave themselves up; and then he took the city and the whole kingdom with all its dependencies.

23.—How Joseph vanquished a king and beheaded him.

And now when Joseph had taken the kingdom, the king of Babilonie sent to him that he should give up the kingdom, as it belonged to his own kingdom, and his residence was in it; and because it was not right that he should keep the kingdom, as he was not noble and would be a bad vassal. Joseph sent back word that there must be a ruler in the kingdom, and that he should confirm it to him, and sent to say that he would mint in his name, and observe all that was due to him. The king would not do so, because he had a son to whom he wished to give the kingdom; and he attacked Joseph with fifty thousand men. Joseph went to meet him with sixty thousand men, and they fought with each other at a plain called Achtum.* (¹) The king fled to a city near the plain. Joseph followed, and took the king and beheaded him, and occupied the kingdom as before.

* In all probability Nachdschowan, or Nachidschewan, the Naxuana of Ptolemy. The plain and the town are of the same name. *N*.

24.—How Schiltberger came to Aububachir.

And after that Miraschach, Tämerlin's son, was taken in battle and beheaded, I came to his son Aububachir, with whom I remained four years. And after the king of Babiloni was also killed by Joseph, as is already written, Abubachir took a country called Kray; it belonged to the kingdom of Babiloni. Abubachir had also a brother called Mansur,(1) who had a country called Erban. He sent [word] that he should come to him. This, Mansur would not do; so he went and took him, put him into prison and strangled him, and took his country. It is also to be noted, that Abubachir was so strong, that he shot through a ploughshare with an Infidel bow; the iron went through, and the shaft remained in the ploughshare. This ploughshare was sent as a marvel to Thämerlin's capital, called Samerchant, and fixed to the gate. When the king-sultan heard of his strength, he sent to him a sword that weighed twelve pounds. It was worth one thousand guldens. And when the sword was brought to him, he ordered that an ox, three years old, should be brought to him, as he wished to try the sword. When the ox came, he cut it into two parts at one blow. This happened during Tämerlin's lifetime.

25.—Of a king's son.

With Abubachar, was the son of a king of Great Tartary. To him came messengers, wanting him to go home, that he might be responsible for the kingdom. He asked Abubachir to allow him to go; this he did, and so he went home with six hundred horsemen; I was one of five [Christians?] who went with him into Great Tartary. You must notice through which countries he passed. First, through the country called Strana, where silk grows; then through a country called Gursey, where there are Christians, and they believe in the Christian faith, and Saint Jörig is patron there. After that, he passed through a country called Lochinschan; there, also, silk grows; then through another called Schurban, where silk grows of which the good stuffs are made at Tamasch and at Kaffer, and also at Wursa, the capital of the Infidels, situated in Turkey; this silk is also taken to Venice and to Lickcha, where good velvet is worked; but it is an unhealthy country. Afterwards he passed through a country called Samabram;(¹) then through one called in the Tartar tongue, Temurtapit,*(²) which is as much as to say, the Iron Gate. This divides Persia and Tartary. Then he passed through a city called Origens; it is powerful, and lies in the middle of a river called Edil.(³) Then he travelled through a mountainous country called Setzulet, where there are many Christians who have a bishop there; their priests belong to the Order of the Shoeless, who do not know Latin, and they sing and read their prayers in the Tartar tongue. It is found that thus the laity become stronger in the faith, and also many Infidels are confirmed in the Christian faith, because they understand the words that the priests sing and read. After that, he went into Great Tartaria, and came to the lord named Edigi, who had written and sent messengers to him, as he wanted him to come and rule the kingdom. And when he arrived, Edigi was waiting, having prepared to go into a country called Ibissibur.* It is to be noted, that it is the

* Derbend, *i.e.*, the closed gate or barricade, called by the Turks Timurcapi, or the Iron Gate. *N*.

† This, undoubtedly, is Siberia, here mentioned for the first time. It so happens that the name of Siberia appears in the Russian annals of about the same period, 1450.— See Lehrberg's *Zur Erläuterung der älteren Geschichte von Russland*, St. Petersburg, 1816. Schiltberger probably looks upon the Buddhists as Christians, as has frequently been the case. *N*.

custom for the king, in Great Tartary, to have a Chief to rule over him, who can elect or depose a king, and has also power over vassals. Now at that time Edigi was the Chief. The vassals in Tartary wander about in winter and summer, with their wives and children, and their cattle, and when the king encamps, there must be erected one hundred thousand huts. Now when the son of the above-named king of Tartary, and who was named Zegre, (⁴) had come to Edigi, he went with him into the above-named country, Ibissibur, and they travelled two months before they arrived there. There is a mountain in that country, which is thirty-two days' journey in extent. The people there, themselves say, that at the extremity of the mountain is a desert, and that the said desert is the end of the earth; and in this same desert nobody can have an habitation, because of snakes and wild beasts. On the same mountain there are savages, who are not like other people, and they live there. They are covered all over the body with hair, except the hands and face, and run about like other wild beasts in the mountain, and also eat leaves and grass, and anything they can find. The lord of the country sent to Edigi, a man and a woman from among these savages, that had been taken in the mountain.(⁵) The horses are of the same size as donkeys, and there are many wild beasts that are not in Germany, and of which I do not know the names. There are also in the above-named country, dogs, that go in carts and in sledges; they are also made to carry luggage, and are as large as donkeys. Dogs are eaten in this country. It is also to be noted, that the people in this country believe in Jesus Christ like the III kings who came and brought offerings to Christ at Bethlaem, and saw him lying in the manger; and they have a picture, which is a representation of our Lord in a manger, as the three holy kings saw him, when they brought offerings to him. They have this also in their temples, and say their prayers before it; and the people who are of this faith are called Ugine.(⁶) In Tartaria there are many people of this religion. It is also the custom in the country, that when a young man, who has not had a wife, dies, he is dressed in his best clothes, and players carry him, and he is laid on a bier, and a canopy is placed over him. And all the young people, also dressed in their best clothes, go before, and the players with them. The father and mother, and friends, also follow the bier, and it is taken to the grave by the young people and by the players, with singing and much merry-making. But the father and mother and friends, go near the bier and weep; and when they have buried him, they bring their food and drink, and the young people and the players sit down, and eat and drink by the grave with much rejoicing. The father and mother and friends, sit on one side, and lament, and when they have done, they take the father and mother to the place where they live, and there they lament; and so they end the ceremony which was as if they had had a wedding, because he had no wife. In this country they have nothing but millet, and they do not eat bread. All this I have seen, and was there with the above-named king's son, Zeggra.

26.—How one lord succeeds another lord.

And after that Edigi and Zeggra had subdued the country Ibissibur, they went into the country Walher, and conquered it also, and afterwards they went back to their country. At that time, there was a king in Great Tartaria who was called Sedichbechan, and kan is as much as to say a king, in the Tartar tongue. When he heard that Edigi had come into his country, he took to flight. Edigi sent after him, that he should be brought as a prisoner, but he was killed in a battle.(¹) Then Edigi elected a king named

Polet, who reigned one year and a half.(²) Then there was one named Segelalladin, who expelled Polet; and after this, Pollet's brother was king, and he reigned fourteen months. Then came his brother, named Thebachk, who fought with him for the kingdom, and killed him,(³) and then there was no king. But he had a brother called Kerumberdin, who became king, and reigned five months. Then came his brother Theback, and he expelled Kerimberdin and became king. Then came Edigi and my lord Zeggra, and they drove away the king, and Edigi made my lord the king as he had promised. He was king for nine months. Then came one named Machmet, and he fought with Zeggra and with Edigi. Zeggra fled to a country called Distihipschach, and Machmet became king. Then came one named Waroch; he expelled Machmet and became king. After that, Machmet recovered, and he drove away Waroch and was again king. Then came one named Doblabardi, who drove away Machmet and became king, and was king for three days only. Then came the same Warach, who expelled Dobladbardi, and again became king. Then came my lord Machmet, and he overcame Warach and again became king. After that, came my lord Zeggra, and he fought with Machmet and was killed.(⁴)

27.—Of an Infidel woman, who had four thousand maidens.

During the time that I was with Zeggra, there came to Edigi, and also to Zeggra, a Tartar woman named Sadurmelickh,(¹) with four thousand maidens and women. She was powerful, and her husband had been killed by a Tartar king. She wanted to be revenged, and therefore came to Edigi, so that he should assist her to expel the king. And you must also know, that she and her women rode to battle and fought with the bow, as well as men; and when the women rode to battle, they had on one side a sword, and on the other a bow. In a battle she had with a king, there was the king's cousin who had killed the husband of this woman, and he was made a prisoner. He was brought before the woman; she ordered him to kneel, and drew her sword, and cut off his head at one blow, and said: "Now am I revenged." I was present there, and I also saw this.

28.—In what countries I have been.

Now I have described the battles and the fights which took place, during the time that I was with the Infidels. Now I will also write and name the countries that I have been in, since I left Bavaria. At first I went into Ungeren, before the great expedition against the Infidels. There I remained ten months, and after that we went amongst the Infidels as is described. I have also been in Wallachy and in its two chief cities; one is called Agrich,* the other Türckisch; also in a city called Übereil, situated on the Tunow. There were the kocken([1]) and the galleys, in which merchants bring their goods from the land of the Infidels. It is also to be noted, that the people in Little and in Great Walachy hold to the Christian faith, and they also speak a particular language; they also allow their hair and beard to grow, and never cut it. I have also been in Little Walachy, and in Sybenbürgen which is a German country; the capital of this country is called Hermenstat. Also in Zwürtzenland; the capital is called Bassaw.†([2]) These

* Agrisch, now better known as Ardschisch in Walachia. For Türckisch we should read Bukurescht. *F.*

† Brasowa or Burzelland in Siebenbürgen. Wurzerland was also written Burzerland and Burzelland. It is to the south-east of Siebenbürgen, its capital being Cronstadt, Brasowa in Slav, called Bassaw by Schiltberger. *F.*

are the countries on this side of the Tonow, in which I have been.

29.—In which countries I have been, that lay between the Tonow and the sea.

Now will be noted the countries that are between the Tunow and the sea, in which I have been. First, I have been in three countries, which three countries are all called Pulgrey. The first Pulgrey is where people cross from Hungern to the Iron Gate; the capital is called Pudem. The other Pulgery lies opposite to Walachy; the capital is called Ternau. The third Pulgery lies where the Tunow flows into the sea; the capital is called Kallacercka.*(¹) I have also been in Greece; the capital is Adranapoli, which city has fifty thousand houses. There is also a large city by the White Sea in Greece, and it is called Salonikch; (²) and in this city lies Saint Sanctiniter, from whose grave oil flows.†(³) In the middle of the church there is a well, and on his day the well is full of water, but it is dry on every other day in the year. I have been in this city. There is also a mighty city in Greece, called Seres; and all the territory that lies between the Tünow and the sea, belongs to the Turkish‡ king. There is a city and a fortress called Chalipoli; there the high sea is crossed. I myself crossed there, over to Turkey. This same sea is crossed to go to Constantinoppel. I was three months in the said city where

* Kallacercka is the old Bulgarian port Callat, Callatis, or Callantra, to the north of Varna, which has taken the place of Callat. *F.*

† The miracle of the exudation of oil from the body of Demetrius, is related by Nicetas, i, 7, 193, Edit., Paris. The similarity in the statements made by the Bavarian and by Nicetas, leave no room whatever for doubting that this is the correct name of the Saint, and not that of Theodora, as given by a transcriber's error in the Anagnosta, *De excidio Thessalonicensi. Il.*

‡ "Tütschen", in the text.

people go over into Great Turkey. The capital of Turkey is called Wursa. The city contains two hundred thousand houses, and eight hospitals where poor people are received, whether they be Christians, Infidels, or Jews. Three hundred castles are dependant on this city, without excepting the chief towns which are hereafter described. The first is called Asia,*(¹) in which is the grave of St. John the Evangelist; it is in a fertile country called Edein in the Infidel tongue; but the natives call it Hohes. The other city and country that belongs to it, is called Ismira, and Saint Nicholas was bishop there.(⁵) There is also a city and a country called Maganasa,(⁶) which is a fertile country. There is also a city called Donguslu; (⁷) the country that belongs to it is called Serochou, and there the trees bear fruit twice yearly. There is a city called Kachey, situated high up a mountain, and has a fertile country called Keunan. There is also a city called Anguri; it has a fertile country also called Siguri.† In this city are many Christians who hold to the Ermenian faith; and they have a cross in their church that shines day and night; even Infidels go to the church, and they call the cross the bright stone. The Infidels also wanted to carry it off and put it in their temple, but whoever touches it, his hands become distorted. There is also a city called Wegureisari,(⁸) and the country is called by the same name. There is also a country called Karaman, the chief city being called Laranda. There is also in this country a city called Könia, in which lies the saint, Schenisis, who was first an Infidel priest, and was secretly baptised; and when his end approached, received from an Armenian

---

* Asia is a mistake for Ephesus. To this belongs the passage, "hie zeland heiszet es Hoches". The Turkish Aisulugh, *i.e.*, "Ἅγιος·Θεολόγος, as the Byzantines called St. John. *F.* and *H.*

† Printed editions give Sigmei, which is nearer to the true reading, Sultan Öni or Ögi. Anguri or Ancyra, belongs to the province of Sultan Ögi or Öni. *F.*

priest, the body of God in an apple. He has worked great miracles. There is also a city called Gassaria, and the country is of the same name. In this country Saint Basil was bishop.(⁹) I have also been in Sebast, which was once a kingdom. There is a city on the Black Sea called Samson; it is in a fertile country called Zegnikch. The above-named countries and cities all belong to Turkey, and I have been in them all. Item, there is a country called Zepun; it is on the Black Sea. In this country they sow millet only, and they make their bread of this millet. There is the kingdom of Tarbesanda; it is a small and well protected country, and fruitful in vineyards, and is on the Black Sea, not far from a city called Kureson (¹⁰) in the Greek tongue.

30.—Of the castle of the sparrow-hawk, and how it is guarded.

There is on a mountain a castle, called that of the sparrow-hawk. Within, is a beautiful virgin, and a sparrow-hawk on a perch. Whoever goes there and does not sleep but watches for three days and three nights, whatever he asks of the virgin, that is chaste, that she will grant to him. And when he finishes the watch, he goes into the castle and comes to a fine palace, where he sees a sparrow-hawk standing on a perch; and when the sparrow-hawk sees the man, he screams, and the virgin comes out of her chamber, welcomes him and says: "Thou hast served me and watched for three days and three nights, and whatever thou now askest of me that is pure, that will I grant unto thee." And she does so. But if anybody asks for something that exhibits pride, impudence, or avarice, she curses him and his offspring, so that he can no longer attain an honourable position.

31.—How a poor fellow watched the sparrow-hawk.

There was also once a good poor fellow, who watched for three days and three nights before the castle; and when he had watched, he went into the palace, and when the sparrow-hawk saw him, he screamed. The virgin came out of her room and welcomed him, and said: "What dost thou require of me. Whatever is of this world and that is honourable, I will grant unto thee." He asked her for nothing more than that he and his family might live with honour; this was granted. There also came the son of a king of Armenia, who also watched for three days and three nights. After that, he went into the palace where stood the sparrow-hawk. The sparrow-hawk screamed, the virgin came out, welcomed him and asked: "What dost thou want that is of this world and that is honourable." He asked for nothing, and said he was the son of a mighty king of Armenia, and had silver and gold enough, and also precious stones, but he had no wife, and he asked her to be his wife. She answered him and said: "Thy proud spirit that thou hast, must be broken in thee and in all thy power"; and she cursed him and all his kindred. There also went a lord of the Order of St. John, who also watched and went into the palace. The virgin came out, and asked him also what he desired. He asked her for a purse that would never be empty, which was granted. But after this, she cursed him and said: "The avarice thou hast shewn, brings great evil to thee. Therefore I curse thee, so that thy order may diminish and not increase." Then he left her.([1])

32.—More about the castle of the sparrow-hawk.

During the time that I and my companions were there, we asked a man to take us to the castle, and gave him money; and when we got to the place, one of my companions wanted to remain and keep watch. He who brought us advised him against it, and said that if he did not carry out the watch, he would be lost, and nobody would know where he went; the castle is also hidden by trees, so that nobody knows the way to it. It is also forbidden by the Greek priests, and they say that the devil has to do with it, and not God. So we went on to a city called Kereson. There is also a country that belongs to the above-named kingdom, called Lasia,(¹) and it is fertile in vineyards. Greeks are in that country. I have also been in Lesser Armenia; the capital is Ersinggan. There is also a city called Kayburt, *(²) and it has a fertile country. Also a city called Kamach,(³) situated on a high mountain, and below the mountain flows a river called the Eufrates; it is one of the rivers that flows out of Paradise. This river also flows through Lesser Armenia, and then courses through a desert ten days' journey across; then it is lost in a marsh, so that nobody knows where it goes.(⁴) It courses also through Persia. There is also a country called Karasser; it is fertile in vineyards.(⁵) There is also a country called Black Turkey; the capital is called Hamunt, and the people are warlike.(⁶) There is also a country called Churt, the capital of which is Bestan.(⁷) Item, a kingdom called Kursi, where the people hold to the Christian faith, have a distinct language and are a warlike people. There is a country called Abkas, its capital Zuchtun;(⁸) it is an unhealthy country, and men and women wear flat caps on their heads, which they do because the place is unhealthy. There is also a small country called Megral, the capital is Kathon,†(⁹) and in which country they hold to the Greek faith. Also a country called Merdin;(¹⁰) this is a kingdom where there are Infidels. I have been in all the above-named countries, and have learnt their peculiarities.

    * Baiburt. *N*. Byburt, in edition of 1811.
    † Possibly Gori in Mingrelia. *N*.

33.—In which countries silk is grown, and of Persia and of other kingdoms.

The chief city of all the kingdoms of Persia is called Thaures.(¹) The king of Persia has a larger revenue from the city of Thaures, than has the most powerful king in Christendom, because a great many merchants come to it. There is also a kingdom in Persia, the capital of which is called Soltania. There is also a city called Rei,(²) in a large country where they do not believe in Machmet as do other Infidels. They believe in a certain Aly who is a great persecutor of the Christian faith; and those of this doctrine are called Raphak.* (³) There is also a city called Nachson; (⁴) it lays near the mountain where the ark stood in which was Noah, and the country is fertile. In it are also three cities, one called Maragara,(⁵) the other Gelat,(⁶) and the third Kirna.(⁷) All three are in a fertile country. There is also, on a mountain, a city called Meya; it is a bishop's see where they hold to the Roman religion; the priests are of the Order of Preachers, and sing in the Armenian tongue.(⁸) There is a rich country called Gilan, where rice and cotton only is grown, and the people wear knitted shoes. There is a large city called Ress,(⁹) in a good country where good silk kerchiefs are made. Also a city called Strawba,(¹⁰) in a good country. Another called Antioch ;(¹¹) the city wall is stained with the blood of Christians, so that it is red. And a city called Aluitze.† (¹²) Tämerlin besieged it for sixteen years before he took it. There is also a country called Massandaran, which is so wooded, that nobody can go into it. There is a city called Scheckhy; it is in a fertile coun-

---

* Raschedi. *N.*

† This is the castle of Alandschik, mentioned by Scherifeddin.—*Hist. de Timurbec,* ii, 391. *H.*

try near the White Sea.*(¹³) In this country also is silk grown. Item, a country called Schuruan, and the capital is called Schomachy; it is a hot and unhealthy country, but the best silk is grown there. There is also a city called Hispahan, which is in a good country. There is also in Persia the kingdom Horoson,† and its capital is called Hore,‡(¹⁴) which has three hundred thousand houses. In this same country and kingdom, during the time that I was amongst the Infidels, there was a man three hundred and fifty years old. So the Infidels said. The nails on his hands were one inch in length, his eyebrows hung down from his eyes over his cheeks. He was without teeth, which had fallen out twice, and for the third time two grew, but they were weak and not as strong as they should be, and he could not masticate nor eat with them; they had to feed him. The hair in his ears went down to his jaw; the beard reached to his knees. He had no hair on his head, and could not speak, but he made himself understood with signs. They were obliged to carry him as he could not walk. This man was held to be a saint by the Infidels, and they went to him on a pilgrimage as people do to a saint, and said that Almighty God had chosen him, because for a thousand years no man had lived so long as this man; and who honours him, honours Almighty God, who had wrought such miracles and signs in him. This man was called Phiradamschyech.(¹⁵) There is a city called Schiras; it is large and in a good country, where no Christian is allowed to trade, especially in the city. A city called Kerman (¹⁶) in a good country, and a city called Keschou which lies near the sea; there pearls grow, and it is a good country. Item, a city called Hognus; it is large and lies near the sea where one goes to Great India, and great merchandise comes there from India. It

---

* By White Sea is here understood (in contradistinction to the Black) the Caspian, and Scherki is intended to indicate its western coast. *H.*

† Chorasan. *N.* ‡ Herat. *N.*

is a good country, wherein are found many precious stones which are peculiar to it. There, also, is the city called Kaff,(¹⁷) also a good country, where all kinds of spices are found, and whence also one goes to Great India. There is a country called Walaschoen; it has a high mountain where many precious stones are found; but nobody can take them because of the serpents and wild beasts. When it rains, it is the torrent that brings them down, then come the experts who know them, and pick them out of the mud. There are also unicorns in those mountains.(¹⁸)

34.—Of the tower of Babilony that is of such great height.

I have also been in the kingdom of Babilonien. Babilonien is called Waydat in the Infidel tongue. The great Babilonie was surrounded by a wall, twenty-five leagues broad, and one league is three Italian miles; the wall was two hundred cubits high and fifty cubits thick, and the river Euffrates courses through the middle of the city; but it is now all in ruins, and there is no longer any habitation in it. The tower of Babilonien is distant fifty four stadia, and four stadia is an Italian mile, and in several places it is x leagues in length and in breadth. The tower is in the desert of Arabia, on the road when one goes into the kingdom of Kalda; but none can get there because of the dragons and serpents, and other hurtful reptiles, of which there are many in the said desert. The tower was built by a king who is called in the Infidel tongue, Marburtirudt.(¹) It is also to be noted, that a league is three Lombard miles, and four stadia is one Italian mile. One Italian mile should have one thousand full paces, and one pace should have v feet,* and

* "schuch", in text.

one foot should have nine inches, and one inch is the first member of the thumb.(²) Now I will also take note of New Babilonien. New Babilonien is separated from Great Babilony by a river called Schatt; (³) it is a large river, and in it are many sea monsters that come from the Indian sea. Near the river grows a fruit tree called the date, but the Infidels call it kiuna,(⁴) and nobody can pick the fruit until the storks come and drive away the serpents, which live under the tree and on it; for this reason nobody can get the fruit which grows twice during the year. It is also to be noted, that in the city of Babilony two languages are spoken, the Arabic and Persian. There is also a garden in Babilony, in which are all kinds of beasts; this garden is ten miles long and enclosed by a wall, so that none can get out. In this garden, the lions have a place to themselves in which they can move about. I have also seen the garden. In this kingdom the people are not warlike.(⁵) Item, I have also been in Lesser India, which is a fine kingdom. The capital is called Dily. In this country are many elephants, and animals called surnasa, which is like a stag, but it is a tall animal, and has a long neck four fathoms in length or longer. It has long fore legs, and the hinder are short.(⁶) There are many animals in Lesser India. There are also many parrots, ostriches, and lions. There are also many other animals and birds, of which I cannot give the names. There is also a country called Zekatay;(⁷) the capital is called Samerchant, and it is a large and mighty city. In this country the language is distinct; it is half Turkish and half Persian, and the people are warlike. In this country they do not eat bread. It is also to be noted, that an Infidel lord named Tämerlin had conquered all the country during the time that I was with him. I have been in all those countries; but he conquered many other countries in which I have not been.

35.—Of Great Tartaria.(¹)

I have also been in Great Tartaria, and of the custom of the country it is to be noted, first, that nothing besides millet is sown. They do not eat bread, and they do not drink wine, but they drink the milk of mares and of camels, and they also eat camel and horse flesh. It is also to be noted, that the king of these countries and his vassals pass winter and summer in the fields, with their wives and children, with cattle and all that belongs to them; and they go from one pasturage to the other, because it is a flat country. It is also to be noted, that when they choose a king, they take him and seat him on white felt, and raise him in it three times.(²) Then they lift him up and carry him round the tent, and seat him on a throne, and put a golden sword in his hand. Then he must be sworn as is the custom. It is also to be noted, that when they eat or drink, they sit on the ground, as all Infidels do. There is not a more warlike people among the Infidels than the Great* Tartars, who can fight and perform journeys as they do. I myself have seen them bleed [their horses] and drink the blood after they have cooked it. This they do when they are in want of food. I have also seen when they are long on a journey, that they take a piece of flesh, cut it into slices, place it under the saddle, and ride on it, and eat it when they were hungry; but they salt it first and think that it will not spoil, because it becomes dry from the warmth of the horse, and becomes tender under the saddle from riding, after the juice has gone out of it. This they do when they have no time to prepare their food. It is also the custom, that when the king rises in the morning, they bring to him some mare's milk in a golden goblet, which he drinks fasting.

* The word is "roten" in the text, doubtlessly for "grossen".

36.—The countries in which I have been, that belong to Tartary.

Here is to be noted in which countries I have been, that belong to Great Tartary. A country called Horosaman;* the name of the capital is Orden, and it lies in a river called Edil, which is a great river.([1]) There is also a country called Bestan; its capital is Zulat, and it is a mountainous country. Item, a city called Haitzicherchen, which is a large city,([2]) and in a good country. Another city called Sarei; there, is the residence of the kings of the Tartars. There is also a city called Bolar, in which are different kinds of beasts.([3]) Also a city called Ibissibur,([4]) and a city Asach, which the Christians call Alathena.([5]) It has a river, called Tena, and much cattle. They send large kocken and galleys full of fish from this country, and they go to Venice, Genoa, and the islands that are in the sea. Item, there is a country called Ephepstzach; its capital is Vulchat.†([6]) In this country every kind of corn is cultivated. A city called Kaffa, which lies by the Black Sea, and is surrounded by two walls. Within one wall are six thousand houses, in which are Italians, Greeks, and Armenians; it is a chief city on the Black Sea, and has within the outer walls, xi thousand houses, in which are many Christians; Romans, Greeks, Armenians, and Syrians. There are also three bishops; a Roman, a Greek, and an Armenian. There are also many Infidels who have their particular temple. The city has four towns subject to it; they are by the sea. There are also two kinds of Jews in the city, and they have two synagogues, and four thousand houses are in the suburbs.([7]) Item, a city called Karckeri,([8])

* Chowaresm, whence we have Chiwa, its capital being Orgens or Urgendsch. *N.*

† Selgath or Sorgathi, which Abulfeda calls Crimea or the Fortress, whence the entire Tauric peninsula has received its name. Schiltberger is wrong in saying that it was the capital of Kiptschak. *N.*

E

in a good country called Sudi; but the Infidels call it
That;(⁹) there are Christians of the Greek faith in it, and
there are good vineyards. It lies near the Black Sea, and
in this country Saint Clement was thrown into the sea.
Close by, is a city, called in the Infidel tongue, Serucherman.(¹⁰) Item, a country called Starchas, which also lies
by the Black Sea, where the people are of the Greek faith;
but they are a wicked people, because they sell their own
children to the Infidels, and steal the children of other
people and sell them; they are also highway robbers, and
have a peculiar language. It is also their custom, that when
one is killed by lightning, they lay him in a box and put it
on a high tree. Then all the people in the neighbourhood
come, and bring their food and drink under the tree; they
dance and enjoy themselves under it; they kill oxen and
lambs, and give them away for the sake of God. This they
do for three successive days, and at the end of a year they
come to where the dead man lies, near the tree, and again do
what they did before, until the body putrefies. This they
do, because they suppose that a man struck by lightning is
a saint.(¹¹) Item, the kingdom of Rewschen, which is tributary to the Tartar king. It is to be noted, that there are three
tribes amongst the Great* Tartars. One is called Kayat,† the
other Inbu,‡ the third Mugal.(¹²) It is also to be noted, that
Tartary is a three months journey in extent, in which no wood
or stones are to be found, only grass and shrubs. The countries described all belong to Great Tartary, in all of which I
have been. I have also been in Arabia; there the capital is
called in the Infidel tongue, Missir.§ The city in this kingdom has twelve thousand streets, and each street has twelve
thousand houses. In the city, is the residence of the king-

* The word "roten" is here repeated. See p. 48.
† Kajat, Kerait. *N*.　　　　　　　　　　　　‡ Uighur. *N*.
§ Missir, Miser, we are informed in chap. 40 and chap. 44, was called
Cair by the Christians; we should therefore here read Egypt for Arabia.

sultan, who is king over all Infidel kings, and lord of all Infidels. He is a mighty lord in silver and gold, and in precious stones, and has daily twenty thousand men at his court.(¹³) It is also to be noted, that no person can be made king-sultan unless he has been sold.(¹⁴)

37.—How many kings-sultan there were, whilst I was amongst the Infidels.

You should know, and take note, how many kings-sultan there were during the time that I was there. The first king-sultan was named Marochloch ; then there was one named Mathas, king; he was made a prisoner, and placed between two planks and sawn in two parts, lengthways. After him, was a king named Jusuphda, with whom I was for eight months; he was made a prisoner and beheaded. After him was one named Zechem ; then one called Schyachin, who was fixed on an iron spike; for it is the custom in this kingdom, that when two fight for that kingdom, whichever overcomes the other and brings him to prison, takes him when convenient and dresses him like a king, and leads him to a house made for the purpose, in which there are iron spikes, and he is put on one of those spikes, so that it comes through at the neck, and on the spike he must rot.(¹) There was a certain king named Malleckchafcharff; this king invited to a marriage, [those] in Rom, in all Christendom, and also in all lands. Now you must note what is his title and superscription.(²) We, Balmander,* the all-powerful of Carthago,(³) Sultan of the noble Saracens, Lord of Zuspillen, Lord of the highest God† in Jherusalem,(⁴) in Capadocie,(⁵) the Lord of Jordan, the Lord of the East whence flows the boiling sea; the Lord of Bethlahen where your

* This letter and all these titles are inventions, related to Schiltberger in all probability by the Armenian. *N.*
† "ain herr des obristen gots."

Lady our niece was born, and her son our nephew* of
Nazareth. (⁶) The Lord of Synay, of Talapharum, and
of the valley of Josaphat. The Lord of Germoni, around
which mountain are seventy-two towers all embellished with
marble.(⁷) The Lord of the great forest, four hundred
miles in length, and inhabited by seventy-two languages.(⁸)
The Lord of Paradise and of the rivers that flow from there,
situated in our country of Capadocie; the guardian of the
caves,(⁹) the mighty emperor of Constantinoppel, Amorach
of Kaylamer, the mighty emperor of Galgarien, the Lord of
the withered tree, the Lord where the sun and the moon
rise and set, from first to last; the lord [of the places] where
Enoch and Helyas are buried. Item, the protector of the
first Prester John, in enclosed Rumany, and guardian of
Wadach. Guardian of Alexander, Founder of the fortified
city of Babilonie, where the seventy-two languages were invented. Emperor king of all kings. The Lord of Christians, Jews, and Infidels. Destructor of the Gods.(¹⁰) Thus
did he write to Rom when he wanted to have his daughter's
marriage, at which marriage I also was present. It is
also to be noted, that it is the custom in the country of the
king-sultan, that during the week of their feast, married
women are at liberty to be wanton with men if it be their
desire, without their husbands or anybody else having anything to say, because it is the custom. It is also the custom
for the king-sultan, when he rides into a city, or when
people from strange countries come to him, to cover his face
that none may see it; and if it be a great guest, he must
first kneel three times† and kiss the ground, then stand
up and go near him. If he is an Infidel, he kisses his bare
hand, but if he is a Christian, he draws his hand into his
sleeve, and puts out the sleeve which he must kiss. When
the king-sultan sends a messenger, he has at the several
stations on the road, horses ready with all that is needed.

* " neff."   † " stunt."

His messenger, whom he sends, has a bell at his girdle; he covers it with a cloth until he gets near a station, then he removes it and lets it ring. When it is heard at the station, a horse is prepared for him, and he finds it ready. He rides to another station, and there he again finds one ready. This he goes on doing, until he gets to the place to which he was sent. This is done on all the roads of the king-sultan.(11) It is also to be noted, that the king-sultan also sends letters by pigeons, because he has many enemies, and is afraid that they might stop his messengers. They are sent mostly from Archey to Tamasgen, between which places is a great desert. It is also to be noted, how the pigeons are sent to any city to which the king-sultan wishes to have them sent. Two pigeons must be put together, and sugar must be put into their food, and they are not allowed to fly; and when they know each other well, the hen-pigeon is taken to the king, and he keeps it, and marks the cock-pigeon that it may be known from which city it is; it is then put into a separate place that is prepared, and the hen-pigeon is no longer allowed inside. They no longer give him so much to eat, and no more sugar as he used to have; this is done that he may wish to return as soon as possible to the place where he was before, and where he was trained. When they wish to despatch him, the letter is tied under a wing, and he flies away straight for the house where he was trained. There he is caught and the letter taken from him, and they send it to whomsoever it belongs.(12) When a guest comes to the king-sultan, whether he be a lord or a merchant, they give him a pass; and when the letter is shewn in his country, they kneel when it is read, and they kiss it, and shew the guest great honour and attention, and they take him over the country from one place to the other. It is also to be noted, that when the ambassador of a king, or of some other lord of a foreign country, comes, it is the custom among the Infidels to attach to him a chief with three or four hundred, or with six hundred horsemen; and when the king-sultan becomes aware of him, he is seated on his throne in attire ornamented with precious stones, and having seven curtains before him. And when the lord who is sent on the embassage wants to enter, one curtain is withdrawn after the other, and each time he must bow and kiss the ground. When the last is withdrawn, he kneels before the king, who holds out to him his hand; he kisses it and then delivers his message. There is a bird in Arabia called sacka,([13]) which is larger than a crane, and has a long neck, and a broad and long beak. It is black and has large feet, which are much like the feet of a goose in the lower parts; its feet are also very black; its colour is the same as that of a crane; it has a large crop in front of its neck, in which it has quite a quart of water. It is the habit of this bird, to fly to a river and fill its crop with water; then it flies away to the desert where there is no water, and pours it out of its crop into a hole in the rock. Then come the little birds of the desert to drink, when he attacks those birds for his food. This is the same desert that people cross, who go to the tomb of Machmet where he is buried.

38.—Of the mountain of St. Catherine.

The Red Sea is two hundred and forty Italian miles broad; it is called the Red Sea, but it is not red, but the land around is in some parts red. It is the same as other seas, and is near Arabia, and is crossed to go to Saint Catherine, and by whoever wishes [to go] to Mount Sinay, where I have not been; but I have heard about it from Christians and Infidels, because Infidels also go there. The Infidels call the mountain Muntagi,*([1]) which is the same as calling it the mountain of the apparition, because God appeared before Moysi on this mountain, in a flame of fire, when he spoke to

* Muntagi should be called Huschan-Daghi, Mountain of the Apparition. *F.*

him. On the mountain there is a monastery, in which are Greeks who form a large brotherhood; they do not drink wine, and live like recluses; they do not eat meat, and are a religious people, and fast always. Within, are many burning lamps, and of the oil for burning and eating, they have enough sent to them by a miracle from God, which happens in this way. When the olives are ripe, all the birds that are in the country come together, and each bird brings a branch in its beak to the mount of Saint Catherine, and they bring so many, that they have enough for the lamps and for food. In the church, behind the altar, is the place where God appeared to Moysi in the burning bush; when the monks go near it they are bare-footed, because it is a holy place; because our Lord commanded Moysi to take off his shoes because the place is holy, and the place is called the place of God. Three steps higher up, is the high altar where lay the bones of Saint Catherine; the abbot shows this sanctuary to pilgrims, and he has a silver thing with which he touches the sanctuary and the bones. In this way he obtains an exudation of oil, which is neither like oil nor balsam; this he gives to the pilgrims, and shows there the head of Saint Catherine and many other sacred things. A great miracle takes place in this monastery, where there are as many lamps that are always burning, as there are monks. When a monk is about to die, his lamp becomes dim, and when it goes out, he dies. When the abbot dies, he who sings the mass finds on the altar a letter, in which is written the name of the man who is to be the abbot, and his lamp relights itself. In the same abbey is the spring where Moysi caused the water to flow, when he struck the rock with his staff. Not far from the said abbey, is the church built in honour of our Lady, where she appeared to the monks; higher up, is the chapel of Moysi, to which he fled when he saw our Lord face to face. There is also on the mount, the chapel of the prophet Helyas; the mount is called Oreb; close to the chapel of Moysi, is the site where our Lord delivered to him the tables with the ten commandments, and on this same mountain is the cave in which Moysi remained, when he fasted forty days. From this valley one gets to a larger valley, and gets to the mountain to which Saint Catherine was carried by angels. In the same valley is a church, built in honour of the forty martyrs, in which the monks often sing the mass. The valley is cold, and the place on Saint Catherine's mount where she was carried by the angels, is nothing but a heap of stones; but there has been a chapel which is destroyed. There are also two mounts called Sinay, which are near each other, except for the valley which is between them.

39.—Of the withered tree.

Not far from Ebron is the village of Mambertal,([1]) where is the withered tree which the Infidels call kurruthereck; it is also called carpe,* and has been since the time of Abraham, and was always green until our Lord died on the cross; since His death it has withered. It is found in prophecy, that a prince will come from the Occident towards the sun, and will with the Christians take possession of the holy sepulchre, and will cause the celebration of the mass under the withered tree; then will the tree become green and bear fruit. The Infidels hold it in great honour, and take good care of it. It has also the virtue, that when anybody suffers from epilepsy, and he passes by it, he falls no more; and it possesses many other virtues, so that it is well taken care of.([2]) Item, it is two full days journey from Jherusalem to Nazereth where our Lord was brought up, which was formerly a considerable city; but now it is a small village, the houses are far from each other, and mountains are

* Selvy is the Turkish for cypress tree. This word appears as Sirpe in edition of 1814.

around it. There was a church where our Lady received the salutation of the archangel Gabryel, but now there is only a pillar.(³) The Infidels guard it well, because of the offerings which the Christians bring there; these they take away because they are enemies, but they dare not do anything to them, because it is forbidden by the sultan.

40.—Of Jherusalem and of the Holy Sepulchre.

When I was at Jherusalem, I was there during a great war, and our thirty thousand [men] were encamped near the Jordan on a beautiful meadow; this is the reason why I could not see all the holy places well; but I will relate some things. I went twice to Jherusalem with a koldigen(¹) named Joseph. Jherusalem lies between two mounts, and there is great want of water. The Infidels call Jherusalem, Kurtzitalil.(²) The church in which is the holy sepulchre is a fine church, high and circular; it is covered all over with lead, and is outside the city. In the middle of the church, in the chapel on the right hand, is the holy sepulchre, wherein nobody can enter, unless he is a great lord; but a stone of the holy sepulchre is let into the wall of the tabernacle, and the pilgrims can kiss and touch it.(³) There is a lamp that burns all the year until Good Friday, then it goes out, and re-lights itself on Easter day. There is also on Easter eve a brightness above the holy sepulchre, that is like fire; (⁴) many people come there from Ermenia, from Siria, and from the country of Prester John, to see this brightness in the church. On the right hand is Mount Calvarie where is *an altar* (?) ;* there, is the pillar to which our Lord was bound whilst he was scourged. Near the said

---

* The word *altar* is omitted in the edition of 1859. Neumann states that several editions give different substitutes for this word. In those of 1475(?) and 1549, the word "altar" is inserted.

altar, are forty-two steps under ground; there, were found the holy cross and those of the two thieves. In front of the gate of the church, are eighteen steps; there, our Lord on the cross said to his mother: "Woman, behold, that is thy child"; and he said to Saint Johannsen: " Behold, that is thy mother." He went up those very steps when he carried the cross; and on the same side, but a little higher, is the chapel in which are the priests from the country of Prester John.([5]) In front of the city is the church of Saint Steffan, where he was stoned; ([6]) and against the valley of Josophat, is the golden gate before the church where is the holy sepulchre. Not far from there is the great hospital of Saint Johanns, in which they receive sick people. The hospital has one hundred and thirty-four columns; there is another hospital that rests on fifty-four marble columns.([7]) Below the hospital is a fine church, called that of our great Lady, and between them is another church called that of our Lady, where Mary Magdalen and Mary Cleophas tore out their hair when they saw God on the cross. In front of the church where is the holy sepulchre, is the temple of our Lord; it is very fine, high, and circular; it is also wide and covered with tin; there is also a fine open space with houses around, and it is paved with white marble; the Infidels do not allow either Christians or Jews to enter it.([8]) Near to the great temple is a church covered with lead, and called the throne of Salomon; ([9]) and on the left hand is a palace, called the temple of Salomon. A church there, is in honour of Saint Annen, in which is a well; whoever bathes in it is healed, whatever be his disease. It was there our Lord healed the bed-ridden man.([10]) Not far from this is the house of Pilate, and close by, is the house of Herod([11]) who ordered the children to be killed. A little further, there is a church called that of Saint Annen, in which is an arm of Saint Johannes Crisostimus, and the greater portion of the head of Saint Stephen.([12]) There is a street which leads to

Mount Syon, where is the church of Saint James. Not far from the mount, is the church of our Lady, where she lived and also where she died. When one is on Mount Syon, there is a chapel in which is the stone that was over the holy sepulchre; there is also a pillar to which our Lord was bound, when the Jews scourged him. In the same place was the house of Annas, who was the Jewish bishop. At the top of thirty-two steps, is the place where our Lord washed the feet of his disciples; near the same place, Saint Stephen was buried. This is also the place where our Lady heard the angels sing the mass; in the same chapel, near the high altar sat the twelve holy apostles on the day of Pentecost, when the Holy Ghost came upon them. At this same place, our Lord celebrated the Passover with his disciples. Mount Syon is in the city of Jherusalem, and stands higher than the city.([13]) Below the mount is a beautiful castle which was built by the king-sultan.([14]) On the mount are buried King Soldan ([15]) and King David, and many other kings. Between Mount Syon and Salomon's temple, is the house where our Lord raised the maiden from death; it is also the place where Isayas the prophet was buried. In front of the city of Jherusalem, lies buried the prophet Dayel. Between the mount of Oliueli and Jherusalem, is the valley of Josophat which reaches to the city. There is a brook in the valley of Josophat where is the sepulchre of our Lady, XL steps below ground. ([16]) Not far off is a church where Jacob and Zacharias the prophets are buried.* Above the valley is the mount of Olives, and close to the mount, is the mount of Galilee.([17]) From Jherusalem *two hundred stadia are counted to the Dead Sea, which is one hundred and fifty stadia wide,*([18]) *and into which flows the river Jordan, at the source of which,*† and at no distance, is the church of Saint Johannes;

---

* " da sint begraben Jacob und Zacharyas, die propheten."

† The words in italics are wanting in the edition of 1859, and are substituted from that of 1814, a reproduction of the passage in the editions of 1475 (?) and 1549.

and a little higher up, Christians usually bathe in the Jordan,([19]) which is neither broad nor deep, but there are good fish in it; its source is from two springs on the same mountain, one spring is called the Jor, the other, Don, and from these it has its name; ([20]) it flows through a lake, then under a mountain, and comes up on a beautiful plain, where the Infidels often have a fair during the year.([21]) In this same plain is the grave of Saint James, and on this same plain we encamped with our young king, with thirty thousand men sent to him by the Turkish king. There are many Christians on the Jordan, and they have many churches there. It is to be noted, that the Infidels took possession of the holy sepulchre, twelve hundred and eighty years from Christ.([22]) Ebron lies seven leagues from Jherusalem, and is the chief city of the Philistines; on Ebron are the graves of the patriarchs, Adam, Abraham, Isaac, and Jacob, and of their wives Eva, Sara, Rebecca, and Lia. There is a fine church which the Infidels take great care of, and hold in great honour, because the holy fathers lie there; they do not allow either Christians or Jews to enter, unless they have the permission of the king-sultan, and they say, we are not worthy to enter so holy a place. In front of the city of Miser, which the Christians call Cair, there is a garden where balsam grows; it grows there only, and in India. The king-sultan enjoys a large income from this balsam. The Infidels often adulterate it, and merchants and druggists also mix it, and this they do that they may make more profit.([23]) Genuine balsam is pure and clear, and has a pleasant taste, and is yellow; but when it is thick and red, it is not genuine. Take a drop of balsam in the hand, and expose it to the sun; if it is good, you cannot keep it long in the sun, because you feel the great heat. Take a drop of balsam on a knife, and put it near a glowing fire; if the balsam burns, it is genuine. Take a silver cup or goblet full of goat's milk, stir it quickly and put a drop of balsam into it; if it is good, the milk will immediately curdle, and so the balsam is proved.

41.—Of the spring in Paradise, with IIII rivers.

In the middle of Paradise there is a spring, from which flow four rivers that course through different countries. The first is called Rison and flows through India; in this river are found many precious stones and gold. The other is called Nilus: it flows through the country of the Moors and through Egypt. The third is called Tigris, and flows through Asia and Great Armenia. The fourth is called the Eufrates, which flows through Persia and Lesser Armenia. Of these four rivers I have seen three.(¹) One is called Nilus, the other Tigris, the third, Eufrates. I have been many years in the countries through which these rivers flow, and have there experienced many things that are good and bad, of which a great deal more might be said.

42.—How pepper grows in India.

I have not been in Great India where the pepper grows, but I have heard in the Infidel country from those who have seen it, where and how it grows. In the first place, I have understood and heard, that it grows near the city of Lambe, in a forest called Lambor;(¹) this forest is quite XIIII days journey in length. In this forest are II cities and many villages in which are Christians; it is very hot where the pepper grows. The pepper grows on trees which are like the wild vine, and is something like the sloe when it is green; and they bind them to poles as they do the vine, and the trees bear a great deal. When it is green it is ripe, then they cut it as they do grapes, and expose it to the sun until it is dry. Three kinds of pepper grow; the long and black grows with the leaves. There is the white, which is the best, and they keep it in the country; but not so much of this grows as of the other. There are also many serpents there, produced by the heat. Some people say, that when the pepper is to be gathered, fires are made in the forest to drive away the serpents, therefore the pepper becomes black; but this is not the case, because if they made a fire, the trees would wither and bear no more fruit; but the truth is, that they wash their hands with the juice of an apple which they call liuon,(²) or of some other plant; the serpents escape from the smell, and then they gather the pepper without trouble. In the same country they also grow good ginger, and many spices and aromatics.

43.—Of Allexandria.

Alexandria is quite seven Italian miles long, and three broad, and is a fine and pretty city, and the river Nilus flows past the city into the sea; and the city has no other drinking water, and it is conducted into the city by means of cisterns. Many merchants come there from over the sea, from Italian countries, from Venice and from Genoa. Those from Genoa have their own counting-houses at Alexandria, and those from Venice likewise.(¹) It is the custom at Allexandria, that at the hour of vespers, all the Italians must be in their counting-houses, and no longer without, about the city, which is strictly forbidden. Then an Infidel comes and locks up the counting-house, and takes away the key until the morning, when he comes and opens it again. Thus they take care that the Italians shall not take their city, because they were once conquered by the king of Zipern.(²) Near the port of Alexandria there is a fine high tower, on which there was not long ago a mirror, in which one could see from Alexandria toward Cipern those who were on the sea ; and whatever they were doing, all could be seen in this mirror at Allexandria, so that at the time that the king of Zypern went to war with Allexandria, he could do them no harm. Then came a priest to the king of Ziperen, and asked what he would give him if he broke the mirror. The king replied, that if he would break the mirror, he would give him whichever bishopric he might choose to have in his country. The priest then went to Rome to the Pope, and said : That he would break the mirror at Allexandria, if he would allow him to abjure the Christian faith. He gave him permission that he might do so in words, and not in deeds nor with the heart. Now he did this for the sake of the Christian faith, because the Christians at sea suffered many injuries from the Infidels, through this mirror. The priest returned from Rome to Alexandria, and was converted to the faith of the Infidels, and learnt their writing, and became an Infidel priest and their preacher, and taught them the Infidel faith against the Christian faith, and they held him in great honour, and wondered, because he had been a Christian priest, and they trusted in him very much. They asked him which temple in the city he wished for, as they would give it to him for his life time. There was also a temple in the middle of the tower where the mirror was ; this temple he asked for, for his life time ; they gave it to him together with the keys of the mirror. There he remained nine years, and then one day he sent to the king of Zypperen that he should come with his galleys, and he would break the mirror which was in his power, and he thought, that, after breaking the mirror, if the galleys were there, he would go on board. One morning many galleys came, he struck the mirror three blows with a hammer before it broke, and from the noise all the people in the city were frightened, and ran to the tower and fell on him, so that he could not get away ; then he jumped out of a window of the tower, into the sea, and was killed. Soon afterwards, the king of Zyperen came with a large force, and took Allexandria, and remained in it three days.([8]) Then came the king-sultan, and he marched upon him so that he could not remain; and he burnt the city, and took away with him many people with their wives and children, and much booty.

44.—Of a great giant.

It is to be noted, that in Egypt there was a giant, who was called in the Infidel tongue, Allenklaisser. In this country is the city called Missir, but the Christians call it Kayr, and it is the capital of the king-sultan. In this same city are twelve thousand baking ovens. Now the said giant was so strong, that one day he brought into the city a bundle of wood to heat all the ovens, and one bundle was enough; each baker gave him a loaf, which makes twelve thousand loaves. All these he ate in one day. The shin-bone of this giant is in Arabia, in a valley between two mountains. There is a deep valley between the rocks, where flows a river at such a depth that no person can see it, one only hears its rush. It is in this same valley that the shin-bone of the giant serves as a bridge; and whoever comes there, whether they are riding or on foot, must pass over this shin-bone. It is also on a road where traders pass, coming and going, because the defile is so narrow, that people cannot pass by any other way; and the Infidels say that this bone is one frysen * in length, which is equal to an arrow's flight, or more. There, a toll is taken from traders; with the same, they buy oil to anoint the bone that it may not rot. It is not a long time since a king-sultan had a bridge built near the bone; it is about two hundred years [ago], according to an inscription on the bridge. When a lord comes there with many people, he passes over the bridge, and does not pass

* Farsang or fursak = 3 m. 787½ yds.

over the bone; but whoever wishes to pass over this wonder, may do so, that he may say of it that in this country there is an incredible thing, and which is nevertheless surely true. And if it were not true, or had I not seen it, I would not have spoken or written about it.(1)

45.—Of the many religions the Infidels have.

It is to be noted, that the Infidels have five religions. First, some believe in a giant called Aly, who was a great persecutor of Christians. Others believe in one who was called Molwa,(1) who was an Infidel priest. The third believe, as the three kings believed, before they were baptised. The fourth believe in fire, because they say that Abel, the son of Adam, brought his offering to Almighty God, and the flames of the fire were the offering; therefore they believe in this offering. Among the fifth, some believe, and the largest number among the Infidels believe, in one who is called Machmet.

46.—How Machmet and his religion appeared.

It is here to be noted of Machmet, how he came and how he brought his religion. Item, his father and mother were poor people, and he is a native of Arabia. When he was thirteen years old he went away from home, went to [some] merchants who wanted to go to Egypt, and asked them to take him with them. They took him, agreeing that he must look after the camels and horses, and wherever Machmet went, or stood, there stood always a cloud over him, which was black; and when they came to Egypt, they encamped near a village. Now at that time there were Christians in Egypt; the pastor of the village came to the merchants, and invited them to dine with him. They did so, and told Machmet that he must look after the horses and camels. This he did. And now when they came into the pastor's house, the pastor asked them if they were all there? The merchants said: " We are all here, except a boy who is guarding our camels and horses." Now this priest had read in a prophecy, how one, born of two persons, would spread a doctrine against that of Christianity, and that as a sign who the man was to be, a black cloud would stand over him. The pastor went out, and saw a black cloud over the little boy, who was Machmet. When he had now seen him, he asked the merchants that they should bring the boy; they brought him. The pastor asked him his name. He said, "Machmet". This, the priest also found in prophecy, and more [than this], that he would be a mighty lord and man, and that he would greatly trouble Christianity; but that his doctrine would not last one thousand years, and then it would decrease. When the pastor knew that he was named Machmet, and saw the black cloud stand over him, he understood that he was the man who would introduce this doctrine, and he placed him at his table above the merchants, and showed him great honour. After the meal, the pastor asked the merchants if they knew the boy. They said; "No, but he came to us, and asked us to take him with us into Egypt." Then the pastor told them how he had read in a prophecy, how this boy would introduce a doctrine against Christians, through which they would suffer much, and for a sign [of this], a black cloud would be always over him; and showed them the cloud and said, that when he was in the galley, the cloud was there also. He said to the boy: "Thou shalt be a great teacher, and shalt introduce a particular doctrine amongst the Infidels, and thou shalt overpower the Christians by thy might, and thy descendants will also acquire great power.([1]) Now I pray thee that thou wilt leave my race, the Armeny, in peace." This he promised him, and then went with the merchants to Babiloni, and became a great scholar in Infidel writings, and preached to the Infidels that they should believe in God who had created heaven and earth, and not in the idols that were the creatures of men; they have ears and hear not; they have eyes and see not; they have a mouth and speak not; they have feet and walk not; nor can they save either the body or soul; and he converted the king of Babilony and many people with him. Then the king took him, and gave him power over the land; this he exercised; and when the king died, he took the king's wife, and become a mighty Calpha, which is as much as to say, a Pope. He had four men with him who were well learned in Infidel writings, and to each he gave an office. To the first, he gave charge of ecclesiastical jurisdiction; to the other, lay jurisdiction; the first, was named Omar, the other, Otman; the third was named Abubach, to whom he gave charge of weights and manufactures, so that he was over them, and each one should be faithful in his work. The fourth was named Aly; he made him chief over all his people, and sent him into Arabia that he should convert Christians, because Christians were there at the time; but if any would not be converted, then he should compel them by the sword. We read in the Infidel book, Alkoray, that in one day ninety thousand men were killed for [the sake of] Machmet's doctrine, and the whole of Arabia was converted. Machmet gave them a law, how they were to conduct themselves before God, who had created heaven and earth. And the law of the Infidels begins in this way. First, when a boy was born, when he comes to be thirteen years old, he must be circumcised, and he has instituted five daily prayers, which must be daily repeated. The first prayer is when the day breaks; another, in the middle of the day; the third, at the time of vespers; the fourth, before the sun goes down; the fifth, when day and night part. With the first four, they praise God, who has made heaven and earth; with the fifth, they pray to Machmet, that he will intercede for them with God. And they must go into the temple at certain times of the day; and when they want to go into the temple, they must wash the mouth, then the hands, feet, ears, and eyes. And when any one has sinned with his wife, he cannot go into the temple, until he has washed his whole body; this they do in the same belief as we Christians who confess; and the Infidels believe that, after they have washed, they are as pure as Christians, who, with full penitence, have confessed to the priest. And when they want to enter the temple, they take off their shoes and go in bare footed; they cannot take in any arms, or weapons that cut, and they do not allow any woman in the temple, so long as they are inside; and when they go into the temple, they stand near each other, with their hands close to each other; and they bend and kiss the ground, and their priest sits on a seat before them, and begins a prayer which they repeat after him. It is also to be noted, that in the temple no one speaks to another, nor looks at another, until the prayer is ended. In the temple they do not put one foot far from the other, but keep them close together; they do not go to and fro, nor look here and there, but they stand still in one place, and keep their hands together until they have quite finished their prayer; and when they have quite finished, they bow to each other, and only then go out of the temple. It is also to be noted, that no door of the temple is left open. They have no painting and no picture inside, only their writings, plants, roses, and flowers. They do not willingly allow Christians to enter, and more than this, it is to be noted, that Infidels must not spit, cough, or do anything of the sort in their temple; but if some one does so inside, he must go out and wash himself, and, added to this, must suffer much reproach from the Infidels; and when one coughs, sneezes, or ....., he must go out of the temple and wash himself after it. It is also to be noted, that they keep Friday as we keep Sunday, and whoever does not go to the temple on their holy-day, is taken and tied to a ladder, and carried about the town from one street to the other, and tied in front of the temple until their prayer is finished; and then they beat him twenty-five times with a rod on the naked body, whether he is rich or poor. Item, all the young dropped by their cattle on the Friday, are given to the hospital. Their priests also say, that when prayer is finished on a holy-day, people may work, because work is holy, and that man commits more sin by being idle than with work, and therefore they allow their people to work on holy days after they have finished their prayer. And when they finish their prayers on holy-days, they raise their hands towards God, and all pray with common voice for vengeance on Christendom, and say : "Almighty God, we pray thee not to suffer Christians to be united," and say, that if Christians are united and have peace amongst themselves, they must succumb. It is also to be noted, that they have three kinds of temples; one, to which they all go, is Sam, a parish church; the other, into which priests go, is a monastery, and in which they also go through their probation; the third, is where their kings and mighty vassals have their burial, and in it poor people are received for the love of God, whether they be Christians, Infidels, or Jews, and the temple is like a hospital. The first temple is also called Mesgit, the other Medrassa, the third, Amarat.([2]) It is also to be noted, that they do not bury their dead either in the temples, or around them; they bury in the fields and on the high roads; this they do that those who pass by, may pray to God for them. And when one is about to die, they stand around him, and tell him that he must think of God, and call to God to have mercy upon him ; and when he dies, they wash him, and then their priests carry him, singing, to the grave, and bury him. It is also to be noted, that the Infidels fast one month in the year, and this fast changes every year to another month, and they fast one whole day without eating or drinking, until they see the stars in the sky. Then the priest goes up the tower, and calls the people to prayer, and they go into the temple and say their prayers, and only when they have finished their prayer, they go home and eat all night until the morning, meat, or whatever they may have. Also, they do not lay with their wives during their fast; and when a woman is pregnant or in child-bed, she may eat during the day, and the sick may do the same. They do not take payment during fast, either for houses or for any thing that pays interest.

47.—Of the Infidels' Easter-day.([1])

It is also to be noted of the Infidels' Easter day, that, after they have fasted four weeks, they have Easter for three days following, and on the morning of Easter day they go to the temple, and finish their prayer as is their custom; and when they have done, the common people put on their arms, and then come to the high priest's house, with the chiefs of the town and the soldiers, and then take out of the priest's house, the tabernacle, and ornament it with cloth of gold and velvet, and the chiefs and the principal [people] carry it in front of their temple, and in front of the tabernacle they carry their banners, and all the musicians they can find also go before it; and when they bring it to the temple, they put it down, and the chief priest goes into the tabernacle and preaches inside it. When he has preached, they put a sword in his hand; he draws it and speaks to the people, and calls upon God that he should give us might and strength against all the enemies of Machmet's faith, so that we may overcome them with the sword. Then they all put out their hands, and pray to our Lord that it may so happen, and after this, the mighty lords go into the temple and pray, and during that time, the people must guard the tabernacle and the lords. When their prayer is finished, they take the tabernacle with the priest inside, and carry him back to his house, with the musicians and banners. Afterwards, they go to their houses and have great rejoicings for three days.

48.—Of the other Easter-day.

And then, after a month, they have another Easter day in honour of Abraham. On this [day] they kill lambs and oxen, and give to the poor, by the will of God, [and] to the honour of Abraham, because he was obedient, and wanted to sacrifice his son to God. At this time, the Infidels go to the grave of Machmet, and to the temple which Abraham built and which lies in front of the city, and Machmet has his grave in it, and it is called Madina. On Easter day the king-sultan covers the temple of Abraham with velvet, which is black, and then their priest cuts off a small piece for each Infidel pilgrim that comes, that he may take it away as a sign that he has been there.

49.—Of the law of the Infidels.

It is also here to be noted, what Machmet has forbidden in the laws he has given to the Infidels. First, he has forbidden the Infidels that they should dare to cut the beard, because it would be against the will of God when he created Adam, the first man, in his Divine image; and the Infidels also say, that he who would have a face different to that he received from God, does it against God's command, whether he be young or old. They also say that whoever cuts his beard, he does it from vanity and pride, and to please the world, and scorns the creation of God; it is particularly the Christians who do this to please their women, and this is a great misfortune for them, because, for the sake of vanity, they disfigure the image in which God created them. Then Machmet forbade that any one should lift his hat or uncover his head to another, whether he be king, emperor, noble or plebeian, which they also observe; but when they go before a mighty man, they bow and kneel before him. They say, when one's father, and mother, or another friend dies, they should uncover the head before him. This they also do. When they lament for one, they take off their hat, and lift it high and throw it on the ground, and then they lament. This also has Machmet allowed, that a man may take as many wives as he can support. It is also their law, that when a woman is pregnant, they do not go near her until the child is born, nor for fourteen days after; but they may have a concubine. The Infidels also say that after the last day they will have wives, with whom they will lie; but they will always remain virgins. They also say that God has established marriage only for those who die in the faith of Machmet. He has also ordered that they must not eat any animal, or bird, unless they cut its throat and let the blood flow, which they observe. They do not eat pig's flesh, because Machmet has also forbidden it.

50.—Why Machmet has forbidden wine to Infidels.

It is also to be noted, that Machmet has forbidden wine to Infidels, because as the Infidels say: One day he was passing, with his servants, a public-house, in which were many people making merry. He asked why those people were so merry; one of his servants told him it was caused by wine. Machmet said: "Is it such a drink that people become so merry from it!" Now in the evening Machmet went out again, and there was a great noise because a man and his wife were fighting, and two persons were killed. He spoke and asked what was the matter? One of his servants said that the people who were merry have now lost their senses, because they have taken too much wine, and they knew not what they did. Then Machmet forbade wine to all, under a heavy penalty, whether ecclesiastic or lay, emperor, king, dukes, barons, counts, knight and varlet, servants, and all those who were of his faith, and that they should no longer drink wine, whether they be well or ill, and this is why he has forbidden wine to them, as the Infidels have told me. He has also ordered that the Christians and all those who are against his faith, should be persecuted day and night, except the Armeny who are to be free amongst them; and where there are Armeny amongst them, then they should not take from them a monthly tax greater than two pfennings, because Machmet had promised the Armenian priest, as has been stated. He has also ordered, that when they overcome Christians, they should not kill them; but they should pervert them, and should thus spread and strengthen their own faith.

51.—Of a fellowship the Infidels have among themselves.

It is also to be noted, that during the time he was on earth, Machmet had forty disciples. They have a special fellowship and have made an alliance against Christendom, and this is their law. Whoever wants to be of their fellowship, must swear that if he meets a Christian, he will not let him live nor take him a prisoner, whether from favour or for the sake of profit; and if it should happen that in a battle which Infidels [might] have with Christians, he cannot succeed to take one, he must buy a Christian and kill him. Those who are in this fellowship are called

They ;*(¹) there are many of them in Turkey, and they always go against the Christians because it is their law.

52.—How a Christian becomes an Infidel.

It is also to be noted how a Christian, from the beginning, becomes an Infidel. When a Christian wants to become an Infidel, he must before all men raise a finger, and say the words: "La il lach illallach;" Machmet is his true messenger.(¹) And when he says this, they take him to the high priest; then he must repeat the above written words before the priest, and must deny the Christian faith, and when he has done that, they put on him a new dress, and the priest binds a new kerchief on his head; and this they do that it may be seen he is an Infidel, because Christians wear blue kerchiefs, and the Jews, yellow kerchiefs, on the head. Then the priest asks all the people to put on their armour, and who has to ride, rides; also all the priests who are in the neighbourhood. And when the people come, they put him on a horse, and then the common people must ride before him, and the priests go behind him, with trumpets, cymbals and fifes, and two priests ride near him; and so they lead him about in the town; and the Infidels cry with a loud voice and praise Machmet, and the two priests say to him these words: "Thary wirdur, Messe chulidur, Maria cara baschidur, Machmet kassuldur": which is as much as to say; There is one God, and the Messiah his servant, Mary his maid, and Machmet his chief messenger.(²) After they have led him everywhere in the city, from one street to another, then they lead him into the temple and circumcise him. If he is poor, they make a large collection and give it to him, and the great lords shew particular honour to him, and make

* To those who are unfamiliar with the name, the title of Ghasi would scarcely be recognised in that of They. *N.*

him rich; this they do, that Christians may be more willing to be converted to their faith. *If it is a woman who wants to change her religion,** she is also taken to the high priest, and must say the above words. The priest then takes the woman's girdle, cuts it in two, and makes of it a cross; on this, the woman must stamp three times,† deny the Christian faith, and must say the other words above written. The Infidels have a good custom among their merchants, when one wants to buy from another, whatever be the merchandise. The buyer says to the seller, that he should make a just profit on what he buys, so that he also might live; so that he takes no more profit than one pfenning in forty pfennings, which is equal to one gulden in forty guldens, and no more; this they call a right purchase and profit, and this Machmet has also commanded them, so that the poor, like the rich, might live. The priests also always say in their sermons, that they should help each other and be subject to their superiors, and the rich are to be humble before the poor, and when they do this, God Almighty gives them strength and might against their enemies; and whatever their priest says to them about spiritual things, they are obedient and submissive to it. This is the faith of Machmet which he has given to the Infidels as his law, such as it is, as I then heard it from them.

53.—What the Infidels believe of Christ.

It is also to be noted, that the Infidels believe that Jesus was born of a virgin, and that after the birth, she remained a virgin. They also believe that when Jesus was born, he spoke to his mother and comforted her, and they believe that

---

* The words in italics are wanting in Heidelberg MS. Penzel has it —" Ist die übertüten wollenden ein Frauenzimmer." In edition of 1549, we find—" Ist aber ein frau." † " stunt."

Jesus is the highest prophet of God amongst all prophets, and that he has never committed sin; and they do not believe that Jesus was crucified, but that it was another who was like him; therefore Christians have a wicked faith, because they say that Jesus was crucified, who was the highest friend of God, and has never committed any sin, therefore God would not have been a just judge if Jesus was crucified and innocent. And when one converses with them of the Father, and Son, and Holy Ghost, they say that they are three persons, and not one God, because their book Alkaron says nothing of the Trinity. When anybody says that Jesus is the word of God, they say, this we do know, that the word of God has spoken, otherwise he would not be God; and when one says that wisdom is the Son of God who was born of the Virgin Mary, from a word which the angels announced to her, and on account of which word we must all rise and come to judgment; they say it is true that no one can go against the word of God. They also say that the strength of the word of God cannot be conceived by any one, and therefore their book Alkoran says, and gives them a sign, by the word which the angel spoke to Mary, that Jesus was born of the word of God. They say that Abraham was the friend of God, Moyses the prophet of God, Jesus the word of God, so was Machmet the true messenger of God. They also say, that Jesus, of the four, was the most worthy, and was the highest with God, and it will be he also who will judge the last judgment of God over all men.

54.—What the Infidels say of the Christians.

The Infidels also say that whatever territory they possess of the Christians, they do not owe it to their power, nor to their wisdom, nor to their holiness, but they have it because of the injustice, perversity, and arrogance which Christians have against them; therefore Almighty God has decreed, that they should take the land from Christians, because they do not conduct their affairs, whether spiritual or temporal, with justice, because they look to wealth and favour, and the rich treat the poor with haughtiness, and do not help them either with gifts or with justice, and do not hold to the doctrine which the Messiah has given them. They also say, that they find it and read it in their prophecies, that the Christians will yet expel them out of the country, and will again possess the country; but so long as Christians are such, and are perverse, and their spiritual and temporal lords live such a disordered life, we are not afraid that they will expel us out of our country; because we fear God, and do always what is right and just, and worthy, according to our faith, for the love of God and in honour of our prophet Machmet, who is the highest messenger of God, who has given us the right doctrine by his teaching; to him we are obedient, and always willingly follow his commandments which are in the book called the Alkoran, which has been touched upon often before.

55.—How Christians are said not to hold to their religion.

The Infidels also say that Christians do not hold to the commandment, nor to the doctrine of the Messiah, which the Messiah has commanded them, and they also do not observe the law of the book Inzil, which is called Ewangely, nor the rules which stand in that book. They hold to particular laws, spiritual and temporal, which are against the laws of the book Inzil, and the commandments and laws contained therein are all holy and just; but the law and belief which they have set up and invented, are all false and unjust, because the laws which they have made are for profit and favour, which is all against God and his dear prophets; and whatever misfortunes and troubles they have, are all decreed to them by God for their unrighteousness.

56.—How long ago it is since Machmet lived.

Item, it is to be noted, that the time Machmet was born counts from Christ's birth, six hundred and nine years, and the Infidels say, that on the day he was born, one thousand and one churches fell of themselves, and that happened as a sign of the injury he would do to Christianity in his time. It is also here to be noted, how many tongues there are in the Greek faith. The first is the Greek tongue, in which their books are written; the Turks call them Vrrum. The other is the Rivssen tongue, which the Infidels call Orrust. The third, Pulgery, which the Infidels call Wulgar. The fourth, the Winden tongue, which they call Arnaw. (¹) The fifth, the Walachy tongue, which the Infidels call Vfflach. The sixth, the Yassen tongue, which the Infidels call Afs. (²) The seventh, the Kuthia tongue, which the Infidels call Thatt.* The eighth, the Sygun, which the Infidels call Ischerkas. The ninth, Abukasen, and the Infidels call them Appkas. The tenth tongue, Gorchillas, and the Infidels call them Kurtzi. The eleventh, the Megrellen tongue, also so called by the Infidels. Item, between the Zurian and Greek faith, there is but one difference, therefore they say the Schurian tongue is also of their faith; but the Schurians are of Jacob, and have the faith of Saint Jacob, and have it that each must make the wafer with his own hands, into which God's body will be changed. And when he has made the paste, he takes a hair from his beard and puts it in the wafer, and changes it into God's body. And there is a great difference between what the Greek and

* For this name, see chap. 36, note 9.

what the Schurian priest reads, or sings, in the church, because it is the Schurian and not the Greek tongue. (³)

57.—Of Constantinoppel.

Constantinoppel is a fine large city and well built, and is quite ten Italian miles in extent at its walls, about which it has fifteen hundred towers. The city is triangular, having the sea on two sides. The Greeks call Constantinoppel, Istimboli, but the Turks call it Stampol; and opposite to the city, is a city called Pera, which the Greeks call Kalathan, and the Infidels call it the same. (¹) Between the two cities is an arm of the sea, quite three Italian miles in length, and half [a mile] or more in breadth; and the arm is crossed from each side, because the distance by land is far. The said city belongs to Genaw. The great Alexander cut through high rocks and mountains fifteen Italian miles in length, and caused two seas to flow into each other;(²) and that which flows is called and is the Great Sea, and it is also called the Black Sea, and the Tunow and many other great rivers flow into it. In the said sea one goes to Caffa, to Alathena, to Trabessanda, and to Samson, and to many other cities and countries that lay around. The arm of the sea [at] Constantinoppel is called Hellespant by the Greeks, and the Infidels call it Poges. The Turks also have a shore across the sea, opposite to Constantinople, which they call Skuter; there, the Turks cross the sea. Also not far from Constantinoppel by the sea, was Troya, on a fine plain, and one can still see where the city stood. (³) The emperor of Constantinoppel has two palaces in the city; one is very beautiful, and is much decorated inside with gold, lapis-lazuli, and marbles. In front of the palace is a fine square for tilting, and for all [kinds of] pastime that might be desired in front of the palace. (⁴) In front of the palace is the statue of the emperor Justian on a horse; it is placed upon a high piece of marble, which is a pillar. I asked a burgher of the city of what this statue was made; he told me it was of bronze, and that both the horse and the man was entirely of one casting. Some people of the country say that it is of leather, and yet it must have stood there quite a thousand years; had it been leather, it would not have stood so long, it would have rotted. At one time the statue had a golden apple in the hand, and that meant that he had been a mighty emperor over Christians and Infidels; but now he has no longer that power, so the apple has disappeared.([5])

58.—Of the Greeks.

Not far from Constantinoppel there is an island called Lemprie; in it is a mountain that is so high, it reaches to the clouds.([1]) At Constantinoppel is the most beautiful church, so that nothing like it can be found in India; it is called Sancta Sophya, and is covered all over with lead, and one can see one's self on the walls inside the church as if in a mirror, because the marble and lapis-lazuli on the wall is clear and clean. In this same church is their patriarch with his priests, and the Greeks and all those who are under the patriarch go in pilgrimage, as we, for our sins, go to Rome. When Constantine had finished the churches, he placed as an improvement in the church, high up in the middle of the dome, five golden discs, and each disc is as wide, large, and thick as a mill-stone;([2]) but the emperor took down two during the great war which the Turkish king Wyasit had with him, when he besieged Constantinoppel for seven years. I myself was at that same time with the king in Turkey,([3]) and I have also seen the three discs [left] in the church. The church of Sancta Sophia has three hundred gates, which are all of brass. I was III months at Constantinoppel in the house of the patriarch, but I and my comrades were not allowed to walk about the city, because they were afraid that the Infidels would recognise us, and would take us before the emperor. I would gladly have seen it (the city), but it could not be, because the emperor had forbidden it, but even then we sometimes went out with the patriarch's servants.

59.—Of the Greek religion.

It is to be noted, that the Greeks do not believe in the Holy Trinity; they do not believe in the Chair at Rome, nor in the Pope. They say that their patriarchs have as much power as the Pope at Rome. The sacrament they make of leavened bread, and take it with wine and warm water; and when the priest changes the body of God, they all fall down on their faces and say: "No man is worthy to look at God." And when the priest has finished the Mass, he takes the bread that remains, of which he had prepared the sacrament, and cuts it into small pieces on a dish, and then men and women sit down. Then the priest or his assistant takes the bread round, and so every one takes a piece and eats it, and this bread they call prossura. This bread is not baked by any man or woman, only by a virgin or a nun. They also give the sacrament to young children, but they do not give the sacred oil to any body; and they also say that nobody is wise, and that no one goes into heaven or hell before the day of judgment; then each man will go into heaven or into hell as he has deserved. They have no Mass, unless it is asked for. They say that only one Mass is to be celebrated at the same altar in the day, and they do not let Mass be said at their altars in Latin, and Mass must not be said in any language but in the Greek language, because the Greek language is of their faith. They say also that their faith is the true Christian faith, and the others are not true. They also have the Mass on feast days only, and not on week days, because all their priests are craftsmen and must work, and all have wives and children, and their priests take one wife only; and when she dies he cannot take any more, either in marriage or otherwise. If he has anything to do with a woman, and the bishop becomes aware of it, he takes away from him his priestly charge, so that he cannot say the Mass any more. And when a bishop consecrates a priest, he girds him with a girdle, and when the priest does anything against his priestly order, the bishop takes away the girdle, so that he cannot say Mass any more, and is fallen from his office. The best and the richest marry the priests, and when they are in a house, the priests' wives sit at the upper [end] of the table, and when women walk together, the priests' wives go first. Their churches are not independent. When a man builds a church and dies, his heirs inherit the church like other property, and sell it as any other house. They say, it is not a sin to have to do with unmarried women, because it is not a deadly sin, as it is natural. They also say, that when one takes a monthly profit of two pfennings for one hundred pfennings, it is goodly gain, and not usury. On Wednesdays, they do not eat meat; and so, on Friday, they eat fish and oil only, and say that Saturday is not a fast-day, and one may well eat meat on that day. In the churches, the women stand separately, and neither men nor women dare to go near the altar. And when they make [the sign of] a cross, they do it with the left hand. And when one is about to die, they baptise him again, and there are many who are baptised every year. They have no font in their churches; and when their bishop stands in the choir, he stands in the middle of the church and in the choir, and the priests stand around him. Their bishop eats no meat throughout the year, and during the fasts he eats no fish nor anything that has blood, and all their clergy do the same. When they baptise a child, they have x or more godfathers; men and women bring to the child a christening shirt or a candle. They also say, that our priests sin if they have a Mass every day, because they cannot always be worthy. They also say, that our priests commit mortal sin when they shave their beard, because it is not godly, because it happens from unchastity, and to please the women. And when one dies, and prayers for the dead are sung for him, boiled wheat to eat is given to the priests and to the people, after an old usage, and this same wheat they call coleba. They wash their dead before they bury them. Their priests sell and buy like other merchants. They fast during Lent for fifty days; and the priests and the laity also fast forty days in Advent, and for the twelve holy apostles they fast thirty days; they also fast fifteen days for our Lady's Assumption; they have only three days in the year for our Lady, because they do not keep Candlemas. Item, the Greeks do not keep the resurrection of Jhesus xpi at the same time with us; they keep it on the next Friday after Easter. Then they sing Xristos anesti, which is as much as to say, Xristus is risen.([1])

60.—How the city of Constantinoppel was built.

It is also to be noted, that the emperor of Constantinoppel himself creates the patriarchs, and also gives all God's gifts to the church, and is lord of spiritual and temporal matters as far as his territory reaches. I have heard much and often from their learned men, that Saint Constantine came from Rome with many kocken and galleys to Greece, to the place where Constantinoppel lies, and then there appeared to him an angel from God, who said to him: "Here must thy dwelling be; now sit on the horse, and do not look back, and ride to the place from which thou hast begun to ride." He mounted, and rode quite half a day; and when at night he arrived at the same place where he had mounted, he looked back, and saw a wall of the height of a man spring up from the ground; and from the place where he had looked back, to the place from which he had begun to ride, which is quite twenty paces or more, there was no wall; it has been much tried to build a wall, but it will not stand; but it goes towards the sea, so that they can defend themselves better than if it had been towards the land. I have seen it, because in the same place there is a breakwater,*([1]) therefore the Greeks say that the said wall was built by angels; and that the crown with which their emperor is crowned, and which was brought to Saint Constantine by an angel from heaven, is a heavenly crown; and therefore there is no worthier nor more highly born emperor than the emperor of Constantinoppel. And when a priest dies, they put on him everything that belongs to a priest at the altar, and they put him on a seat in the grave, and cover him with earth. The chant, Ayos otheos, which they sing once a year only, they sing upon all other holy occasions; and during Lent they sing the Alleluia every day, when they are in church. They sing Kirieleyson only, in their Mass, and not Xreleyson. They say, there is but one Godhead and no difference, that it is God the Father and God the Son, and therefore it would not be right to sing Christ. They also bow very humbly before their priests. When a layman meets a priest, he takes off his hat, and bows humbly, and says: "Esloy mena tespotha"; which is as much as to say: Bless me, Lord. Then the priest lays his hand on the layman's head and says: "Otheos efflon essenam"; and that means, God bless thee; and this they do always, men and women, when they meet a priest. When a priest takes a wife, he takes her before he becomes a priest; the reason is, because if he does not beget a child,

* "wann es an der selben stat ein getüll hat."

he cannot be a priest, but so soon as he has got a child, he is consecrated to be a priest. Laymen pray only with the Pater Noster, and do not know the Belief nor the Ave Maria. Many priests wear white garments at Mass.(²)

61.—How the Jassen have their marriages.

Inter illas gentes, Gargetter et Jassen, nuptiæ explentur hac conditione, videlicet mater puellam suam intactam esse asserit, sed ni reapse sit virgo, conjugium non conficitur. Quando igitur de nuptiis agitur, cantibus comitantur puellam ante thalamum, et ibi se ponere jubent; succedit inde sponsus cum adolescentulis, et gladio stricto percutit thalamum, et prope illum se se ponit una cum adolescentulis, et comedunt et bibunt, et se oblectant inter choreas et cantus. Et quum ita solatia cesserint, sponsum denudant usque ad subuculam suam, et egredientes relinquunt cum sponsa. Postea venit sponsi frater, et nonnullus ex amicis intimis, et ante ostium excubat stricto ense; et quum sponsus sponsam virginem non invenit, hoc matri ejus palam facit. Deinde mater sponsi cum amicis suis ante thalamum adstat, observant panniculos, et si nullum virginitatis signum inveniunt, omnes incipiunt se contristare; quum vero pater et mater sponsi cum amicis suis mane adveniunt, ut festa conjugalia concelebrent, mater sponsi manu regit poculum in una parte perforatum, et implet vino claudens foramen digito, et inde matrem sponsæ invitat ut libat amovens digitum e foramine, et sic vinum extra fluit; tum mater sponsi dicit matri sponsæ: Ita evenit de filia tua. Hoc summo dedecori est parentibus sponsæ, quam tradunt eis ut secum ducant, dicentes, se velle nubere filis intactam puellam, sed non ita evenisse de eorum filia. Then come their priests and the chief [persons] that are there, and invite the bridegroom's father and mother, and then they go to their son the bridegroom, and ask him whether or no he will have her? If he says, "Yes", she is given to him by the priests, and the other persons who have interceded for her. But if he says, "No", then they are in all things separated; and whatever he has brought to her, she gives the whole back to him; and whatever clothes he has given her, she must give back to him; after which, he can take another wife, and she another husband.(¹) There are many people in Ermenia, who have this custom. The Infidels call the Gorgiten, Kurtzi; and the Jassen they call Affs.

62.—Of Armenia.

I have also been a great deal in Armenia. After Tämerlin died, I came to his son, who has two kingdoms in Armenia. He was named Scharoch; he liked to be in Armenia, because there is a very beautiful plain. He remained there in the winter with his people, because there was good pasturage. A great river runs through the plain; it is called the Chur, and it is also called the Tygris; and near this river, in this same country, is the best silk. The Infidels call the plain, in the Infidel tongue, Karawag.(¹) The Infidels possess it all, and yet it stands in Ermenia. There are also Armenians in the villages, but they must pay tribute to the Infidels. I always lived with the Armenians, because they are very friendly to the Germans, and because I was a German they treated me very kindly; and they also taught me their Pater Noster and their language, and they call the Germans, Nymitsch.(²) In Armenia are three kingdoms; one is called Tiffliss, the other is called Syos, the third is called Ersingen; the Armenians call it Isingkan, and that is Lesser Armenia. They also possessed Babylon for a long time; but they now have it no longer. The son of Tämerlin had Tyfflis and Ersing at the time that I was there. Sifs belonged to the king-sultan, and was won, counting from Christ's birth, twelve hundred and seventy-seven years; then did the sultan of Alkenier conquer it.([3])

63.—Of the religion of the Armenians.

The Armenians believe in the Holy Trinity. I have also often heard their priests preach in their churches, when I had gone to Mass, and been in their churches, that Saint Bartlome and Saint Thaten of the twelve holy apostles, converted them to the Christian faith, but that they have often been perverted again. There was a holy man named Gregory, and the king of Armenia was his cousin, and he lived in the time when Saint Silvester was Pope at Rome.([1]) The king of Armenia died, and he was a good Christian, and his son was king, and he was named Derthatt; he was very strong, because he had the strength of forty oxen; what they could drag and lift, that he could lift alone. It was this same king who built the large church at Bethleen, as has been already stated.*([2]) And when he became king after his father, he turned Infidel, and persecuted the Christians, and took hold of his cousin Gregory, and told him he must worship his idol. This the blessed man would not do, so he put him into a pit where there were adders and serpents and many other hurtful reptiles, that they might eat him. But they did nothing to him. He lay there twelve years. About the same time, several saintly maidens came to Ermenia from Italy, and preached the Christian religion instead of the Ermenen religion. The king heard this, and ordered that they should be brought to him. There was one amongst them who was named Susanna, who was very beautiful; she was taken to his room, when he wished to urge her to

* No such previous statement appears either in the Heidelberg MS. or in Penzel.

unchastity, but strong as he was, he could do nothing with the young woman, nor win her with all his power, for God was with her. This was told to him in the prison, and he said: "Oh, the wicked pig!" At the same time, the king fell from his throne, became a pig, and ran away to the woods. Then there was great disorder in the land, but the vassals of the country consulted, and took Gregory out of the pit, and asked him if he could help the king. He answered them and said, that he would not help him, unless they and he became Christians. The vassals promised him this, also for the king. Then said Gregory: "Ride into the wood, look for him, and bring him." They rode into the wood, and brought him to Gregory; and as soon as he saw Gregory, he ran to him, and kissed his feet. Gregory knelt on his knees, and prayed to Almighty God that he would have mercy on the man, and make him whole. The king again became a man, and was, with all his people, again a Christian,(³) and went against Babiloni and the Infidels, and conquered Babilonia and the whole country, three kingdoms, and converted them to Christianity, and appointed Gregory over the clergy and all ecclesiastical orders. In this way, their religion was established by the King Derthat and the man Gregory.(⁴) They also took much territory that belonged to the Infidels, and forced them to Christianity by means of the sword; but now they have lost all their kingdoms, although they are a fighting people. It is not long since they lost a kingdom, and a good capital called Siss; it was taken by the king-sultan. It is also their patriarch's seat, but he must pay great tribute to the sultan. The king of Zypern has many nobles of Armenia at his court, because it is near. Then was Gregory told of the great miracle which Pope Silvester had performed on Constantine, during the time that he was emperor at Rome, because he had made him clean of an eruption, and that he had saved from death the children that had been brought together to be killed, because the doctors informed the emperor that he should wash in the blood of children, so that he might get well of his eruptions.

64.—Of a Saint Gregory.

Gregory thought over it, and said to the king: "The power that thou has conferred upon me, has no influence, unless I have it from the holy father Silvester"; and he told the king of the great miracle performed by the holy father on the emperor Constantine. The king said that he would willingly see him, and would go with him, and prepared and made arrangements for [the government of] his kingdom. He took with him forty thousand men, good horsemen and foot-soldiers; he also took with him many valuables and many precious stones, with which to do honour to the holy father, Saint Silvester.([1]) Gregory took with him the most learned men that he had under him, and went from Babiloni through Persia, through Greater Armenia, and through many other countries, and went through the Iron Gates which lie between two seas, and reach into Great Tartary towards Ruwschea; through Walchi, Pulgeri, through Ungeren, Frigaul, through Lamparten, through Duschkan, and so they came dry-footed to Rome, as they had not passed over the sea. And when they were near Rome, Silvester sent to them all the blind, lame, and sick, that Gregory might heal them, as he wished to test his sanctity. When the king, Derthat, saw the people, he was angry, and thought the Pope was making fun of him. Gregory, without being angry, said: "I know well what he means"; and ordered that water should be brought to him; and he knelt on his knees, and prayed to Almighty God that those who will be sprinkled with the water, will become sound. He then took a sponge on a stick, and sprinkled the people with it;

and he who was touched by it, was healed. The blind received sight. The Pope, Silvester, heard of this, and went with all his clergy, and with the whole city of Rome, to meet him, and shewed him deference and honour. They were a whole year going by land, from Babilony to Rome. Gregory asked the Pope Silvester to give him power to free his clergy and his people from the jurisdiction of Rome, because he was so far that he could not always go to the Chair; then he gave him the power of a patriarch, and whoever wished to have this power, could not obtain it elsewhere than at Rome, and would have to send an embassy to Rome every three years. This he vowed to him, and arranged that all those who were of his faith, ecclesiastical or lay, should be subject to the Chair at Rome, and whoever would not be so, should be under the ban of the Pope, be he bishop, lord, or menial, rich or poor, in his land, and this oath the king and all his knights also took. This lasted three hundred years after the time of Gregory, that they were subject to the Chair, after which they no longer went to the Chair, and themselves chose a patriarch. Their patriarch they call Kathagnes, and a king they call Takchauer.([2])

65.—Of a dragon and a unicorn.

There was also at that same time on a mountain near Rome, a dragon and a unicorn, that did much harm to the people in the streets, so that none could pass. Then the holy father, Saint Silvester, asked the king of Armenia, as he was a powerful man, whether he would not try, with God's will, to kill the dragon and also the unicorn; the king went alone, and saw where they were, and when he got there, he saw them biting each other, and he looked at them until the dragon escaped, and the unicorn chased him to a hole in the rock; the dragon turned himself in the hole, and defended himself against the unicorn. The unicorn struck at the dragon with his tongue, and tried to draw him outside. The dragon seized the unicorn, and they struggled together, until the unicorn pulled the dragon out as far as his neck, and the one would not let the other go. At that moment, the king ran up and cut the dragon's neck, and with the tugging that the unicorn gave it, the head rolled down the rock; the king then sprang up and killed the unicorn also. He then returned to Rome, and ordered that the heads should be brought; now the waggon had enough to do to carry the head of the dragon; and so the King Derthat delivered the Romans of the reptiles, for which the city, and especially the holy father, shewed him great honour. Then Gregory went to the Pope, and asked him for the articles which belonged to the faith, which he gave him, and then they returned to their own country, and Gregory taught the Christian faith as he received it from the Pope, which they do not hold any more, as is above stated.[1] Now, they themselves elect their patriarch, and when they wish to make one, twelve bishops and four archbishops must be present, and he is elected. Many of the articles that Gregory brought from Rome, have been changed, and they are now separated from the church of Rome. Their priests make the sacrament with unleavened bread, and nobody else prepares the bread, but the priest who is to celebrate the Mass, and he prepares one only. Whilst he is making it, other priests must read the psalter right through, and if there are no priests, then he must say it himself, right through.[2] They say that it is a great sin that a man or woman should make the bread for the Holy Sacrament; they also say that it is not right to sell this bread like other bread. They communicate the Holy Sacrament with wine, and not with water. When they want to have the Mass, they all stand together, and none communicate until he who is at the high altar has communicated, so that they all communicate together. They also read the gospel [looking] towards the rising of the sun, and whichever priest celebrates the Mass, does not dare to sleep that day after midnight; and for three nights previously, and one night after, he must separate himself from his wife. They do not allow any deacon or any of a lower grade to be at the altar, only the priest; and no man or woman can attend the Mass unless they have confessed; and no woman can go into the church whilst she is unwell. Whoever has hatred or enmity towards another, must stand before the church, and is not allowed to go in until he has become reconciled. Woman and man sing the Pater Noster and the Belief, with the priest, when he celebrates the Mass. They give the Sacrament also to young children. The priests do not shave their hair nor their beard. Instead of consecrated oil, they have balm, and the patriarch gives the sultan a large price for the balm, which he sends to his bishopric. When one wants to be a priest, he must be forty days and nights in the church; and when the XL days are passed, he sings his first Mass, and he is led out with singing, dressed for the Mass. Then come his wife and child, and they kneel before him, and he gives them his blessing; then come the priest's friends and those of his wife, and they bring their offerings; also those who are invited; and there is great rejoicing in his honour, more even than when he was married, but he cannot be with his wife until he has said the Mass for forty days in succession. When they baptise a child, a man receives it, not a woman, because they say that our Lord had only a man to baptise him, and not a woman. It is also a great sin to take a woman to a baptism. They hold baptism in great honour, and whoever comes into the presence of his godfather, must kneel on the ground before him. They hold, that in sponsorship, marriage is forbidden to the fourth generation. They place much confidence in our religion;(³) they also willingly go to Mass in our churches, which the Greeks do not. They say, that between their religion and ours, there is only a hair's breadth, but that there is a great division between the Greek and their religion. During the week, they fast on Wednesday and on Friday. They do not fast in Advent, and may eat oil, but on those days they eat as often as they like after midday. They fast one week for Saint Gregory. They have a saint named Aurencius,(⁴) who was a doctor, for whom they also fast one week. They fast also on the day of the Holy Cross, which is in September; they fast also one week for Saint James the Great;(⁵) and they fast xv days in August, for our dear Lady. They fast one week for the three holy kings. They have a saint who was a knight; his name is Zerlichis;(⁶) they call upon him loudly when they are at war or in other necessity; they fast one week for him. There are many knights and nobles who fast for him for three days in January, so that they do not eat or drink, because he is a great helper in need. Their saints' days they keep on Saturday. On Easter eve, they celebrate the Mass after vespers, because that is about the time when the light shines on the holy sepulchre at Jherusalem. They also celebrate Easter, Trinity, and Ascension day with us; the other holy days they keep separately. Christmas and the Epiphany they keep at one and the same time, and on that evening, after vespers, they have the Mass. They say, that God was born on that day, and was baptised thirty years after, on that same day, and therefore they keep Christ's birth and his baptism on the same day, and that is the sixth of January. They fast one week for the twelve holy apostles, and keep their feast-day one day only, and that is Saturday. They pray with the Ave Maria once a year only, and this they do upon our Lady's day in Lent, which they do not hold as we do.(⁷) When two married persons quarrel with each other, and the one will not have the other, they are separated at bed and board; but, if neither wishes to have the other, they are separated so that each can take another spouse. If they have any children, they are given to the father. Their churches are all free, as no one can inherit or sell them. When a priest wants to build a church with his own money, he must give it to the parish, so that after his death no one may dispose of it, or he is not allowed to build it; and the same if a lord or layman builds one, so that nobody shall interfere, because it has been the custom amongst them. When a priest or layman founded a church, his heirs inherited it as they did his other property, and let it out on usury, or sold it like other property. This they have changed, and will not allow it any more, and say that every house of God should be free. Their priests go to matins every night,* which the Greek priests do not. They allow the prayers for the dead to be said for their rich people during their lifetime, and say that it is better to light a candle with one's own hand, than to let another person light it, by which they mean that he who does not care for his soul in his lifetime, will scarcely be cared for by his friends afterwards, because the friends get the money and do not care for the soul. They say, that when a man himself does good to his own soul, it is agreeable to God. When a poor man dies without confessing or without [having received] the body of God, a place in the churchyard is obtained for him by his advocate, and they lay him in the churchyard, and place a large stone on the grave, and write on it the name of God and the name of the dead man who lies there, and this they do for a sign that he is dead. And when a bishop or priest dies, they dress him as he stands before the altar, and the priests make his grave, then carry him out of the church, and put him on a seat in the grave. The first day they bury him up to his girdle, and go every day to the grave, and sing and read the psalter over him, and each

* "Und es gond ir priester och all nächt ze mettin."

priest throws a spadeful of earth over him, and this they do every day until the eighth day, and then they bury him altogether.(⁸) When a young man or a virgin dies, [they put on] silk and velvet clothes, and gold rings on the ears and fingers, and so they bury young people who have not been married. And when one marries a young woman who should be a virgin, and [he] finds that she is not a virgin, he sends her back to her father, and will not take her unless more fortune is given to her, than was arranged at the contract. They have only one cross in their churches, and not more, and say, it is a sin to crucify our Lord more than once in a church. They have no paintings on their altars, and their patriarchs and bishops grant no indulgence in their churches, and say, that pardon and remission belong to the living God, and if a man goes into the church with repentance and devotion, God, in his compassion, will grant him pardon and remission of his sins. When the priest finishes the Mass, he does not give the blessing; he descends from the altar, and men and women go up to him, and he touches one after the other on the head, and says: "Asswatz thogu thu miechk"; which means: God forgive thee thy sins.(⁹) They read low Mass aloud, that everybody may hear, and they pray for those who are entrusted to them, and for everything for which they ought to pray; for the ecclesiastical and lay authorities over all Christendom, and they pray for the Roman emperor, and all kings, dukes, barons, counts, and knights, who are subject to him;(¹⁰) and while he thus prays, all the people kneel, and raise their hands to God, and say: "Ogornicka"; which means: Lord have mercy upon us. And whilst the priest prays, these words are continually repeated by the women and men. They behave with much devotion in their churches; they do not look here and there, and do not speak, especially while they are at Mass. They decorate their churches beautifully, and have fine vestments of velvet and of silk of all sorts of colours. None of their laity dare to read the gospel as our own learned laity do, who, when they come across a book, read what they find in it; no one dares to do so, for, should he read the gospel, he would be under the ban of the patriarch, because they say that no one is to read the gospel but a priest. They incense their houses every Saturday, and on the eve of every feast-day, and no one has any other incense than the white incense which grows in Arabia and in India. Priests and laymen eat like the Infidels, sitting on the ground. They have not many preachers amongst their priests, because everyone is not allowed to preach. Their preacher must be well read in the Holy Scriptures, and must have power from the patriarch to preach, and when he has the power, he may punish a bishop. Such a preacher they call Varthabiet, which is the same as being a legate; and there are more than one, and they move from one city to the other and preach. When a priest or bishop does wrong, they punish him for it, and say, that if a priest teaches the Word of God, but does not understand and attend to it, he commits a sin.([11])

66.—Why the Greeks and Armani are enemies.

The Greeks and Armeni are always enemies, and I will tell you why it is so, because I have heard it from the Armenians. The Tartars came into Greece with forty thousand men, and did much harm to the country, and then lay siege to Constantinoppel. Then the emperor of Constantinoppel sent to the king of Armenia for forty knights, the best he had in the land, and asked him to help him. The king asked how many there were [of the enemy]; the ambassador replied to him, that there were forty thousand. Then the king of Armenia selected forty knights, the best he had in his land: "I will send forty knights to the emperor, who will, with

God's help, exterminate the Infidels, and drive them by force out of the country. When the knights came near Constantinoppel to the emperor, then the ambassador told him what he was ordered to say. The emperor thought that the king of Armenia wanted to make fun of him; and on the third day, the knights went before the emperor, and asked to be allowed to go at the enemy. The emperor asked them if they meant to overcome forty thousand men? They asked to be allowed to go out, and that the gate should be shut after them, for they should have Almighty God on their side, and would fight with Him for the Christian faith, to do which they had come, or else they would die. He gave them leave, and they went out amongst the enemy, and killed eleven hundred of them, besides the prisoners they brought to the gate; but the emperor would not let them come in, unless they also killed the prisoners, so they killed them all in front of the gate. The emperor was frightened at this, and took great care of them, and treated them very well, and they fought with the enemy every day, and every day did them much harm in the fight, and in a short time expelled the enemy from the city, and drove them out of the country. And when the devoted knights had driven away the Tartars, they went to the emperor, and wanted leave to return to their king; but the emperor took council how he was to put them to death, and invited them to stay with him three days longer; he would shew them great honour and consideration, and called out aloud: "Whoever wishes to eat and drink and live well at the emperor's court for three days, let him come." He sent a pure virgin to each knight at his separate lodging, and this he did that the virgins might be got with child by the knights, and that they should leave their seed there; because the emperor told his lords that he wanted to take the fruit from the trees and fell the trees, thinking, that after he had killed the knights, the king of Er-

H

menia would become subject to him. On the third night, he ordered that all the knights should be killed in their lodgings, which was done, with the exception of one who had been warned by the young woman he had with him. He returned and complained to the king that all his companions had been killed by [order of] the emperor. The king was terrified, and grieved much for his devoted knights, and wrote to the emperor that he had sent to him forty men who were worth forty thousand; and he must know that I will come to him, and for each of my forty knights will kill forty thousand men. Then the king of Ermenia sent to the Kaliphat of Babilony to ask his aid to march against the Greek emperor. The Kalipha himself came to help him with a great many people, and then they advanced together against the emperor with four hundred thousand men. This the emperor of Constantinoppel heard of, and went out to meet them with a great many people, and fought with them, but it was not long before he fled into the city of Constantinoppel. They followed him as far as the sea opposite to Constantinopoli, and encamped there. Then the king asked the Calypha to give him all the men he had made prisoners, and he would give him all the booty he had taken from the Greek. This was done. The king took the prisoners opposite to the city, and killed forty-times forty thousand men; and he made the arm of the sea red with blood, because he had sworn that he would give to the sea the colour of blood; and after all this was done, he still had so many prisoners, that thirty Greeks were given for an onion; this was done to insult the emperor, that it might be said that thirty Greeks were given for an onion.(¹) The Armenians are a brave people, those that live amongst the Christians, [as well as] those that live amongst the Infidels. They are also clever at work, because all the clever work the Infidels can do, in gold, purple, silver, and velvet, the Armenians can also do, and they also make good scarlet.

I have described and named the countries, cities, and religions, that I have been in amongst the Infidels. I have also written about the fights in which I have been, and of the religion of the Infidels of which I have experience, and with many other marvels which are already touched upon. Now you will hear and understand how and through which countries I have come away.

67.—Through which countries I have come away.

When Zegra was defeated, as is already related, I came over to a lord named Manstzusch; he had been a councillor of Zegra. He was obliged to fly, and he went to a city called Kaffa, where there are Christians; it is a strong city in which there are [people of] six kinds of religion. There he remained five months, and then crossed an arm of the Black Sea, and came to a country called Zerckchas; there he remained half a year. When the Tartar king became aware of this, he sent to the lord of the country, and asked that he should not allow the lord Mantzuch to remain in his territory, and he would do him a great favour. Mantzuch went into another country called Magrill; and, as we now came into the country of Magrill, we, five Christians, agreed, that we should go to our native country from the land of the Infidels, as we were not more than three days' journey from the Black Sea; and when it appeared to us opportune and right to get away, all five of us escaped from the said lord, and came to the chief town of the country, which was called Bothan, on the Black Sea shore, and begged that we should be taken across [the sea], but it was not granted to us. Then we left the city, and rode along the sea-shore, and got to a mountainous country. There we rode until the fourth day, and came to a mountain from which we saw a kocken on the sea, at about eight Italian miles from the coast. We remained on the mountain until night, and made a fire, and when the captain saw the fire, he sent some men in a skiff that they might see who we were near the fire on the mountain, and when they came towards us, we made ourselves known. They asked what sort of people we were? We said we were Christians, and were made prisoners when the king of Ungern was defeated at Nicopolis, and had come so far with the help of God; therefore, might we not go over the sea, as we had dependance and hope in God, that we should yet return to our homes and to Christianity. They would not believe us, and asked if we could repeat the Pater Noster, the Ave Maria, and the Belief? We said, "Yes", and repeated them. They then asked how many of us there were? We said, "Five". They told us to wait on the mountain, and went to their master and told him how we had spoken to them. He ordered that we should be brought, and they came with the skiff, and took us to the kocken. On the third day that we were on board the kocken, pirates came in three galleys, and would gladly have done us harm, because they were Turks. They chased us three days and two nights, but could do us no harm. We got to the city of Sant Musicia;(¹) there we remained until the fourth day, then the Turks went their own way. After that, we went to sea. We wanted to go to Constantinoppoli; but when we got out to sea, so that we could see nothing but sky and water, there came a wind which threw back the kocken about eight hundred Italian miles, to a city called Synopp. There we remained eight days, and after that we went further, and were one month and a half on the sea without being able to get to the land; and we ran short of food, and we had no more to eat and drink, until we got to a rock in the sea, where we found snails and crabs, which we picked off, and upon which we lived for four days, and were one month on the sea before we got to Constantinoppoli. And when we got there, I and my companions remained, and the kock passed through the strait for Italy. And as we were passing through the gate into Constantinopel, they asked us where we came from? We replied, that we had been prisoners amongst the Infidels, and that we had escaped, and wanted to return to Christianity. Then they took us before the Greek emperor, who asked us how we had escaped from the Infidels? We related to him from the beginning to the end, and when he heard it all, he told us not to be anxious; he would take care to send us home; and he sent us to the patriarch, who also lives in the city, and ordered us to wait until he sent a galley for his brother, who was with the queen of Unger, when he would help us into Walachy. Thus we were three months at Constantinoppel, which is surrounded by a wall eighteen Italian miles [in extent], and the wall has fifteen hundred towers. There are one thousand and one churches in the city, and the principal church is called Sant Sophia, which is built, and is also paved, with polished marble, so that when one who has not been before, goes into the temple, he imagines that the church is full of water, the marble shines so. It has a large dome covered with lead. It has three hundred and sixty gates, of which one hundred are quite of brass.(²) After three months, the Greek emperor sent us in a galley to a fortress called Gily, where the Tunow flows into the Black Sea. At this fortress I separated from my companions and joined some merchants, and went with them to a city called in German the White City, situated in Walachy. Then I came to a city called Asparseri;(³) then to a city called Sedschoff, the capital of Little Walachy; then to a place called in German, Limburgch, the chief city in White Reissen the Lesser.(⁴) There I lay ill for three months. After that, I came to Krackow, the capital of

Polan. After that, to Neichsen in Saxony, and to the city of Bressla, which capital is in Slesy. I then came to a city called Eger; from Eger to Regenspurg; from Regenspurg to Lantzhut; from Lantzhut to Frisingen, near which place I was born; and, with God's help, I returned to my home and to Christianity. Almighty God be thanked, and all those who have helped me. And when I had almost despaired of coming [away] from the Infidel people and their wicked religion, amongst whom I was obliged to be for XXXII years, and of any longer having fellowship with holy Christianity, God Almighty saw my great longing and anxiety after the Christian faith and its heavenly joys, and graciously preserved me from the risk of perdition of body and soul; therefore, I ask all who have read or have heard this book read, that they should think kindly of me before God, so that they should be eternally freed, there and here, from such heavy and unchristian captivity. Amen.

This is the Armenian Pater Noster.

Har myer ut Gegnikos surpoitza annum chika archawt-nichw iogacy kam thw hy ergnick yep ecgary hatz meyr anhabas tur mies eis or yep thawg meis perdanatz hentz minck therog nuch meinrock per danabas yep mythawg myes ypbwertzuchm heba prigo es mies ytzscheren. Amen.

This is the Tartar Pater Noster.

Atha wysum chy chockta sen algusch ludur senung adung kel suū senung hauluchūg belsun senung arcchung aley gier da vk achta wer wisum gundaluch otmak chumuseu wougū kay wisum iasochni alei wis dacha kayelle nin wisū iasoch lamasin dacba koina wisni sunamacha illa garta wisni gemandan.*(⁵)

The end of Schiltberger.

* These prayers, from the edition of 1475 (?), are omitted by Neumann, who considered their insertion as being superfluous; nor do they appear in Penzel's edition.

NOTES

TO

THE TRAVELS

OF

JOHANN SCHILTBERGER.

NOTES.

CHAPTER I.

(1.) "Then came many people from all countries to help him." —The army of King Sigismund, made up of contingents from various states, consisted of about 100,000 men at the siege of Nicopolis, 60,000 being horsemen. An Eastern writer has estimated the number of fighting men at 130,000 (Aschbach, *Gesch. K. Sigmunds*, i, 101, Saad-eddin, *Bratutti edition*). In his narrative of the action, Bonfinius (*Rer. Hung. Decad. III.*, ii, 403) repeats the proud boast of the king of Hungary, that not only should he turn the Turks out of Europe, but were the sky itself to fall, he was prepared to support it on the points of his lances.   ED.

(2.) "Pudem."—In the middle ages, this city was called Bdin or Bydinum (Schafarik, *Slawische Alterthümer*, etc., ii, 217), transformed by Schiltberger into Pudem, and by Marshal de Boucicault (Petitot *Collect.*, vi, 448) into Baudins. According to Mannert, quoted by Hammer (*Hist. de l'E. O.*, i, 416), Widdin was situated on the site of the ancient Bononia, now called by the people Bodon; but he makes no mention of the Βιδύνη of the Byzantines, which he would have found on consulting Acropolita. Widdin, the capital of Western Bulgaria, was inherited by J. Sracimir upon the death of his father, the King John Alexander, in 1365; and Eastern Bulgaria was bestowed by this sovereign on his younger son, Shishman III. The former was under the necessity of acknowledging the suzerainty of the Porte, in the reign of Amurat I; and there is every reason for supposing that it was he whom Boucicault (448) designates the lord of the country, in saying, that he was a Greek Christian, forcibly subjected to the Turks.   BRUUN.

(3.) "The king took possession of this city also."—Hammer (328) and Engel (*Gesch. d. U. R.*, ii, 198) are of opinion, that Schiltberger here refers to the city of Orsova; but the former allows, that the city believed by Engel to be Orsova, was the Aristum of Bonfinius (*Rer. Hung. Decad. III.*, ii, 377), called Raco by the French Marshal (449); it may therefore be conceded that the city in question was Rahova, on the road taken by the Christian army, which would have been retracing its steps, had its aim, after the capture of Widdin, been the siege of Orsova. BRUUN.

(3A.) "Nicopoly."— In my *Geographische Anmerkungen zum Reisebuch von Schiltberger (Sitzungsberichte d. Kön. Bay. Akad.*, 1869, ii, 271), I have endeavoured to shew that, in stating that the Infidels knew the city of "Schiltaw" by the name of "Nicopoly", Schiltberger does not call attention to the city of Nicopolis on the Danube, near the estuary of the Osma, but to ancient Nicopolis founded by Trajan, the ruins of which are still to be seen near the village of Nikup, on the Rushita, a tributary of the Yantra. I was formerly of opinion that the battle which decided the Eastern question at that period, was fought near the village, and this opinion, adopted by several authors of merit, has recently been supported by M. Jirecek in his admirable work, *Geschichte der Bulgaren*, wherein reference is made to an ancient Servian Chronicle in which it is recorded, that the battle took place "na rece Rositê u Nikopolju". It would appear, however, that the author of this notice, through some misapprehension, confounded the Rushita with the Osma; and M. Kanitz (*Donau-Bulgarien*, ii, 58-70) having lately, on just grounds, condemned my hypothesis, I am now persuaded that the Christians were defeated by Bajazet in the neighbourhood of the present town of Nicopolis, which was in existence at that time, though from what period is not known; nor are we able to determine when the ancient Nicopolis "ad Hæmum", disappeared.

If Schiltberger's contemporaries sometimes designated the one city by the name of Great Nicopolis, they did so simply to distinguish it from a fortress on the opposite, the left bank of the Danube, called Little Nicopolis, that was taken by the Christians in the preceding campaign (Jirecek, 354). It is, therefore, just possible, that the sultan, having passed Trnov, or Ternova, when on his way to the besieged city, had also entered Tchunkatch (see trans. of the Turkish historiographer, Neshry, in *Zeitschr. d. D. Morgenl. Gesellsch.*, xv, 346), the name possibly given by Neshry to the castle of Tchuka, the ruins of which are to be seen in the upper part of the city, called now as it was then, Shvishtov, Shistov, Sistova, situated at a distance of fifteen miles to the south-east of the field of battle. If such were indeed the case, I would venture to suggest, until some better explanation is offered, that our author may, by mistake or through some misconception, have given to the besieged city the name of Shistov, corrupted by him to "Schiltaw". BRUUN.

(3B.) Nicopolis, the city besieged "by water and by land for XVI days", must, unquestionably, have been the place of that name on the right bank of the Danube, and not ancient Nicopolis, "ad Istrum", as believed by some authors, the site of which, distant nearly forty miles from the river, has been satisfactorily determined by M. Kanitz, from an inscription he has been fortunate enough to disinter out of a mass of its ruins. The present Nicopolis, built on a limestone cliff, fills a ravine formed by two heights commanding the town. Sigismund may, or may not, have occupied those heights; but, when surprised at his dinner, at ten o'clock in the morning on the day of the battle, by being informed that the Turks were making their appearance (Froissart, iv, c. 52), he advanced one mile only from his encampment outside the beleaguered city, for the purpose of encountering Bajazet; and the French assumed the offensive immediately after the "Duke of Walachy" had reconnoitred the enemy's position. If a further advance was made at all, it could scarcely have covered much ground, seeing that the 12,000 foot-soldiers routed by Sigismund had advanced to oppose him; and when the king was about to follow up his victory by attacking a body of horse, the sultan being on the point of taking to flight, the timely aid of the latter's ally, the despot of Servia, changed the fortunes of the day. The battle, says Froissart, lasted three hours only, and the result, so disastrous to the Christian army, he attributes to the impetuosity of Philippe d'Artois, Comte d'Eu, who disregarded the instructions of the king of Hungary. "Nous perdons hui la journée", said the latter to the Grand Master of Rhodes, "par l'orgueil et bobant (vanity) de ces François; et s'ils m'eussent cru, nous avions gens assez pour combattre nos ennemies."

The Christian soldiers fled in disorder, and being hard pressed by Bajazet's troops, many were killed on the mountain, one of the heights near Nicopolis, as they hurried to the Danube, many others being drowned in their unsuccessful efforts to reach the shipping —probably some of the vessels of the Venetian blockading squadron, under the command of Giovanni Mocenigo, on board of which, Sigismund, and Philibert de Noillac, Grand Master of the Order of St. John of Jerusalem, were received; the latter being conveyed to Rhodes, whence the ships sailed for Dalmatia to land the king. It seems pretty clear, from Schiltberger's narrative, that the battle of Nicopolis was fought in the immediate vicinity of the city on the Danube, and therefore at a considerable distance from the ancient Nicopolis, the city of Trajan. Details of the action will be found in Aubert de Vertot d'Aubeuff's *Histoire des Chevaliers Hospitaliers de St. Jean de Jerusalem*, etc., 1726.

There is no evidence that Schiltberger set foot in Shistova, but the name had doubtlessly become familiar to him, both before and after his capture, at a time that he was totally unacquainted with the language of the people amongst whom he had fallen. If the incidents of his eventful career were indeed dictated from memory, his statement that the Infidels knew Nicopolis as "Schiltaw", for Shrishtov, Shishtovo, may be accounted for, by the accidental confusion of names.   ED.

(4.) "Werterwaywod."—Schiltberger evidently alludes here to John Mirca (John Mirtcha), prince or voyevoda of Walachia, called John, by Mme. de Lusson (Engel, *Gesch. d. U. R.*, iv, 160 : iii, 5), and Marcus, by the Byzantines (L. Chalco, 77). He was the son of the voyevoda, J. Radul, and having succeeded his elder brother, J. Dan, added the Dobroudja to his domains after the short reign of Ivanko or Iuanchus, "filius bonæ memoriæ magnifici domini Dobrdize", as he is styled in the treaty concluded with the Genoese in 1387 (*Not. et Extr.*, etc., xi, 65 ; and *Mem. de l'Inst. de France*, vii, 292-334). There is no difficulty in recognising the Bulgarian despot, Dobrotitch, in the person of the father, who, after the death of Alexander, declared his independance in the Dobroudja, whence, in all probability, its name.

(Bruun, *Journ. du Minis. de l'Instruc. Pub.*, St. Petersburg, Sept. 1877.)
BRUUN.

(5.) "he had come a great distance with six thousand men."—The force commanded by the Comte de Nevers, son of Philip, Duke of Burgundy, consisted of 1000 knights, 1000 soldiers, and 6000 mercenaries. The Count was supported by the flower of the French nobility. Aschbach (*Gesch. K. Sigmund's*, i, 98) places the total at 10,000 men.
ED.

(6.) "Duke of Iriseh, known as the despot."—Stephen, prince of Servia, is here designated the despot of "Iriseh", because Servia at that time was also known as Rascia. Thus —" ipsum regnum Rasciæ—regno Hungariæ ab antiquo subjectum", etc. (Engel, *Gesch. d. U. R.*, iii, 370). Windeck, the contemporary biographer of Sigismund (Aschbach, *Gesch. K. Sigmund's*, i, 234), likewise states, that the king advanced "gegen Sirfien und Raizen, und bedingte mit dem Tischbot", that is to say, the despot. As the Turks are in the habit of preceding with an I, all foreign names commencing with a consonant, so may Schiltberger's comrades, as Magyars, have converted Rascia into Iriseh.
BRUUN.

(7.) "Duke of Burgony."—This Duke of Burgundy was the valiant Comte de Nevers, aged 22 years only, afterwards surnamed Jean sans Peur; he was uncle to Charles VI. "Hanns Putzokardo" is easily recognised as the John Boucicault already noticed. As to the lord "Centumaranto", Fallmerayer believes this person to have been Saint Omer, without, however, stating any reason for this belief; it is, therefore, more probable that Châteaumorant should be substituted for the name given by Schiltberger.

We read in Boucicault, that one Jean Chasteaumorant arrived in Turkey, with the money for the ransom of the French knights. It is very possible that a namesake, and even a near relative of this Châteaumorant, was among them, to whom the marshal afterwards entrusted the defence of Constantinople against the Turks, upon his own return to France.
BRUUN.

CHAPTER II.

(1.) "Hannsen of Bodem."—The Marshal Boucicault (Petitot *Collect.*, 465, 471) confirms Schiltberger's statement, to the effect that Bajazet consented to spare the lives of a certain number of great lords, hoping "to receive from them much treasure and gold". Henri and Philippe de Bar, cousins-german of the king, the Constable Count d'Eu, the Count de la Marche, and the Lord de la Trémouille, were of the number. No clue is given to the correct name and nationality of Stephen Synüher, but as he and the lord of Bodem (Widdin) are distinguished from the twelve French nobles whose lives were spared, it is pretty certain that allusion is made to Stephen Simontornya, nephew to Stephen Laszkovitz, voyevoda of Transylvania (Hurmuzaki, *Fragm. zur Gesch. der Rum.*, 225). Aschbach informs us, that the uncle and nephew, who had both assisted at the battle of Nicopolis, were the first to take to flight; but it is very possible, that the nephew happened to be among those who failed to reach the river in time to enable him to embark, and was thus made a prisoner. John of Bodem was undoubtedly John Sracimir, king of Western Bulgaria, whose capital was Widdin. BRUUN.

(2.) "Kalipoli."—Gallipoli, is mentioned (Ducas., *Hist. Byz.*) as being the first town occupied by the Turks (1356) on the European continent. By the treaty of Adrianople, 1204, upon the fall of the Empire, Gallipoli, which had been strongly fortified by the Byzantine emperors, fell to the Venetians; but the possession of an important stronghold commanding the entrance to the Marmora and Black Sea, was continually disputed by the Italians and Greeks, until the year 1307, when the Genoese and Greeks having, as allies, vanquished the Catalans in the Sea of Marmora, laid siege to Gallipoli, to which place those mercenaries of the Empire had been sent, who, after destroying the town and devastating the country around, withdrew into Attica and Bœotia. The Turks rebuilt the fortifications, which were greatly strengthened by Bajazet, who also constructed a port for his galleys. The Count de Nevers and 24 of his illustrious companions in arms, were detained in captivity at Gallipoli, and afterwards at Broussa, until ransomed for the sum of 200,000 golden ducats. (Heyd., *Le Colonie Commer.*, i, 347; Hammer, *Hist. de l'E. O.*, i, 106.) ED.

(3.) "Windischy land."— According to Froissart (iv, c. 52), Sigismund embarked at Constantinople on board of a vessel that had just discharged a cargo of provisions. It is stated in the *History of Cyprus*, that the king arrived in Dalmatia by way of Rhodes. Thwrocz (Schwandtnerus, *Script. Rerum Hung.*, iv, 9) adds, that he afterwards landed in Croatia, the country alluded to by Schiltberger as "Windischy land". See "Windische Mark", in *Cosmographey*. BRUUN.

CHAPTER III.

(1.) "and the people he took away, and some he left in Greece." —Baron Hammer points out, that Styrian historians have not noticed this fact, with which, in all probability, is connected the origin of certain Slave settlements in Asia Minor. M. Lamansky (*O Slav. v. Mal. Asii*) however, believes, they are of more ancient date. BRUUN.

(2.) "king-sultan."—Schiltberger styles the sultan of Egypt, king-sultan, because, having the caliph at his court, he was considered as being at the head of all Mahomedan monarchs. The sultan at the period indicated was Barkok, the first of the dynasty of Circassian Mamelouks, if we except Bibars II, whose reign, 1309-1310, was of the shortest duration. Twenty years before his accession (1382), Barkok was carried as a slave into Egypt, from the Crimea, whither he had gone from his own native country in the Caucasus. BRUUN.

(3.) "king of Babylony."—This king of Babylon was Ahmed, son of Oveis, son of the Jelarid Hassan the Great, the descendant of Abaka, the son of Houlakou, the son of Tuly, son of Jengiz

I

Khan. Timour drove Ahmed from Baghdad, but he returned upon several occasions, notably in 1395, and remained until 1402. Previously to the battle of Nicopolis, Bajazet had written to tell him that, in his opinion, the expulsion of Timour was of greater moment than that of the Takfour, that is to say, of the Greek emperor (Hammer, *Hist. de l'E. O.*, ii, 466, note xv). BRUUN.

(4.) "king of Persia."—Even before the battle of Nicopolis, nearly the whole of Persia had been subjugated by Timour, and divided between his sons, Omar Sheykh and Miran Shah, and other amirs. The Shah Mansour, who had also appealed to Bajazet for succour, perished in 1393 at the battle of Sheeraz; the other princes of the house of Mouzzafer had been put to death, with the exception of Zein Alabin, and Shebel, the two sons of the shah Shoudja, who ended their days at Samarkand (Weil., *Gesch. d. Chalifen*, ii, 40); it is, consequently, somewhat puzzling to determine, to which sovereign of Persia the Christian captives were sent. BRUUN.

(5.) "White Tartary."—According to Neumann, Schiltberger here seeks to distinguish the free Tatars from the Black Tatars, that is to say, the vanquished and paying tribute. Erdmann (*Temud. d. U.*, 194), on the authority of Rashid uddin, considers that by White Tatars were meant the Turk tribes, who were afterwards known as Mongols, the Black Tatars being the real Mongols. He tells us, that after having subdued the White Tatars and other Turk people, the Black resumed their ancient name of Mongols, and extended their sway to Eastern Europe, including under the name of Tatars even the Turks in the West, with the exception of those by whom they were opposed in Asia Minor, and who afterwards became known in Europe as the Ottoman Turks.

This, however, does not explain to us where the White Tatars, repeatedly mentioned by Schiltberger, dwelt. We learn from him, first, that a powerful lord from their country was the son-in-law of Kady Bourhan uddin, sovereign of Sebaste, who was put to death by Kara Yelek or Oulouk, chief of the Turkomans of the White Sheep: secondly; that, having laid siege to the city of

Angora, which belonged to Bajazet, they were forced to yield to him; and, thirdly, that at the battle of Angora, 30,000 of them went over to Timour, and were the cause of his gaining the day.

Taking into consideration these several facts, is it not possible, that the White Tatars of Schiltberger are to be identified with those of the White Horde of Eastern writers; the Blue, as they were sometimes alluded to by Russian annalists, perhaps because of their encampments on the shores of the Blue Sea, the Lake Aral? This Horde, as the patrimony of the elder branch of the house of Jujy, whose chief town was Ssaganak, near the upper Syr Darya, was dependent to a certain extent on the Golden Horde, ruled over by the descendants of Batou, the second son of Jujy. But this state of dependence was not of long duration, for towards the close of the 14th century, the famous Toktamish, a prince of the elder branch, succeeded in annexing the whole of the Golden Horde to his possessions, after having, with the assistance of Timour, rid himself of his uncle Ourous Khan. Having quarrelled with his protector, this ambitious man was under the necessity of courting the friendship of Bajazet, who was only too pleased to secure another ally against the threatening domination of the ruler of Jagatai; there is, therefore, nothing surprising in the fact of the sultan sending a certain number of Christian captives to Toktamish, were it only to console him for the unfortunate termination to his war with Timour in 1395. At all events, the partisans of Toktamish, who effected their escape under the leadership of Timour Tash, upon the defeat of the former near the banks of the Terek, were received by the sultan with open arms. Savelieff (*Mon. Joud.*, 314) gives it as his opinion, that Timour Tash who held the Crimea under the suzerainty of Toktamish, was himself a member of the Jujy family; in which case the sovereign of Sebaste might well have given his daughter in marriage to him, without contracting a misalliance, and the very nature of this alliance, may have incited Timour Tash to treat his benefactor with ingratitude in laying siege to Sebaste, his whole household being in his suite, after the custom of the country. Having necessarily become reconciled with the sultan, he might easily have treated him with treachery at the battle of Angora, by passing over to the ranks of his countrymen; in such a case they would have obtained a victory, in consequence of defection amongst the Tatars in the service of Bajazet, as we are informed by Arabian authors, and not, as Persian and Turkish historians have imagined, through defection among "the Turk princes of Asia Minor".

It is, nevertheless, no easy matter to reconcile this hypothesis with the statement made by Clavijo (*Hakluyt Soc. Publ.*, 75). After alluding to the capture of Sebaste by Timour, the Spanish envoy continues:—" Before he arrived there, he met with a race called the White Tartars, who always wander over the plain; and he fought and conquered them, and took their lord prisoner; and took away as many as fifty thousand men and women with him. He then marched to Damascus," etc., etc.

In another passage, he returns to the Tartaros Blancos subdued by Tamerlane, and says that they were encamped between Turkey (Asia Minor) and Syria. These White Tatars were evidently identical with the White Tatars of Schiltberger, who had nothing in common with the Tatars of the White Horde, frequently designated as being of "Great Tartary". It may therefore be assumed that the White Tatars mentioned by both travellers, were Turkomans, inhabitants of the eastern parts of Asia Minor, whose descendants have to this day preserved the Mongol type, and the same mode of living as the White Tatars of Schiltberger and Clavijo (Viv. de Saint-Martin, *Desc. de l'A. M.*, ii, 429). East Cilicia was at that time actually divided between two Turkoman dynasties, which had not been vanquished by the Ottoman arms; small states that had existed from the year 1378, the date at which the Lusignans, who had succeeded the Roupenian dynasty of Little Armenia in 1342, were expelled from Cilicia by the Baharite Mamelouks of Egypt. The one reigned at Marash, the other at Adana; the latter being known as the Ben Ramazan, the former as the Soulkadyr or Joulkadyr, the name by which Marash was afterwards known amongst Turkish geographers. Both dynasties were in existence until 1515, when they were subjugated by the sultan, Selim, and their territories incorporated with the empire (Viv. de Saint-Martin, *Desc. de l'A. M.*, i, 529).

It would appear that the rulers of the White Tatars, alluded to by Clavijo, belonged to the family of the Joulkadyr. It was, at any rate, against that dynasty, Timour despatched a force after the capture of Sivas, to punish it for its hostility towards himself, when besieging that city (Weil., *Gesch. d. Chalifen*, v, 82); and the Mongols soon afterwards carried off all the herds belonging to a prince of this house, whose encampment was near Palmyra (*ibid.*, 91). As was the case with the White Tatars of Clavijo, those mentioned by Schiltberger drew their rulers, at least in part, from princes of this house. It was Bajazet's desire, that his son should marry the daughter of Nazr uddin Joulkadyr, who would not have been forgotten at the distribution of prisoners taken at Nicopolis. This Nazr uddin had received his fugitive relative, the son of Bourhan uddin, the brother-in-law, according to Schiltberger, of the ruler of the White Tatars. It appears to me that the seeming diversity in the statements made by various authors, with regard to the nationality of the troops who went over to Timour at the battle of Angora, is to be explained by admitting, that the Tatars who betrayed the cause of Bajazet, were Turkomans who acknowledged the authority of the Ben Ramazan and the Joulkadyr; that is to say, that their rulers were princes holding possessions in Asia Minor. Our author's recital enables us to understand, why Oriental writers would seem to be at issue as to the nationality of the "Tatar Regiments" (Weil., *Gesch. d. I. V.*, 437) which deserted their colours at the battle of Angora. BRUUN.

(6.) "Greater Armenia."—Armenia proper is here called Greater, to distinguish it from the Lesser, which was understood to be the eastern part of Cappadocia, near the Euphrates. In the middle ages, the denomination Lesser Armenia included the whole of Cappadocia, inasmuch as it was inhabited by Armenians who had been expelled their own country by the Seljouks and Turkomans (11th and 12th centuries). At a subsequent period, the Armenians occupied nearly the whole of Cilicia and the west of Syria, anciently called Commagen, and afterwards known as Euphrates. All these new acquisitions were included under the name of Lesser Armenia. BRUUN.

CHAPTER IV.

(1.) "Karanda."—This city, on the site of ancient Laranda, is now known as Karaman, so named after the son of a certain Sophy, upon whom it was bestowed (1219-46) by Ala uddin, sultan of Iconium, together with a portion of Cappadocia and of Cilicia, that is to say, of Lesser Armenia. Mohammed, the son of Karaman, extended the limits of his states in every direction, and even took possession of Iconium or Konieh. His son Ali Bek, surnamed Ala uddin, was married to Nefise, the sister of Bajazet, an alliance, however, that did not restrain him from invading Ottoman territory, an act which resulted in war between the brothers-in-law, and he was made a prisoner by the Turks after the fall of Iconium, in 1392. According to Saad uddin (Zinkeisen, *Gesch. d. O. R.*, i, 350), Karaman was killed by Timour Tash, governor of Angora, without the knowledge of Bajazet, who would have spared his brother-in-law. Ahmed and Mohammed, the sons of Karaman, were afterwards reinstated by Timour in their possessions, which included, besides Laranda, evidently the "Karanda" in the text, the cities of Alaïa, Derendeh, Sis, Veysheher, Konieh, Aksheher, Akseraï, and Anazarba. BRUUN.

CHAPTER V.

(1.) "Sebast."—Sebaste, called Sivas by the Turks, and Sepasdia, Sevasdia, Sevasd, by the Armenians—the capital of Lesser Armenia, after being long subject to Constantinople, was ceded, in 1021, by the emperor Basil to Senekharim, king of Armenia, in exchange for Vasbouragan. It was taken in 1080 by the Greeks, who lost it to the Seljouks (J. Saint Martin, *Mem. sur l'Arménie*, i, 187). ED.

CHAPTER VI.

(1.) "Wirmirsiana."—According to Chalcocondylas, Orthobulus or Ertoghrul, the eldest son of Bajazet, was made a captive by

Timour at Sebaste, in 1400, and shortly afterwards put to death; but no Arabian or Persian chroniclers have asserted this, nor does Shereef uddin allude to the circumstance. Arabshah (Weil., *Gesch. d. Chalifen*, ii, 82) says that Souleiman, the son of Bajazet, was governor of Sebaste, which he must have quitted before its conquest by the Mongols. BRUUN.

CHAPTER VII.

(1.) "city of Samson."—This is the ancient Amisos, still called Samsoun by the Turks. Fallmerayer (*Gesch. d. K. v. T.*, 56, 289) observes, that the Byzantines frequently added a prefix to a name, such as εἰν, which, in time, became contracted to ες and σ, and in this way Ἄμισον was turned into σ' Ἄμισον—Σάμσον. This city, the chief town of Janyk, was then under the dominion of another Bajazet, surnamed the Impotent, who perished in his struggle with Bajazet about 1392. BRUUN.

(1A.) Fallmerayer's explanation may be further illustrated, by quoting the names of ancient cities in the Morea and in the island of Crete, that have undergone change through the probable corruptions of a prefix. Hierapytna has become Tzerapetra; Itanus is now Tzetana, Tsitana, and even Sitana. Etea has become Setea, while Stamboul, Istamboul, itself is a corruption of 'Εἰς τὴν πόλιν. The modern Greeks would also appear to be in the habit of thus corrupting words in ordinary use, as, for instance, ampelon, vineyard, they call tsembela; kampos, a field, tzecampo, etc. (Spratt, *Researches in Crete*, i, 55, 200). ED.

CHAPTER VIII.

(1.) "Italians of Genoa."—It is not known when the Genoese founded a colony at Samsoun, which they called Simisso. Heyd (*d. Ital. Handelscolon*, etc., in the *Zeitschrift f. d. gesam. Staatswissenschaft.*, xviii, 710) justly observes, that they must have been there previously to the year 1317, because the existence of a

Genoese consul at Simisso at that date, is proved by the records of Gazaria. In the Regulations for Gazaria, 1449 (*Zap. Odess.*, v, p. 629), no mention whatever is made of a consul being at Simisso; I cannot therefore agree with M. Heyd that the consulate was maintained until 1461, when Mahomet II drove the Genoese out of Samastris (Amastris), their principal port, and took possession of Sinope, where, to the year 1449, those Italians still had a consul (*ibid.*, 809). The Genoese were driven out of Samsoun, in all probability in 1419, when that quarter of the town "occupied by infidels" was taken by Mahomet I (Hammer, ii, 180, 472, note xiv). At this period Schiltberger was still in Asia, and he appears to have been aware that the Genoese were obliged to quit the town. At any rate, in saying that the Italians of Genoa were still in possession of it, in the reign of Bajazet, he probably wished to intimate that they had quitted it at a later period. BRUUN.

(2). "Ternowa."—Trnovo or Ternov, the capital of Eastern Bulgaria, was taken and destroyed by the Turks in 1393, at a moment that Shishman happened to be absent. Turkish authors have recorded, that at Nicopolis he surrendered at discretion, and died, according to some, in confinement, and at an advanced age; others, however, state that he was beheaded, which, judging by the narrative in the text, would appear doubtful. Alexander, Shishman's eldest son, having turned Mahomedan, was appointed governor of Saroukhan, as we are informed by Rehm (*Gesch. d. Mittelalt.*, iv, 2, 584); and it is possible that he was transferred to Samsoun after the conquest of the province of Janyk, in the province-general of Trebizond. His younger brother Fruzin remained a Christian, and died at Kronstadt in 1460. BRUUN.

CHAPTER IX.

(1.) "Wurchanadin."—It has already been noticed that Bourhan uddin was prince of Sebaste or Sivas. The Turkish lord named Otman in this chapter, was Kara Yelek, chief of the Turkoman Horde of the White Sheep. BRUUN.

(2.) The death of Bourhan uddin.—Oriental writers are at issue as to the date of the death of Bourhan uddin, and of the incorporation of his domains with those of Bajazet. Saad uddin (Weil., Gesch. d. Chalifen, ii, 60, note i) observes, that various dates are given, from the year 794 to 799 of the Hegira = 1391-96. In his History of the Ottoman Empire (i, 226), Hammer expresses himself in favour of the opinion of Nishandi, an Arabian author, who fixes the date at 795 = 1392. This opinion is supported by Zinkeisen (Gesch. d. O. R., i, 353), who states he has no doubt that "the course of events and the most reliable authorities testify in favour of the year 1392", although Weil makes it clear, that the death of Bourhan uddin could not have taken place before the year 800 = 1398. German historians are guided by the statements of Oriental writers, who have apparently confounded two wars between Bajazet and the sovereign of Sebaste, the one having taken place before, and the other after the battle of Nicopolis. Indeed we learn from Schiltberger, that previously to the war in which he himself was engaged (see page 17), the younger son of Bajazet had driven Bourhan uddin out of "Marsiiany", a city which, from being situated on the borders of Karaman, must have been identical with Marsivan (Viv. de Saint-Martin, Desc. de l'A. M., ii, 448) or Merzyfoun, as it was called by Hadjy Khalpha (Jihan-Numa, etc., ii, 407), and was perhaps the village of Morivazou, the birth-place of St. Stephen of Sougdaia (Zap. Odess., v, 625). In the introduction to his edition of 1859, Neumann submits that Amasia is here intended; but he is in error, because that place had already been taken by Bajazet, not from Bourhan uddin, but from Bajazet the "Impotent", together with Samsoun, Kastamouny, and Osmandjyk (Hammer, i, 312-315).

Neumann is certainly not justified in supposing that Schiltberger would have alluded upon two occasions to the campaign in which he took part—first, in chap. 5, casually; again in chap. 9, wherein we have all the details as they are related by an eye-witness; for, in reference to this, the second campaign, we are informed that it was conducted by the eldest son of Bajazet, and that this son was not Mouhammed; indeed, we are previously told by Schiltberger, that Mouhammed was appointed by the sultan to command the forces sent to "Marsüany", it being the first expedition of that prince, who was aged 14 in 1392, for he died in 1421, in his 43rd year.   BRUUN.

CHAPTER X.

(1.) "Malathea."— Malatia, the ancient Melitene, on the Euphrates, was the station of the xiith Legion. Marcus Aurelius surnamed it "Fulminatrix", in consequence of a miracle that was there operated (Ritter, *Die Erdkunde*, etc., x, 860). Hammer (*Hist. de l'E. O.*, 345), and Zinkeisen (*Gesch. d. O. R.*, 356), assert, on the authority of Saad uddin, that the Ottomans took this and other cities subject to the sultans of Egypt, between the years 798 and 800 of the Mahommedan era. Weil (*Gesch. d. Chalifen*, 70-73), however, does not think that this occupation could have taken place earlier than 801, founding his opinion on the authority of Arabian writers, who have recorded Turkish aggression as having occurred after the advent to the throne, of Faradj, who succeeded his father in 801 = 1399 (June 20). In support of this argument, Weil quotes the testimony of one of those writers who had himself seen the letter, in which was announced to Itmish, the atabek of the new sultan, the capture of Malatia ; but it is also possible that the great dignitary had received this same letter in the time of Barkok, by whom he must have been highly esteemed, for, when on his death-bed, the sultan nominated him his executor. This view of the case agrees with Schiltberger's recital, whilst his observations, towards the end of this chapter, on the taking of Adalia, will serve to explain the strange passage that occurs in the Italian translation of the book of Saad uddin. " Et havendo spedito al Conquisto di Chianchria" (Kiankary the ancient Gangra) " Timurtas-Bassa" (Bajazet's general) " però tutto quel Paese insieme con la Città d'Atena (la qual' è patria de' Filosofi) col suo Distretto pervenne in poter del Rè ; il quale prese anco dalle mani de' Turcomani la Città di Bechsenia" (Behesna) " e di

Mallatie", etc. " There is clearly a mistake in the text or in the translation", says Weil (70), after showing that Hammer and Zinkeisen are greatly in error in supposing, upon the authority of this defective passage, that the city of Socrates could have been taken by the Turks in the course of the same campaign as that in which Malatia fell into their hands; but there would have been nothing extraordinary in the fact of their attacking Angora after the fall of this city, and then Satalia, near the ruins of the ancient Attalia in Pamphylia, in which Neumann fancies that he recognises the Adalia of Schiltberger, because it was situated on the sea-shore opposite to the island of Cyprus. In support of this, the esteemed editor of the edition of 1859 might have quoted another passage, from the *Acta Patriarchatus Constantinopolitani* (*Zap. Odess.*, v, 966), wherein we find it asserted, that the city of Satalia, having been occupied by the Infidels in 1400, the bishop of that city took his departure for Aenos. Notwithstanding these arguments, it appears to me that the Adalia of Schiltberger could not have been Satalia, but rather Adana in Cicilia, for the following reasons.

This city of Adana, Adena, or Adan, is nearer to the island of Cyprus than is Satalia, although not actually on the sea-shore, a situation not attributed to his Adalia by Schiltberger. It belonged to the sultans of Egypt, which was not the case with Satalia, a city that from the year 1207 had been subject to the sultans of Iconium, to the Seljouk principality of Tekke, and to the kingdom of Cyprus, and was already incorporated in the Ottoman Empire (Weil, i, 505; Heyd, xviii, 714). Finally, Schiltberger's notice that the people about Adalia were exclusively employed in the rearing of camels, is applicable to Adana rather than to Satalia; for in those days it was one of the chief centres of commerce in the East, and was encircled by the superb gardens for which it is so celebrated in our own times. It may, I think, be conceded that Saad uddin, or Bratutti his translator, have possibly confounded Athens with Attalia or Adana, and that this very city might have been subjugated by Timour Tash, soon after his reduction of Behesna, Malatia, and other cities in Cilicia.   BRUUN.

CHAPTER XI.

(1.) " Thus Joseph expelled his rival, and became a powerful king."—Upon the death of the Sultan Barkok, his son Al-Melyk Al-Nazr Abou-Saadat Faradj, aged thirteen, ascended the throne. Schiltberger pronounces one of the names of this monarch after his own fashion, and calls him Joseph, and elsewhere Jusuphda, evidently in place of Abou-Saadat. This prince, soon after his accession, was under the necessity of contending in arms with Itmish (who has already been noticed), one of his father's dependants, as Schiltberger represents Joseph to have done. Faradj perished, as did Jusuphda, for he was made a prisoner and beheaded in 1412 (Weil, *Gesch. d. Chalifen.*, ii, 124).

Eastern writers make no mention of the assistance rendered to Faradj by Bajazet, upon the occasion of his struggle with his father's vassal at the commencement of his reign; but their silence on this point is by no means conclusive as throwing doubt on the statement, twice repeated, of Schiltberger, who was himself serving in the force despatched by Bajazet to the support of the sultan, in whom he hoped to secure an ally against Timour, whose power menaced the safety of both. Had the two sultans been indeed of one accord, the conqueror might have received a check. According to Aboul-Mahazin (Weil, ii, 71), Timour is reported to have said, on hearing of the death of Barkok: " Bajazet is an excellent general, but his troops are not worth much; the Egyptians and Syrians, however, are good soldiers, but they are badly handled". It is very certain that Bajazet, in his turn, soon afterwards (1400) appealed for assistance to the sultan of Egypt, who refused to grant it, because the former's venture against Malatia was not forgotten (Weil, 81, note 42); but the necessity he was under of keeping his troops for protection at home, was the truer cause.   BRUUN.

CHAPTER XII.

(1.) "took the city by force, although there were in it five thousand horsemen sent by Weyasit."—The walls of Sebaste, originally constructed by Aladin Kekobady, a Seljouk king, were of extraordinary strength, being twenty cubits in height, and ten cubits in thickness at the base, narrowing to six cubits at the top. The place was stubbornly defended, the besieged being well supplied with munitions of war; but the besiegers constructed towers of greater height than the town, and planted upon them machines for hurling huge stones, so that, at the expiration of 18 days (the text says 21 days), the besieged sued for quarter. Timour spared all the Mussulmans, but the Christians were sent into slavery. The 4000 horsemen (5000 horsemen in the text) being Armenians, were flung alive into pits and covered with earth (Petis de la Croix, *Histoire de Timur Bec*, liv. v, 268). ED.

(2.) "There were also nine thousand virgins taken into captivity by Tämerlin to his own country."—The contemporary historians, Aboul-Mahazin and Arabshah (Weil, 81), describe in like manner the cruelties practised on the inhabitants of Sebaste in 1400, by Timour, whose admirer even, Shereef uddin, differs but slightly in the horrible details (Hammer, *Hist. de l'E. O.*, ii, 59).

BRUUN.

CHAPTER XIII.

(1.) "Scarcely had Tämerlin returned to his own country."— After the fall of Sebaste, Timour proceeded to Syria, where he took several cities, Damascus being of the number; and having recrossed the Euphrates, he entered Baghdad. Bajazet had in the meantime seized upon Erzingan, which belonged to Taharten, who had already acknowledged the supremacy of Timour; an act on the part of the sultan which accelerated the struggle between himself and Timour, and to which Schiltberger alludes in this chapter. In chapters 14-19, he depicts the above-mentioned campaigns and other expeditions of Timour, imagining that they were conducted after the battle of Angora; but as he reports from hearsay only, he was not in a position to form a correct idea of the chronological order in which they occurred. BRUUN.

(2.) "Tarathan."—It is by the name of Taharten that Eastern writers know this prince, who, at that time, possessed the city of Erzingan; whilst Clavigo, who enters into numerous details on the private affairs of the "gran Caballero", calls him Zaratan. The residence of this ruler was near the Kara-sou, at that time the great western arm of the Euphrates, at a place called by the Turks, Erznga or Eznga, a name derived from the Armenian, Eriza, as I am informed by Bishop Aïvazoffsky of the Armenian church at Theodosia. According to Marco Polo, who called it Arzinga (Yule, 2nd edit., i, 47), it was the capital of Greater Armenia, Sis being that of Lesser Armenia. The apparent contradiction in our author's statements arises from the fact that, in another chapter, he represents Sis, Erzingan, and Tiflis, as being the chief towns of the three divisions of Armenia. The first belonged to the sultan of Egypt; the others to the Timourides, actually to Shah Rokh, the son of Timour. In ancient times, Erzingan was celebrated for the temple of Anaïtis (Strabo, xi, 14, 16), destroyed by St. Gregory the Enlightener. Procopius calls the place, Aurea Comana, and tells us that it contained a temple of Artemis, founded, according to tradition, by Orestes and Iphigenia; a temple already transformed into a Christian church at the time he wrote (*De Bell. Pers.*, i, 177; Ritter, *Die Erdkunde*, etc., x, 774).

In quoting, together with Arzes and Erzingan, the fortress of Chliat and Percri, Constantine Porphyrogenitus (*De Adm. Imp.*, 44, 8) referred to Akhlat or Gelath, and the modern town of Pergri on the Bandoumaky, and not, as supposed by Ritter, to the village of Bagaran or Pacaran, near the ruins of Ani, the ancient capital of Armenia, close to the river Arpa-tchaï. Erzingan was destroyed by the Mongols in 1242; in 1387, Taharten acknowledged the suzerainty of Timour, and in 1400 he was expelled by Bajazet, who, in his turn, lost the city to the Tatars. It had not risen out of its ruins in the time of Barbaro, and now they are scarcely to be traced. *Etiam periere ruinæ!* BRUUN.

(3.) "but he died on the way."—Schiltberger's silence with regard to the cage in which Timour confined his captive, agrees, says Neumann, with the result of the researches of Hammer, who seeks to prove that the tale is the invention of a sworn enemy of Timour. The Baron's opinion is supported by the Russian Academician Sresneffsky, in his quotation from a Russian chronicler (Nikitin, in *Hojdenye za try Mory'a*), a contemporary of Timour, who, in alluding to the fate of Ilderim, has not thought it necessary to speak of the cage in which he was made to follow his conqueror. Hammer's argument does not appear to have satisfied Weil (ii, 96), on the grounds that the story of the iron cage does not emanate from Arabshah only, but also from other Arabian chroniclers. Weil equally disputes the assertion that the term cage was intended to signify a litter, and disagrees with Rehm (iv, 3, 151) in his interpretation of the word *kafass*, that it implied a litter as well as a cage, the Arabian word for the former being *handedj*, *mahaffah*, and *kubbet;* and concludes by saying, that if Bajazet was not really carried about in a cage, his litter must have been of most peculiar construction.   BRUUN.

CHAPTER XIV.

(1.) "The cities I have named are chief cities in Syria."— These cities in Syria fell into Timour's hands in the year 1400, but the order of their conquest, as given in the text, differs from the records of Eastern writers. Aboul-Mahazin and Arabshah (Weil, *Gesch. d. Chalifen*, ii, 82) state, that the first to surrender was Behesna, " Wehessum"; then the tower of Aïntab, "Anthap", whence Timour proceeded to Haleb, " Hallapp", now Aleppo, which was taken and dealt with as described by Schiltberger. According to Shereef uddin, Timour Tash, the Egyptian amir and commander of the place, met with the same fate as did the garrison; but Arabshah says, that his life was not only spared, but he also received a robe of honour. Finally, the conqueror seized upon the fortress of Kalat Erroum—Fortress of the Romans—called "Hrumkula" in the text.   BRUUN.

(1A.) Hrhomgla, for "Hrumkula", is the Armenian, as Ourroum Kalch is the Turkish, name of a now miserable village, situated on the western bank of the Euphrates, at the confluence of the river Marzeban. It is surmounted by a castellated building on a high hill. It was a place of some importance from 1150 to 1298, as being the residence of the patriarchs of Armenia. Quoting from Arabshah, Petis de la Croix (*Histoire de Timur Bec*, liv. v, 285) inserts a note to the effect that Timour left Calat Erroum without attacking it, which he dared not do, because the place was very strong.

Having regard to the geographical position of the places in this part of Mesopotamia, taken by Timour in 1400, his road to conquest must have lain thus—Behesna, Aïntab, Aleppo, Ourroum Kalch. Ed.

(2.) " And the city was pillaged."—The Arabian authors, Aboul-Mahazen and Ibn Khaldoun (Rashid-eddin, *Hist. des Mongols, etc.*; by Quatremère, 286), the latter being an eye witness, are agreed that Timour himself ordered the incendiarism of the mosque at Damascus, but they make no mention of the cruelties imputed to him by Schiltberger; they assert, on the contrary, that he very graciously received the deputation headed by the kady, Taky uddin ibn Mouflyk. Other writers have recorded, that Timour was even anxious to save the mosque from the fire which had broken out accidentally and destroyed the entire city. The magnificence of the great "temple" at Damascus, as shown in the text, is confirmed on the testimony of Eastern writers (Quatremère, ii, 262) who state, that this edifice, considered as one of the wonders of the world, had four gates. In saying that there were as many as forty outer gates, Schiltberger no doubt included those of the annexes which, together with the main building, were surrounded by a wall having several entrances; this appears conclusive on consulting an Arabian record quoted by Quatremère (283), which represents that in front of the mosque were many spacious porches, each of which conducted to a large gate, etc. " The view of the buildings, of the domes, of the three minarets, and water courses, as seen from the court, is admirable, and a sight to startle the imagination." There can be little doubt that the gates were numerous, and that Schiltberger should have estimated their number at forty is not to be wondered at, when we consider the practice among Orientals of designating any large

number by the numeral forty, as, for instance, Kyrkyer, Kyrkek-
lesy, etc. BRUUN.

(2A.) In Ibn Haukal's time (10th century), the mosque at
Damascus was considered one of the largest and most ancient in
the land of the Mussulmans. Walid ben Abd-el-Melyk (the sixth
Omniade caliph, 705-715) had beautified it with pavements of
marble, and pillars of variegated marble the tops of which were
ornamented with gold and studded with precious stones. The
ceiling was covered with gold, and so great was the cost that the
revenues of Syria were expended on the work. Porter (*Five Years
in Damascus*, ii, 62) describes the quadrangle as being 163 yards
in length, 108 yards wide, and surrounded by a lofty wall of fine
masonry. The three sides of the cloister, in an adjoining court,
are supported by arches resting on pillars of limestone, marble, and
granite, and on the south side of the court is the *harem* (sacred
place), whose interior dimensions are 431 ft. by 125 ft. Two rows
of columns, 22 ft. in height, extend the whole length of the building and support the triple roof. A transept across the middle, is
supported by eight massive piers of solid masonry, each 12 ft.
square, and a splendid dome, nearly 50 ft. in diameter and about
120 ft. in height, stands in the centre. The interior of the mosque
has a tesselated pavement of marble, and the walls of the transept
and the piers are coated with marble in beautiful patterns. According to Arabshah (*Vattier edition*, v, 169), it was the Raphadites
or Shyites (see chap. xxxiii, note 3, for this sect) of Khorasan who
set fire to this noble mosque, Timour being credited by various
authors, as stated in the preceding paragraph, with having wished
rather to save the edifice from destruction. Much as records may
differ, Schiltberger's relation, so graphic and detailed, merits the
fullest consideration. ED.

(3.) "Scherch."—On March 19, 1400, Timour proceeded from
Damascus by way of Roha (the ancient Edessa near Orfa), Mardin,
and Mosoul to Baghdad (Weil, *Gesch. der Chal.*, v, 91), after having
despatched flying columns hither and thither to forage, some of his
people reaching even to the neighbourhood of Antioch. A portion of
his forces must therefore have crossed the Antilibanus, called Jabal

—mountain—also Shurky, which may have been the "Scherch" mentioned in the text.   BRUUN.

CHAPTER XV.

(1.) "and the king kept his treasure there."—This, in all probability, is the fortress of Alinjy or Alindsha, some miles to the south of Nahitchevan. In 1394, Ahmed ben Oweis sent thither his family and treasure, and it was not until the year 1401 that this fortress was taken by Timour's troops, whilst he himself was laying siege to Baghdad with the bulk of his army. Faradj, who had been left in command by Ahmed, was forced to surrender, after a valorous defence of forty days. All the inhabitants were massacred, and the place was completely destroyed with the exception of the schools, mosques, and hospitals (Weil, *Gesch. der Chal.*, 93). After taking Baghdad, July 9, 1401, Timour passed through Tabreez, on his way to Karabagh, where he purposed spending the winter, occupying the cities of Roha, Mardin, and Mosoul on his march. It would appear that it is to these places Schiltberger refers, but he has fallen into error in saying that they were taken after the capture of Baghdad—a mistake to be accounted for, from his not having served in the expedition.*   BRUUN.

CHAPTER XVI.

(1.) "Lesser India."—Under this name Schiltberger includes the northern portion of the peninsula on this side of the Ganges, giving to the southern part the designation of Greater India. Marco Polo (Yule, ii, 416, 417) employs the same names, but in another sense. His Lesser India included Kesmacoran (Kij-Makran, *i.e.*, Makran), to the whole Coromandel coast inclusive. Greater India extended from the Coromandel coast to Cochin China—Middle India being Abyssinia. Timour's expedition into India (1398)

* See chapter xxxiii, note 12.—ED.

was conducted to the banks of the Indus from Samarkand, by way of Inderab and Cabul. On crossing the river near Kalabagh, he passed by way of Mooltan to Delhi, which he occupied, conducting himself as was his custom on such occasions; but Schiltberger makes no allusion to the cruelties he practised. Perhaps because the details of the expedition were related to him by the Mongols themselves, and not by their enemies, the Arabs and Persians.

BRUUN.

(2.) "and it is of half a day's journey."—We are evidently given to understand here, that the narrow defile through which Timour had to pass, was the famous Iron Gate, at all times considered the frontier limit of India and Turania. In the year 328 B.C., Alexander of Macedon made his way through this passage, described by his historians in language identical to that of Schiltberger......" sed aditus specus accipit lucem, interiora obscura sunt".....(Curtius, viii, 8, 19). Very similar is the testimony of the several Oriental writers quoted in the *Centralasiatische Studien (Sitzungsberichte d. Kais. Akad. d. Wissenschaften*, lxxxvii, 1, 67, 184) by M. Tomaschek, who has availed himself of the results of the Russian expedition to Hissar (*Ysvest. Imp. Geog. Obshtchest.*, xii, 70, 1876, 349-363) to determine the exact locality of the Iron Gate. There may have been near the Iron Gate, in Schiltberger's time, as there is now, a "Winterdorf" (Tomaschek, l.c.) called Darbend or Derbent, but it is not of this "kishlak", but rather of the city of Derbent, in the Caucasus, that Clavijo observes, after stating that the possessions of Timour extended from the Iron Gates situated near Derbent, to those in the land of Samarkand:—" E Darbante es una muy gran ciudad que se cuenta su señorio con una grande tierra, ó las primeras destas puertas, que son mas cerca de nos, se llaman las puertas del Fierro de cerca Darbante, ó las otras postrimeras se llaman las puertas del Fierro cerca Termit, que confinan con il terreno de la India menor." I prefer giving this extract in the original. BRUUN.

(3.) "the lord Tämerlin is come." The correct rendering of this passage is "Amir Timour gheldy."—The Amir Timour is come. ED.

(4.) "and of the elephants many were killed."—This incident is corroborated by Clavijo (*Hakluyt Soc. Publ.*, 153), who places at fifty the number of armed elephants opposed to Timour in the battle near Delhi. The contest being renewed on the second day, "Timour took many camels, and loaded them with dry grass, placing them in front of the elephants. When the battle began, he caused the grass to be set on fire, and when the elephants saw the burning straw upon the camels, they fled. They say that the elephants are much afraid of fire because they have small eyes."

Ed.

CHAPTER XVII.

(1.) "Soltania."—Or Soultanyà—Royal city—so named by Oljaïtou, son of Arghoun Khan, the founder (1305), once the metropolis and largest city in the kingdom. Chardin (*Langlès edition*, ii, 377) tells us that there were not many cities in the world where vaster ruins were to be seen ; and in Kinnear's time (*Geog. Mem. of the Persian Emp.*, 123) the place was reduced to a few wretched hovels. Colonel Yule (Marco Polo, ii, 478) reproduces from Fergusson an illustration of the tomb built for himself by Oljaïtu, or as his Moslem name ran, Mahomed Khodabandah, at Soultaniah, "the finest work of architecture that the 'Tartars of the Levant' have left behind them." Kinnear describes it as being a large and beautiful structure ninety feet in height, built of brick, and covered with a cupola—an edifice that would do honour to the most scientific architect in Europe.

This tomb of Oljaïtou was still magnificent, and especially noted for its colossal gates of damasked steel, even so late as the seventeenth century. "The city was reoccupied by some of the Persian kings in the sixteenth century, till Shah Abbas transferred the seat of government to Ispahan. John XXII set up an archbishopric at Sultaniah in 1318, in favour of Francis of Perugia, a Dominican, and the series of archbishops is traced down to 1425." (*Cathay, and the Way Thither, Hakluyt Soc. Publ.*, 49, note 3.)

Ed.

CHAPTER XVIII.

(1.) "and they were all trampled upon."—This atrocious conduct on the part of Timour, is not the creation of Schiltberger's brain, but it cannot have reference to the capture of Ispahan in 1387, although it is possible that the evolutions of Timour's horsemen against children, was repeated after the fall of Ephesus in 1403; this act of cruelty being imputed to him by several Oriental authors. His return to Samarkand from Ephesus, actually took place after an absence of at least seven, if not twelve years (Rehm, *Gesch. d. Mittelalt.*, iv, 3, 78); and he went there immediately after taking Ispahan in 1387. Schiltberger's details on the revolt of that city under the farrier, Aly Koutchava, and on the construction of the tower of human heads by order of Timour, agree with similar accounts from other sources. BRUUN.

CHAPTER XIX.

(1.) "because it was very cold in that country."—Timour was desirous of adding China to the rest of his conquests, and had even embarked on an expedition, placing himself at the head of a large army; but he fell ill of fever upon reaching Otrar, and died February 19, 1405. BRUUN.

(1A.) Other authorities state Timour's death to have occurred the 17 Shabran, 807 (February 17, 1405). ED.

CHAPTER XXI.

(1.) "with whom I also remained."—Pir Mohammed, son of Jehangir, the eldest son of Timour, died in 1375. Shah Rokh was the youngest of the two sons mentioned by Schiltberger. After the death, in 1410, of Khoulyl son of Miran Shah, the successor of Pir Mohammed who died in 1407, Shah Rokh annexed Transoxana and Samarkand to his possessions, and reigned until 1446. After saying that he had remained with this sovereign at Herat, Schiltberger adds that it was under Miran Shah he served; but he afterwards tells us that he only went over to the latter after Shah Rokh had vanquished Kara Youssouf, ruler of the Turkomans of the Black Sheep. BRUUN.

CHAPTER XXII.

(1.) "Scharabach."—According to Bishop Aïvazoffsky, this plain of "Scharabach" is to be identified with the plain of Karabagh, near the town of Bajazid, in Asiatic Turkey. Neumann is of a different opinion, and points to the district of Karabagh, which extends to the east of Shirwan, as far as the junction of the Kour with the Araxes, anciently called Arzah by the Armenians. Whether the battle of "Scharabach" was fought in Georgia or in Turkey, there is every probability that Schiltberger was made a prisoner upon the occasion, as was also his "lord". It would never otherwise have occurred to him to say, that he was turned over to Aboubekr after the execution of Miran Shah. BRUUN.

(2.) "so that Mirenschach also was put to death."—Miran Shah actually succumbed in his struggle with Youssouf or Joseph (Dorn, *Versuch. einer Gesch. d. Schirwan-Sch.*, VI, iv, 579). His eldest brother, Miszr Khodja (Weil, *Gesch. der Chal.*, v, 46) had defended the city of Van against Timour in 1394, but contemporary authors do not say whether it was he who put Jehangir to death in 1375. Miszr Khodja may have caused the death of another son of Timour, whom Schiltberger has confounded with Jehangir. Perhaps that of Omar Sheykh, upon the nature of whose death authors are not agreed; Rehm (*Tab. gen. des Timurides*, v. iv) stating that he died in 1427 only, and Hammer (*Hist. de l'E. O.*, ii, 37) alluding to his sudden death, as having taken place at about the time of the conquest of Van, by Timour, circa 1394. BRUUN.

CHAPTER XXIII.

(1.) "Achtum."—The author says nothing of the neighbourhood of Nahitchevan, for which Neumann gives him credit, nor of that of Erzeroum, which Bishop Aïvazoffsky believes to be the site of the battle of "Achtum", upon which occasion the Ilkhan Ahmed was defeated by Kara Youssouf. In the plain of "Achtum" we recognise the environs of Aktam, where Timour halted when returning from his last expedition against Toktamish (Dorn, *Versuch. einer Gesch. d. Schirwan-Sch.*, 567; Price, *Chron. Retros.*, iii, 206, who says of Acataem or Actem, that it is a station to the eastward of Moghaun). Neumann agrees with Hammer that Ahmed ben Oweïs was beheaded in 1410, and this is also the opinion of Weil (*Gesch. der Chal.*, v, 141); but Dorn (*ibid.*, 573) has it, that his conflict with Kara Youssouf did not take place until the year 815=1412. BRUUN.

CHAPTER XXIV.

(1.) "Abubachir had also a brother called Mansur."—Besides this Mansour, for whose name I have searched in vain in the various works I have been able to consult, Aboubekr had another brother named Mirza Omar, upon whom Timour bestowed the throne of Houlakou, and who fell out with his elder brother, the said Aboubekr, and had him confined in a fortress (Dorn, *Versuch. einer Gesch. d. Schirwan-Sch.*, 570). Aboubekr afterwards obtained his freedom, and succeeded in ridding himself of "Mansur", to punish him, in all probability, for making common cause with Omar. BRUUN.

CHAPTER XXV.

(1.) "Samabram."—Ibn Haukal describes Shabran as being, in his time, a small place, but "pleasant, and well supplied with provisions". This town appears as Sabran, in Castaldo's map, 1584, and, De Wit's atlas, 1688, and is called Schabran by Olearius (*Voyages*, etc., 1038). It has now totally disappeared, its ruins being on the Shabran-tchaï, a small river flowing into the lake Ak-Sibir on the Caspian shore.

Schiltberger states that the prince passed through "Strana", "Gursey", "Lochinschan", "Schurban", "Samabram", and "Temurtapit"; but as the king's son was sent for, to return forthwith to his own country, it is more probable that he selected a short route, in which case he would have travelled, if the names are here correctly interpreted, through Astara, Shirwan, Shabran, Georgia, Lezghistan, and the Iron Gate, undoubtedly Derbent, which divided Persia from Tatary.

"Strana" I take to be intended for Astara, for the following reasons. It is stated in the last chapter, that Aboubekr took a country called "Kray"; probably Kars, which had been occupied by Timour in 1393, after laying siege to the fortress of Alindsha. Aboubekr than proceeded to "Erban", Erivan, where he seized upon his brother "Mansur", and strangled him. "Zegra", being with Aboubekr, was therefore apparently in Armenia, and must have travelled northwards by keeping close to the Caspian, instead of traversing the heart of the Christian kingdom of Georgia. ED.

2. "Temurtapit."—According to Sprengel (*Gesch. der wichtigsten Geog. Entd.*, etc., 362, 99), the Iron Gate through which the author passed when on his way from Persia into Tatary, was not the Iron Gate at Derbent, in the Caucasus, but the Caspian Gate in Khorasan. Malte Brun (*Précis de la Géog. Univ.*, i, 188) and Sreznevsky (*Hojdenye za try mory'a*, etc., 241) are of similar opinion, while Neumann has no doubt that the Gate of Derbent, called Demyr kapou, Iron Gate, by the Turks, is the "ysen tor" of the text, which, had it been other than that at Derbent, would hardly have been described as being near Georgia and Shabran.

BRUUN.

3. "a river called Edil."—Neumann attempts, but in vain, to identify the city of "Origens", described as being in the middle of the river "Edil", with Astrahan, although it is clear that the author was not ignorant of the real name of the latter place, Hadjytarkhan being included among the cities he visited in Tatary ("Haitzicherchen", see Chapter 36). It is not even necessary to conclude that "Origens", like Astrahan, was bathed by the waters of the Volga, though the Turk name of that river is actually Etel, or Edil, a designation that may have been applied to some other

river, because Schiltberger states elsewhere (Chap. 36) that "Orden", Ourjenj, the chief town of "Horosaman", Khwarezm, was situated near the "Edil", and it cannot be doubted that he there alludes to the Jyhoun, or Oxus, and not to the Volga.

The first large river the author got to after leaving Derbent, was the Terek; we are, therefore, at liberty to suppose that "Origens" was in the delta of that river. Güldenstadt (*Reisen durch Russl.*, i, 166) informs us that the vestiges of the ancient cities of Terki and Kopaï-Kala—now known as Guen-kala, the Burut Fortress, were close to that locality, and that near the mouth of the river were other ruins, which he took to be those of the cities of Tumen and Bortchala, or "the town of the three walls". It is certain that in these parts must have been the residence of the Khozar kings, called Semender, or Saraï-Banou—the lady's palace—Hammer, *Gesch. d. G. H.*, 8) distant a four days' journey only from Derbent, but a seven days' journey from the Itil (Dorn, *Géog. Cauc.* in *Mém. de l'Ac. de St. P.*, vi, ser. vii, 527), which is equal to the twenty farsangs that separated this city from the great river Varshan, or Orshan, alluded to in the celebrated letter of the king of the Khozars to the minister of Abdor-Rahmen III. (D'Ohsson, *Des Peup. du Cauc.*, Par. 828, p. 208.) In these same parts, also, should be placed the residence of the Tchamkal, known to the natives by a name that it was found impossible to pronounce. This name, so difficult of pronunciation, may have been transformed by Schiltberger into "Origens", seeing that Russian annalists have construed it into Ornatch or Arnatch, evidently to be identified with Tenex or Ornacia (Ornatia, Oruntia, Cornax, Tornax). The monk Alberic (*Rel. de Jean du Plan de Carpin*, 114) tells us that this city was taken by the Mongols in 1221, upon the occasion of their irruption into the territory of the Comans and Russians, a city apparently identical with Ornas, "civitas Ornarum", inhabited by Russians, Alans, and other Christians, but belonging to the Saracens. It was completely destroyed by the hordes of Batou, before their invasion of the country of the Russians and Turks (Turcorum, Taycorum, and Tortorum), as we learn from Giovanni dal Piano di Carpine and his travelling companion.

It is to be regretted that, whilst admitting the identity of this city under its various denominations, authors are unable to agree as to its site. Karamsin, D'Avezac, and Kunik are in support of Thunmann's theory, that it was Tana, the modern Azoff. Others, Leontief (Propilei, iv), for instance, are in favour of Frachn's (Ibn Foszlan, 162) opinion that the Oruntia of Alberic, the Ornas of Giovanni dal Piano di Carpine, and the Arnatch of the Russian chroniclers, were all identical with the Ourjenj of Khorasan. I did at one time support these views, but have since sought to prove (*Sitzungsberichte d. Kön. Bay. Akad.*, 1869, ii, 276 *et seq.*) that the city in question was equidistant from Azoff and Ourjenj, or, in other words, that it coincided with " Origens", situated, as we read in the text, on the " Edil", a great river, viz., the Terek. It is pretty clear that " Origens", and Ornatch or Arnatch of the Russians, are corruptions of Anjadz or Anjak, which, according to Khanikoff (*Mémoire sur Khâcâni*, vi, v) was a port in the Caspian Sea near Astrahan, of which the people of the eastern provinces near the Caspian might have availed themselves for the purpose of penetrating into Southern Russia.

There can scarcely, however, be a doubt that the city of " Origens" must be looked for near the Caucasus, seeing that Schiltberger quitted it just before entering the mountains of " Setzulet", manifestly the " Zulat", which we are told in Chapter 36 was the chief city of the mountainous country of " Bestan". We cannot fail to recognise in this "Setzulet", or " Zulat", the city of Joulad, where Timour, in 1395, gained a signal victory over Toktamish, after having annihilated a body of Kaitaks near Terky or Tarkou. Little enough is left to attest to the ancient splendour of Joulad, situated on the Terek, at no great distance from Yekaterynograd ; but Güldenstadt found in its neighbourhood numerous remains, including Christian monuments, chiefly at a place called Tatar Toup—Hill of Tatars. Klaproth (*Voy. au Caucase et en Géorgie*, ii, 161) saw three minarets standing, that greatly resembled others at Joulad ; also the ruins of two churches, which he attributes, as does Güldenstadt, to the 16th century, and to the Greek faith, whilst admitting the assertion of the Circassians, that those edifices were constructed by Franks, that is to say, by

Europeans from the West, who had taken up their residence among the Tatars. This is confirmed by Barbaro (*Ramusio edition*, 109). "Caitacchi i quali sono circa il monte Caspio...... parlano idioma separato da gli altri. sono christiani molti di loro: dei quali parte fanno alla Greca, parte all'Armena, et alcuni alla Catholica." In the face of such evidence, it is not strange that Schiltberger should have met, to the north of the great range of the Caucasus, a Christian bishop and Carmelites who worshipped in the Tatar tongue, although the Carmelites, an order of friars originated at Mount Carmel, were not introduced into Europe by St. Louis until the year 1328 ; and in alluding to the mountainous country of " Bestan", in which was the city of Joulad, the Bishtag—Five mountains— where Ibn Batouta (*Lee edition*, 76) met the Khan Uzbek, Schiltberger must have had in view the environs of Yekaterynograd, still called Beshtamak, because the country is watered by five tributaries to the Terek (Klaproth, i, 327).

BRUUN.

4. " Zegre."—This " Zegre" or " Zeggra", was in all probability Tchekre, coins of whose reign, struck in 1414—1416, at casual encampments—at Bolgar, Astrahan, and Saraï, are preserved (Savelieff, *Mon. Joud.*, ii, 337). BRUUN.

5. " savages, that had been taken in the mountain."—This couple may have been brought from northern Siberia, where the rigorous nature of the climate compelled the natives to wear, by night and by day, as they do now, clothing made of the skins of animals. Schiltberger somewhat assimilates them to monkeys, which reminds us of Herodotus, who described the Neurians as being transformed into wolves, during six months of the year, because they were in all probability clothed in wolf-skins, so long as winter lasted. BRUUN.

6. " Ugine."—One is liable at first sight to identify the " Ugine" with the Ung of Marco Polo (Yule, i, 276), whom he distinguishes from the Mongols proper ; " two races of people that existed in that province (Tenduc) before the migration of the

Tartars. *Ung* was the title of the people of the country, and *Mungul* a name sometimes applied to the Tartars." Pauthier (Marco Polo, i, 218) explains, that by Ung are meant the Keraits, or subjects of Prester John, so named because, like them, he was a Nestorian. A descendant of this Prester John, named George, mentioned by Marco Polo, was converted to Catholicism by Giovanni di Montecorvino, who had numerous partisans in China during the stay in that country of Giovanni de Marignolli (*Reis. in das Morgenl.*, 41); Pauthier is therefore of opinion that, in Schiltberger's time, there were Christian Ung in Northern Asia, who, if not Catholics, were perhaps Nestorians. There could scarcely, however, have been anything in common between the Ung and the "Ugine", for the author says that, although they worshipped the infant Jesus, they were not Christians; and this he makes more explicit in Chap. 45, where he includes them among the five classes of infidels known to him, being those who confessed the three kings before receiving baptism. None of the three kings became the founder of any religion whatsoever. Neumann's views may, therefore, be accepted, viz., that Schiltberger alludes to Buddhism, introduced among the Mongols by Jengiz from Thibet. I should consequently prefer to associate the " Ugine", not with the Keraits, but with the great Turk tribe, the Ung-kut, in whom Colonel Yule (Marco Polo, i, 285) recognises the real Ung of Marco Polo. BRUUN.

CHAPTER XXVI.

(1.) " but he was killed in a battle."—Tchadibek Khan was raised to the throne by Ydegou or Edekou in 1399, upon the death of his brother, Timour Koutlouh. The coins struck during his reign and Russian chronicles show, that his rule lasted until 1407, in the early part of which year Toktamish died near Tioumen, in Siberia, whither he had retired after his defeat by Ydegou and Timour Koutlouh in 1399. Clavijo says that he had effected a reconciliation with Timour, who desired to oppose him to Ydegou, the latter having refused to acknowledge his suzerainty. Upon his return from Siberia, Ydegou quarrelled with Tchadibek, who did not lose his life, but fled to the Caucasus, never again to return to the Horde—a statement which, though at variance with Schiltberger's narrative, is based on a coin of the reign of Tchadibek, struck at Shemahà. Of this coin, Savelieff (*Mon. Joud.*, ii, 225) says, "It certifies that although Tchadibek's influence in the Horde was lost to him, he contrived to enjoy an appanage in the Caucasus." But this unique coin might have been struck when Tchadibek was still at Saraï, for we learn from Dorn (*Versuch. einer Gesch. d. Schirwan-Sch.*, 572) that prayers were offered at Shirwan in the name of Tchadibek, and in the presence of Ydegou so late as the year 1406, and nothing can force us to admit that the same honours would have been paid to the khan after his expulsion by that same amir, or that an appanage would have been bestowed upon him in the Caucasus. BRUUN.

(2.) "Polet, who reigned one year and a half."—Schiltberger may have slightly shortened the duration of the reign of this khan, who was the son of Timour Koutlouh, and was placed on the throne by Ydegou, as successor to Tchadibek. His coins, struck at Saraï, Bolgar, and Astrahan, prove that he must have reigned in Kiptchak from 1407 to 1410, when he was expelled by Jalal uddin, the "Segelalladin" of the text, who was the son of Toktamish.
BRUUN.

(3.) "Thebachk, who fought with him for the kingdom and killed him."—It is stated in Penzel's Edition (1814) of Schiltberger, that Tamir, the brother of Polet, reigned fourteen months and was then expelled by Jalal uddin, who occupied the throne for a like period, fourteen months, and was then deposed by his brother, "Thebachk". Coins and annals establish the fact of the existence of a brother of Poulad, named Timour, who, having ruled in the Crimea in 1407, forcibly seized upon the throne of the Golden Horde in 1411, and was dethroned the following year by Jalal uddin, the Zelenii Soultann of the Russian annalists (Savelieff, *Mon. Joud.*, ii, 329), who would not be entitled to reproach Schiltberger for the free and easy manner in which he deals with the names of the suzerain lords. The brother and murderer of Jalal uddin, named "Thebachk" in the text, was probably no other than Kepak, some of whose coins, struck at Bolgar and Astrahan, are preserved, but the year is unfortunately wanting. Chroniclers make no mention of this prince, attributing the death of Jalal uddin to another brother, Kerym byrdy, who, according to our author, must in his turn have been expelled by "Thebachk"; yet Russian annalists have asserted that Kerym byrdy was killed by another brother, whose name was Yerym ferdyn or Yarym ferden. From the resemblance of the name Jebbar or Tchebbar, by which he was known to Mussulman authors, to that of his elder brother Kepek, Schiltberger may have mistaken the former for the latter, calling him also "Thebachk". BRUUN.

(4.) "and he fought with Machmet and was killed."—It is not determined when and where Tchekre's career terminated, because Eastern and other authors are silent on the disastrous attempt made by this prince to recover the throne from which he had been overthrown by Oulou Mohammed, the great Mohammed, whose origin is uncertain. The author informs us that the death of Tchekre occurred subsequently to the struggle Mohammed had to sustain, first, in his conflict with "Waroch", and afterwards with "Doblabardi". It is evident that in the latter name we have Devlett byrdy, son of Timour Tash, and grandson of Oulou Mohammed, whilst "Waroch" stands for Borrak, son of Ourous Khan, who fled to Oulouk Bek, the son of Shah Rokh in 1424, the same year in which he expelled Oulou Mohammed, that is to say about three years before Schiltberger's return to his own country. It is certain that all the author relates, having reference to the Golden Horde, took place during his captivity, so that the proof of Tchekre's death having taken place between the years 1424 and 1427 is unquestionable; and it is not in the last, but in one of the two preceding years that Devlett byrdy's reign of three days should be determined, notwithstanding that coins of this prince, struck in 1427, have been recovered, for there is little enough likelihood of the opportunity having been afforded him for issuing a fresh coinage during a three days' reign, especially as anarchy pervaded the Horde. There would have been nothing extraordinary in his again dethroning his grandfather after the death of Tchekre, and retaining the sovereignty for a longer period.

The author's relation of his own lot, after Tchekre's first defeat by Oulou Mohammed, is by no means clear, for it is not easy to determine whether he accompanied Tchekre on his flight, or followed the fortunes of Ydegou, upon his being made a prisoner. As to the ultimate fate of this king-maker, opinions are divided. Hammer (*Gesch. d. G. II.*, 382) writes that in 1423 he was still the sovereign of an independent state on the shores of the Black Sea, and must have perished either in the war with Kadyr byrdy, son of Toktamish, or he may have been drowned in the Jaxartes. According to another source (Berezin, *Yarlik Toktamysha*, 61), he was killed by a Tatar of the Barin tribe, from whom his head was stolen by a friend, who, having presented it to Oulou Mohammed, received in recompense that prince's daughter in marriage.

That Schiltberger and Ydegou both actually fell into the hands of Oulou Mohammed, seems more probable, because the author speaks of the latter as his master, "min herr Machmet"; but it is not easy to understand why he should have stated in another place (chap. 67), that after Tchekre's escape he had for his master one of the old councillors of that prince, a certain "Manstzusch", whose name at least reminds us of one of the chief princes of the Golden Horde (Hammer, *Gesch. d. G. II.*, 391), the Manshuk killed in 1440 by Koutchouk Mohammed, Mohammed the Less, the vanquisher of Mohammed the Great.

When, at a later period, Tchekre again sought to dispute the throne with Mohammed, he probably entered into negotiations with this ex-councillor, who would have quitted the country for the express purpose upon the fall of the Pretender. In any case "Manstzusch" left Kiptchak a short time only before Schiltberger's escape, because the latter was never separated from his master until after his return from Egypt, where he had assisted at the marriage of the daughter of Sultan Bourshaï—a sovereign who ascended the throne in 1422 only. If, as I have endeavoured to show, Schiltberger was at that time in "Manstzusch's" service, it is very possible that the latter took him to Egypt, whither he may have been sent by Oulou Mohammed, perhaps to congratulate Boursbaï upon his accession, or for some other purpose. BRUUN.

CHAPTER XXVII.

(1.) "Sadurmclickh."—Sadra, in Arabic, is the feminine of Sadyr—first, foremost. Melyka is queen, and here we have Sadra Melyka, the first of queens; the queen who is prudent above all others. But Sadry is a woman's name in Persia, and amongst Tatars, and malachya signifies literally, in Persian, an angel, so that the heroine in question may have been one distinguished for her exceptional qualities—Sadry, the angel. ED.

CHAPTER XXVIII.

(1.) "kocken."—The koggen was a vessel with rounded bow and stern, perhaps similar to the γαῦλος alluded to by Epicharmus and Herodotus. The kind of vessel actually in question is mentioned in a statute of Genoa, dated 15th February 1340, entitled *De securitatibus super factis naviganti*. " Et de navibus, Cochis, galeis et aliis lignis navigabilibusque vendentur in callegam accipiunt tot asperos qui valeant perperos tres auri ad sagium Constantinopolim......" Cogge, the Anglo-Saxon word for cock-boat, is a name that occurs in *Morte Arthure*.

"'Then he covers his cogge, and caches one ankere."

In the time of Richard II, a coggo was a vessel employed in the transport of troops, and coggle is a name still given to small fishing-boats on the coast of Yorkshire and in the rivers Muse and Humber (Campe, *Wörterbuch;* Jal., *Gloss. Naut.;* Smyth, *Sailor's Word-book*). ED.

(2.) "Bassaw."—This is the Slave name for the city of Kronstadt in Transylvania, the chief city in Burzelland. It is situated near the river Burtzel or Burzel, a name given, according to some geographers (Vosgien, *Dict. Géog.*, i, 157), to the territory through which it flows. This name may, however, owe its origin to Bortz, a Coman chief, who is mentioned in a Brief of Pope Gregory IX., dated 1227, addressed to the archbishop of Gran : "Nuper siquidem per litteras tuas nobis transmissas accepimus quod I. Ch. d. ac d. n. super gentem Cumanorum clementer respiciens, eis salvationis ostium aperuit his diebus. Aliqui enim nobiles gentis illius cum omnibus suis per te ad baptismi gratiam pervenerunt, et quidem princeps Bortz nomine de terra illorum cum omnibus sibi subditis per ministerium tuum fidem desiderat suspicere Christianam." (Theiner, *Vet. Mon. Hist. Hung.*, i, 86.) This prince did certainly seek a refuge in Transylvania, as did many of his countrymen, upon the irruption of the Mongols into Kiptchak. We have it upon the authority of Mussulman writers, that among the eleven Coman tribes settled in this country, were the Bourtch-oglou ; evidently subject to the princes Bourtchevitch mentioned in Russian annals (Berezin, *Nashestvye Mongolov*, ix, 240).

BRUUN.

CHAPTER XXIX.

(1.) "Kallacercka."—The author does not here allude either to Galata, as Jirecek (*Gesch. d. Bulgaren*, 324) supposes, or to Callatis, as believed by Fallmerayer, but rather to the castle of Kaliakra, the ruins of which are still visible on the headland of that name. It is the Τριστρία ἄκρα of the ancients, marked Caliacra in the charts of the 14th century, and known as Γαλιάγρα in the *Acta Patriarch. Constant.*, i, 52, 272. Evliya Effendi (*Travels*, etc., 70-72) having been shipwrecked near the coast of Kilghra, when on his voyage from Balaklava to Constantinople, in 1643, was hospitably entertained by the dervishes of the monastery, near the castle which was then in existence. In 1406, this territory belonged to Mirtcha (Jirecek, 346) ; but ten years later he ceded his possessions south of the Danube to his suzerain lord, the Sultan Mahomet I.

BRUUN.

(2.) "Salonikch."—Schiltberger may have touched at Salonica

when upon his voyage to Egypt, referred to in chap. xxvi, note 4—performed, in all probability, on board of an Italian vessel from Caffa, upon which occasion he passed the island of Imbros, described in chap. 58. There is no evidence whatever that he went to Salonica after his return from Asia to Constantinople, nor is it at all probable that he stopped there when being carried away into slavery after the battle of Nicopolis, notwithstanding that the town belonged to the Turks and not to the Greeks (Zinkeisen, *Gesch. d. O. R.*, i, 287). Bajazet would scarcely have selected so circuitous a route for sending captives to Broussa.

There are good reasons for surmising that the voyage was performed in a Venetian vessel which touched at Salonica. This town, given up in 1403 by Souleiman, son of Bajazet, to the Greeks, was by them sold, in 1423, to the Venetians, who would undoubtedly have taken all necessary measures for putting it into a state of defence and supplying it with provisions, including salted fish from the Sea of Azoff. Another reason for the supposition that Schiltberger's journey into Egypt could not have taken place earlier than 1423, is to be found in the fact that, from Egypt he passed over into Arabia, on a pilgrimage to the holy places of the Mahomedans, having, as it would seem, turned Mussulman through compulsion; and if he has avoided all reference to the journey, it was out of a natural desire not to be reminded of the painful circumstance of his apostacy. BRUUN.

(3.) "from whose grave oil flows."—Hammer observes that Schiltberger confirms the story told of St. Demetrius, and not of St. Theodora, as erroneously related in Anagnosta's *De Thessalonicensi excidio narratio*, the fact being, that the tomb of St. Theodora was close to that of St. Demetrius, from whose foot flowed the oil which was collected annually, and distributed to all believers (*Pout. Rouss. loud.*, 47). Professor Grigorovitch tells us that the well is still shewn beneath the floor of the church, but he was unable to certify that the miracle continued to be operated! BRUUN.

(4.) "Asia."—Fallmerayer and Hammer maintain that Schiltberger was mistaken in saying that the city in which was the tomb of St. John, was called Asia, the correct name being Ephesus, known to the Turks as Aisulugh, and as Ἅγιος Θεολόγος to the Byzantines, who thus styled St. John. The author's learned countrymen might, however, have admitted in his justification the evidence of Codinus (*Urb. nom. imm.*, 316), to the effect that the ancient name of the eparchiate of Ephesus was Ἀσία ἡ Ἔφεσος. Schiltberger may have learnt the ancient name from the monks, who would have employed it in those days. BRUUN.

(4A.) The church at Ephesus, erected over the tomb of St. John the Evangelist, was enlarged by Justinian, and afterwards turned into a mosque (Ibn Batouta). Here, also, as at the grave of St. Demetrius at Salonica, the mortal remains were invested with miraculous powers, for a peculiar kind of dust, in substance like flour, and compared by St. George of Tours to manna, worked its way out of the sepulchre, and being taken about, effected many marvellous cures (Baillet, *Vie des Saints*, viii, 624). ED.

(5.) "Saint Nicholas was bishop there."—St. Nicholas, the patron of Russia, was bishop of Myra in Lycia, which the author confounds with Ismir, the Turkish name for Smyrna. De Lannoy (*Voy. et Ambass.*, 4) commits a similar error in quoting Lisemiere, together with Feule la vielle for Fogliavecchia, and Porspic for porto di Spiga.

Smyrna, a possession of the knights of Rhodes, was taken by Timour towards the close of the year 1402 (Hammer, *Hist. de l'E. O.*, ii, 116), upon which occasion Schiltberger must have visited it, without, however, having been afforded the opportunity of seeing the picturesque valley where Fellows, in 1838 (*Travels and Researches in Asia Minor*, etc.), discovered the imposing ruins of Myra, or Demir, so called by the Turks. It is recorded that in 1087, the relics of St. Nicholas were removed to Bari, and the church in which they were originally laid having fallen to ruins, a small chapel was erected on the site. The restoration of the sacred edifice, completed in 1874 at a cost of 10,000 roubles, was commenced on the initiative of M. Mouravieff. BRUUN.

(6.) "Maganasa".—Magnesia was styled "ad Sipylum", to distinguish it from Magnesia "ad Mæandrum", the remains of which have been discovered near a village called Aïnch-bazar, distant sixteen miles from Ephesus. The former, the Manissa of the Turks, near the Hermus at the foot of Mount Sipylus, has ever been a city noted for its extent, commerce, and population.   BRUUN.

(7.) "Donguslu".—Denizly, a densely populated town in the time of Hadjy Khalpha, was no longer included in the district of Saroukhan, but was added to that of Koutahieh. Near this place, pleasantly situated in a rich and well-watered plain, are the ruins of Laodicea, one of the Seven Churches to which St. John addressed his Revelations.   BRUUN.

(8.) "Wegureisari."—This town, which occupies the site of the ancient Gangra, is the principal in the district. In the days of Hadjy Khalpha, it contained a fortress and an imperial residence, which must have been in existence in Schiltberger's time, and accounts for his addition of the word saraï—palace—to Kiankary, and thus converting the name to "Wegureisari".   BRUUN.

(9.) "In this country Saint Basil was bishop."—It was generally believed that the remains of St. Basil, interred at Cæsarea, were never disturbed; the Abbey of St. Philibert at Tournes in Burgundy, the cities of Bruges, St. Armand in Flanders, and Rome, each claim the possession, but how they came by them is not satisfactorily explained (Baillet, *Vie des Saints*, iv, 710).

ED.

(10.) "Kureson."—Near this city, commonly called Kerasous, Keresoun, situated between Samsoun and Trebizond, are still to be seen the ruins of ancient Κερασοῦς or Parthenium. There was at one time, on the coast near Trebizond, another even more ancient Kerasous, that of Xenophon, of which a lovely valley still retains the name, being known as Kerasoun-derè; but of the city itself, there are no traces.   BRUUN.

CHAPTER XXXI.

(1.) "Then he left her."—Virgin's towers are by no means uncommon in the East. Rich (*Residence in Kourdistan*, i, 172) mentions a Kiz-Kalassi—girl's castle—as being on a hill above the Kizzeljee in Kourdistan. Near a place called Ak-boulak, about twenty-five miles to north-east of Shousha in Transcaucasia, are the ruins of Kiz Kaleh— Virgin's castle—situated on a hill in a perfectly impregnable position. Another Virgin's castle in that part of Asia, is at Bakou ; an inscription on its walls, in Cufic characters, deciphered by Khanikoff (*Ysvest. Geog. Obshtchest.*, ix), records its construction by Masoudi, the son of Daud, one of the "Samiardi fratres" mentioned in the history of Otto, bishop of Freising. Again, there is a tower, erected on the highest pinnacle of the rocky mount upon which stand the fortifications of Soldaya, now Soudagh, in the Crimea, called Kiz-Koula by the Tatars (*The Crimea and Transc.*, ii, 158). The ruins of another fortress, Kaleh Dokhter, are described by Abbott (*Southern Cities of Persia*, MS.) as crowning the height above the city of Kirman ; and visitors to Constantinople are familiar with the construction on the rock off Scutari, unaccountably called by Europeans the Tower of Leander, but known, more legitimately, as the Maiden's Tower, ever since it became the burial-place of Damalis, wife of the Athenian general Chares, who was sent to the assistance of the Byzantines against Philip of Macedon.

The author says, that on quitting the neighbourhood of the mysterious castle, he proceeded to Kerasoun ; it is, therefore, just possible that the legend of the sparrow-hawk was attached to an ancient Kiz-Kalesi seen by Ainsworth (*Travels in Asia Minor*, etc., i, 87) near Tash Kupri, close to the road that leads from Kastamuni to Boiabad, both to the south-west of Sinope. I am unable to discover why the name was so frequently given in the East, to such peculiarly situated strongholds, and would suggest that it was owing to their unassailable position. ED.

CHAPTER XXXII.

(1.) "Lasia."—The territory of the Lazi was part of Colchis, and lay between the Phasis and Armenia. The mountainous country belonged at that time to the empire of Trebizond.　　BRUUN.

(2.) "Kayburt."—Neumann is persuaded that Schiltberger alludes to Baïbourt (or Païpourt), a very ancient fortress to the north-west of Erzeroum, that was restored by Justinian I. Procopius (*De Bell. Pers.*, iii, 253) calls it Baerberdon. Bishop Aïvazoffsky is of opinion that "Kayburt" stands for Kaïpourt, called Kharpert by the natives, situated in a far more fertile country than is Baïbourt. In Marco Polo's time, Paipurth was a castle on the road from Trebizond to Tabreez; and we learn from Barbaro that the fortress of Carpurth, distant a five days' journey from Erzingan, was the residence of Despina Caton, a princess of Trebizond, the consort of Hassan Bey.　　BRUUN.

(2A.) "Kayburt", in a fertile country, is doubtlessly Kharput, distant seventy miles, in a direct line, from Erzingan. The Special Correspondent of *The Times* (January 20th, 1879), has lately described this place as being situated on the edge of a cliff at the top of a mountain in a very picturesque situation; but very difficult to get at, for it takes an hour to ride from the level of the plain to the town. The plain of Kharput is twenty miles long and twelve miles wide, presenting 153,600 acres of splendid land, well irrigated, and in a high state of cultivation.　　ED.

(3.) "Kamach."—Kemakh is on the site of the ancient city of Ani, thirty miles from Erzingan and close to the Euphrates, and not to be confounded with the Ani referred to in Chapter xiii, note 2. Near Kemakh was the temple of Jupiter, constructed by Tigranes, and the city afterwards became the principal seat of the worship of Hormuzd; it was also a state prison, and the burial-place of the Arsacidæ (Ritter, *Die Erdkunde* etc., x, 782-789). Constantine Porphyrogenitus called this stronghold of the Byzantines, Κάμαχα. Kemakh was celebrated among the Turks for its

fine linen, as Erzingan was noted for its good breed of sheep, and
Baïbourt for the beauty of its women. " Kamahoum besy—Erd-
shenshan kousy—Baibourdin kysy." BRUUN.

(4.) " nobody knows where it goes."—This observation on the
peculiarities of the Upper Euphrates, is confirmed by other authors
(Procopius, *De Bell. Pers.*, i, 17; and Ritter, *Die Erdkunde* etc.,
x, 736). On emerging from a narrow valley, the river completely
disappears amongst reeds, which, though annually taken and
burnt, again grow very fast, and so thickly, that carts might be
driven over them to cross the river. BRUUN.

(4A.) The recent survey of the Euphrates shows that the river
really disappears in the Lamloun marshes, its width diminishing
to 120 yards towards the town of Lamloun. It again widens at
Karayem, where the Serayah branch on the western side, and
the Nahr Lamloun branch on the eastern side, reunite with the
main stream. Colonel Chesney makes no allusion whatever to an
overgrowth of reeds, and adds (*Exped. to the Euphr. and Tigris*, i,
58, 59) : "Being thus reunited to its former waters, and at the same
time free from those marshes in which it had been supposed to be
lost, the Euphrates suddenly reappears on its former scale, enclosed between high banks covered with jungle." ED.

(5.) " Karasser; it is fertile in vineyards."—Several travellers
and authors, such as Aboulfeda, Tavernier, Otter, Golius, Ritter,
etc., have represented, that the best wines of the country were to
be obtained at Amadia, fifteen miles from Kohrasar—"Karasser"—
which Hammer (*Denkschr. d. Kön. Akad. d. Wissensch.*, ix) fanci-
fully transfers to Kara-hissar in Armenia. Kohrasar is quite uninhabited and deserted, but the ruins of what were at one time
magnificent churches and other edifices, excited the admiration of
Tavernier (*Six Voy. en Turquie*, etc., en 1642) and Ainsworth
(*Trav. in Asia Minor*, etc., 1842). They indicate the site of the
ancient city of Constantine. It is to be deplored that those
travellers could not afford the time to explore the locality.

BRUUN.

(6.) "the people are warlike".—The warlike inhabitants of Black Turkey were the Turkomans of the White Sheep, who, under Kara Yelek, their chief, seized upon Amid (Amed, Hamith, Karamid), the capital of Dyarbekr, in Mesopotamia, after the death of Timour; it is now known by the same name as the province, but was called Kara Amid—Amid the black—from the colour of its walls. Many traces of its grandeur are left. The academician, Baïer (*De numo Amid.*, 545), shows that it was constructed by Severus Alexander, and fortified by Justinian.

BRUUN.

(7.) "Bestan."—This name is probably intended for Bistan, near the eastern frontier of the pashalik of Soulimanieh. It is now a village of no importance, but near it are the ruins of an ancient castle, also the tumuli known as the Roustan tepe and Shah tepe, in which many objects of antiquity have been found. Judging by its style of architecture, the castle, constructed of bricks, is believed to be of the Sassanian period; but it may have been occupied at a later date, even to the time of Schiltberger, when it was, perhaps, the capital of Kourdistan. The pasha's residence at Soulimanieh is a modern edifice, having been built towards the end of the 18th century (Ritter, *Die Erdkunde* etc., xi, 566).

BRUUN.

(8.) "Zuchtun."—The noxious nature of the climate on the eastern sea-board of the Black Sea, has been fully proved by Russian garrisons to their cost, and especially at "Zuchtun" or Soukhoum Kaleh. Near this place stood the ancient Dioscurias, subsequently called Sevastopolis, after an old Roman fortress in the neighbourhood. It was of great strategic importance to the Empire in the reign of Justinian (*Novell. constit.*, 28; and Procopius, *De Bell. Goth.*, iv, 4), and became a prosperous commercial port after the Black Sea was opened to the Italians. The Genoese established a consulate at Savastopoli, which was maintained until the year 1449 (*Zap. Odess. Obstschest.*, v, 809). BRUUN.

(8A.) "Zuchtun", intended, as shown above, for Soukhoum, and named Soukhoum Kaleh in the year 1578, when Amurat III. as suzerain of Abhase, Mingrelia, Imeritia, and Gouria, arrogated to himself the right to fortify and occupy it as one of two points on the coast (Poti being the other), is the chief town of Abhase, and distant about sixty miles to the north of Poti. The yearly mortality, according to late official returns (1874), was reported as being at the rate of 3 per centum.

The small, square, flat cap seen by Schiltberger, is now in great measure substituted in Abhase by the g'h'tapt or bashlyk, a pointed head-covering of great antiquity, adopted in winter by the troops in Russia, and in fashion among the ladies in that country; but it is still extensively worn by the Imeritians and Mingrelians, who call it papanaky, and consider it sufficient covering for their heads of bushy hair, of which they are very proud, and which they periodically shave to improve the growth. The flat cap, or papanaky, is a small lozenge-shaped piece of leather, cloth, or silk, laid over the fore part of the head, and fastened with strings under the chin. When worn by nobles, the papanaky of velvet is made very ornamental, with gold and silver embroidery. Their Mussulman conquerors used to call the Imeritians, bashashyk—bare-heads (*The Crimea and Transc.*, i, 120; ii, 35, 135). ED.

(9.) "Kathon."—There can be little doubt that Batoum is here intended, a place which appears as Vati or Lovati, in the charts of the 14th century. BRUUN.

(9A.) In the present chapter, the capital of Mingrelia is called "Kathon"; in chapter 67, it is named "Bothan". Neumann suggests that for "Kathon" we should read Gori; Professor Bruun is of opinion that Batoum is intended, and Hammer (*Denkschr. d. Kön. Akad. d. Wissensch.*, ix) thinks that "Kathon" should be Kargwel or Karduel, and "Bothan", Cotaïs; but it may fairly be inferred from Schiltberger's account, that this "Kathon" or "Bothan", as it also appears in the editions of 1475 (?), 1549, and 1814, stands for Poti. In both chapters, the author speaks of the chief town of "Megral", "Magrill"—Mingrelia—as being situated on the Black Sea, and says that on leaving it, he rode along the sea-shore until he reached a mountainous country. Poti, the ancient Phasis, a place of importance from the most remote times, lays in an unexceptionably flat country, from which it would have been necessary for Schiltberger, who was effecting h s escape and must therefore have been travelling south, to ride fully ten miles by the sea-side, before he could have reached a highland. Gori and Koutaïs, being inland towns, are quite out of the question, and had the author got to Batoum, he would already have been in a mountainous country, and need not have described his ride before attaining it. I cannot find any record that Batoum, situated in Lazistan, formerly included in Colchis, ever formed part of the principality of Mingrelia. ED.

(10.) "Merdin".—With the exception of the citadel, which remained in the hands of a prince of the Ortok dynasty, this place, formerly a chief town of Mesopotamia, had to submit, with many others, to the yoke of Timour. Upon the death of the conqueror, his heir, afterwards assassinated by Kara Yelek, called to his assistance Kara Youssouf, chief of the Turkomans of the Black Sheep, and gave to him Mardin, in exchange for Mosoul, where he was poisoned. His son transferred the royal residence to Sindjar, and died of the plague in the year 814 of the Hegira. These were the last members of the Ortok dynasty, which reigned three hundred years. BRUUN.

CHAPTER XXXIII.

(1.) "Thaures."—Tabreez, founded by Zobeide the wife of Haroun-al-Rashid, was long distinguished for the extent of its commercial relations, in which the Genoese and Venetians took part. Although frequently pillaged at the hands of enemies, notably by Janibek in 1357, and by Toktamish in 1387, Tabreez soon recovered from its misfortunes. This capital even became the principal dépôt for merchandise from India and China, after the destruction of the cities of Ourjenj and Astrahan by Timour, who established a commodious route between Tabreez and Samarkand by way of Kashin and Soultanyà. Schiltberger's statement as to the custom's revenue at Tabreez, will not seem exaggerated in presence of the fact, that in 1460 it amounted to 60,000 ducats. Ramusio observes that Tabreez, the great depôt, rivalled Paris in its magnificence, and in the number of its inhabitants. BRUUN.

(1A.) Writing in 1868, Abbott (*Persian Azerbaijan*, MS.) says that Tabreez was the principal seat of commerce in all Persia, and the mart from which nearly all the northern and midland countries were supplied with the produce and manufactures of Europe, conveyed to it chiefly by land transport from the Black Sea; the yearly value was estimated at £1,750,000, the value of goods imported from England being probably three-fourths of that sum. The city contained about 3100 shops of all descriptions; thirty karavansaraïs, occupied by merchants and traders; and about forty others devoted to the accommodation of muleteers and their cattle. Abbott adds, that the commerce of Tabreez had made great advances since 1830, having increased eight-fold in 1860.

ED.

(2.) " Rei."—After passing Tehcran, upon the occasion of his journey from Soultanyà to Samarkand, Clavijo perceived, at a distance of two leagues, a great city in ruins......" but there appeared towers and mosques, and the name of the place was Xahariprey"—Shehri-Rei, the city of Rei, "at one time the largest city in all the land", says Khanikoff, " though it is now uninhabited". But Rey did not remain long thus unpeopled, because the Russian merchant Nikitin (who visited India thirty years before Vasco de Gama), though leaving Tehcran unnoticed, as does Schiltberger, speaks of his stay at Rey, where he witnessed the celebration of the famous Persian festival, instituted in commemoration of the death of Hussein, the son of Ali and grandson of the prophet. (*Poln. Sobr.*, etc., vi, 332.) BRUUN.

(2A.) To the above might be added the evidence of Ibn Haukal, that there was not in the eastern regions any city more flourishing. Rey was celebrated for its gates, for its many remarkable quarters and streets, its numerous bazaars, karavansaraïs, and market-places. The fine linen, camelot, and cotton manufactured at Rey, was sent to all parts of the world. Late travellers have found its site marked by hollows and mounds; mouldering towers, tombs, and wells, constructed of burnt and sun-dried materials (Ker Porter, *Travels in Georgia, Persia*, etc., 1822; Mounsey, *Journey through the Caucasus*, etc., 1872). In the 3rd century of Mahomedanism, Rey was specially noted for its wealth, and was styled, The First of Cities—The Spouse of the World—The Market of the Universe. (Chardin, *Langlès edition*, ii, 411.)　　　　ED.

(3.) "Raphak."—If Schiltberger's companions, when on his journey to Rey or Rhe, were Sunnites, they probably looked upon the people of that city as apostates from the faith; for "Raphak", therefore, we should read Raphadzhy—abjurer—a term applied to renegades. These disciples admit themselves to be Shey—partisans—whence the term Shyites, and in the present instance they were evidently called by the opprobrious name of Raphadzy, as being apostates, by those of a different sect. Ibn Batouta met at Kotaïf (Katiff of Benjamin of Tudela), on the Persian Gulf, some Arabs of the Rafiza sect, who were most enthusiastic, publishing their sentiments everywhere, and fearing no one.

There are Shyite Tatars in Transcaucasia, chiefly in the valley of the Araxes, also in the richly cultivated province of Ouroumych, the seat of the Christian Nestorians, where they people eight villages. These Shyites call themselves Ali Allahy—Worshippers of Ali—and are not averse to drinking wine.　　　　ED.

(4.) "Nachson."—Clavijo (*Hakluyt Soc. Publ.*, 80) sojourned for a time in a city which he calls Calmarin, and attributes its foundation to a son of Noah. This place was probably Sourmalou on the Araxes, taken by Timour in 1385. Tutan, the Turkoman who resided here, might have been the "Tetani, Emperor of Tartary", who, according to Clavijo, had conquered the place, though only a viceroy. There was a Titanus, Vicarius Canlucorum, of the Genoese, in 1449; the Tautaun, Taudoun, of the Avares and Khozars. Two days before reaching Calmarin, Clavijo passed the night in a town called Naujua, where there were many Armenians, which must have been the "Nachson" of Schiltberger, now known as Nahitchevan.　　　　BRUUN.

(5.) "Maragara."— There are numerous remains of ancient fortifications on the heights around Meragha. In a westerly direction, at a distance of thirteen miles to the south-west of Tabreez, are the foundations of a round tower, believed to have been the celebrated observatory of Khodja Nazr uddin—defensor fidei—the friend of Houlakou, who transferred his residence to Meragha after the capture of Baghdad in 1258. To this day is shown his tomb,* and that of his wife Dogous or Dokouz Khatoun, the protectress of Christians, but especially of Nestorians, in whose doctrines she had great faith (Hammer, *Gesch. der Ilchane*, etc., i, 82). Shortly after her death, the patriarch, Iabellasa, agreed to recognise the supremacy of the Pope, the act having been presented to Benedict II. by a Dominican friar named Jacob. Mosheim (*Hist. Tartarorum Eccles.*, 92) pronounces against the authenticity of this document, an opinion shared by Heyd (*Die Colon. der Römisch. Kirche*, etc., 322), on the grounds that it was signed at Meragha. It may, however, be contended that the patriarch might have resided for a time at Meragha, after the fall of Baghdad to the Mongols, considering that his successors had no fixed residence to 1559, in which year the patriarch Elias definitively established the seat at Mosoul; and that a tradition is preserved amongst the Nestorians or Chaldæans of Kourdistan, to the effect that their ancestors, who had resisted Timour, were domiciled between the lakes Van and Ouroumyeh.

In the early part of the 14th century, another brother preacher, Jordanus Catalani, recorded in his *Mirabilia* (*Hakluyt Soc. Publ.*, 9), that those schismatics had adopted the Catholic faith in several cities of Persia, to wit, at Tabreez, Soultanyà, and at "Ur of the Chaldees, where Abraham was born, which is a very opulent city, distant about two days from Tabriz". Heyd says that this Ur cannot be Orfa, a town in central Mesopotamia, which has been identified with the Ur-Khasdim of the Arabians (Ritter, *Die Erdkunde* etc., x, 333); but is more probably the ancient city of Maranda, not far from the lake Ouroumyeh and fifty miles only from Tabreez. But Meragha was, in like

* Abbott says (*Persian Azerbaijan*, MS.) that the tomb of Houlakou, or its reputed site, is pointed out near the town of Meragha.—Ed.

manner, at no great distance from the said lake, and only twenty-four miles, or, according to Hadjy Khalpha, seven farsangs from Tabreez; we are, therefore, justified in concluding, that it was this place the friar designated as Ur of the Chaldees, especially as it was a large city and a bishop's see in 1320 (Galanus, *Concil. Eccl. Arm. cum Rom.*, i, 508; quoted by Heyd, 324). The same cannot be said of Maranda.

Bartholomew of Bologna has given evidence of his zeal, in the fact that many of the Armenian clergy went over to the Church of Rome, and with the view of cementing this union, a new Order, "Fratres prædicatores Uniti", was founded and affiliated to the Dominicans, whose head-centre was at Meragha. But the theory propounded by Bishop Aïvazoffsky is worthy of consideration, viz., that Ur is no other than Urmi or Ormi, a town of some size, hitherto largely inhabited by Nestorian Chaldæans, and that has given its name to the lake Ourmiah, Ormi, or Ouroumych. It is believed to be the birth-place of Zoroaster, who might have been mistaken for Abraham as easily as he has been for Moses.

BRUUN.

(6.) "Gelat."—Khelat was taken in 1229 by the sultan, Jalal uddin, after a three days' siege. Aboulfeda quotes Abou Said, who says that it rivalled Damascus. Bakui (*Not. et Extr.*, ii, 513) extols Khelat for its good water, fruit, and the fish taken from the lake, especially the tamrin, possibly the dorakine found in the Kour, as related by Ystachry (*Mordtmann edition*, 1845). The numerous ruins in the neighbourhood are of the time when Akhlat was the residence of the Shahy Armen—kings of Armenia; they include those of a superb palace, of gorgeous tombs, artificial grottoes, and of a fortress on the shore of Lake Van. Khelat is now a miserable hamlet occupied by Kurds. BRUUN.

(6A.) Khelat, Ghelath, Ashlath, was long the residence of a suffragan bishop of the Armenian Church. ED.

(7.) "Kirna."—On the Gharny-tchaï, a tributary of the Zenga, east of Erivan, is Gharny or Bash Gharny, now an insignificant village, but at one time a place of considerable importance. According to the old Armenian chroniclers, Kharny was founded 2000 B.C. by a prince Keghamè, who named it after himself; but the name was afterwards changed by Kharnig, the grandson of Keghamè, to Kharny. It was here that Tiridates, 286-314, constructed for his favourite sister a superb residence, to which Moses Chorensis (*Whiston edition*, 1736), the Armenian chronicler of the 5th century, thus refers : " Per id tempus Tiridates castelli Garnii ædificationem absolvit, quod quadratis et cæsis lapidibus, ferro et plumbo coagmentatis construxit, atque ibi umbraculum statuit et monumentum mirifica arte cælatum, pro sorore sua Chosroiduchta, in eoque memoriam sui græcis literis inscripsit." This remarkable edifice is alluded to by Kiracos of Gantzac, also an Armenian chronicler, of the 13th century, as "the marvellous throne of Tiridates", in front of the cemetery of Kharny (*Hist. d'Arménie* trans. by M. Brosset, St. Petersburg, 1870). It is now a heap of ruins, known to the natives as Takht Dertad—Throne of Tiridates.

At a short distance above Gharny, also on the Gharny-tchaï in the Goktcha valley, is the venerable monastery of Aïrits vank, Ghergarr or Keghart, noted for its memorial inscriptions of the 12th, 13th, and 14th centuries (*The Crimea and Transc.*, i, 211, 221). ED.

(8.) "the priests are of the Order of Preachers, and sing in the Armenian tongue."—What Schiltberger says with regard to "Meya" — Magou—is confirmed by Clavijo (*Hakluyt Soc. Publ.*, 83). "On Sunday, the first of June, at the hour of vespers, they came to a castle called Maca, belonging to a Catholic Christian called Noradin, and the people who lived in it were Catholic Christians, though they were by birth and language Armenians, and they also knew the Tartar and Persian tongues. In this place there was a monastery of Dominican friars. The castle was in a valley, at the foot of a very high rock, and there was a village on a hill above, and on the top of the hill there was a wall of stone and mortar, with towers, and against the wall there were houses. There was also another wall with towers, and the entrance to it was by a great tower, built to guard it, along steps cut in the rocks. Near the second wall there were houses cut in the rock, and in the centre were some towers and houses, where the lord lived, and here all the people in the village kept their provisions. The rock was very high, and rose above the walls and houses; and from the rocks an overhanging part stretched out, which covers the castle, walls, and houses, like the heaven that is above them." BRUUN.

(8A.) Tradition asserts that Makou, Makouyeh, in the Armenian province of Artazo-Tasht, to the east of Ararat and south of the Araxes, is built over the place where St. Thaddeus suffered martyrdom. The fortress is situated in a gorge above the village (J. Saint Martin, *Mém. sur l'Arménie*, i, 135). ED.

(9.) "Ress."—Resht, the chief town of Ghilan, a place of great commercial importance in Schiltberger's time, is distant six miles from the Caspian Sea. The Genoese and Venetians secured the rich produce of this province, especially the silken stuffs made there or imported from Yezd and Kashan. Marco Polo (Yule, i, 54) speaks of silk called Ghellè, after the name of the country on the Sea of Ghel or Ghelan—the Caspian. BRUUN.

(10.) "Strawba."—Schiltberger changes Astrabad to "Strawba", just as his Italian contemporaries have called the place Strava, Strevi, and Istarba. Its commerce was not considerable, but Astrabad was of some importance as being the depôt for merchandise in transit across the Caspian, from India and Bokhara. BRUUN.

(11.) "Antioch."—Several cities of Asia were in ancient times called Antiochia. Stephen of Byzantium knew of eight, two of which, Edessa and Nisibis, were in Migdonia; and as each, in its turn, had become the foremost bulwark of Christianity, their possession was frequently disputed by the Infidels. Allusion is made in the text to Nisibis, with its ramparts of brick, rather than to Edessa, which was encircled by whitewashed walls. BRUUN.

(12.) "Aluitza."—If the author here alludes to the same fortress (Alindsha?) as is mentioned in chapter 16, of which there can scarcely be a doubt, that is to say, the fortress in which Ahmed ben Oweis kept his treasure; then the story of its siege by

Timour for the space of sixteen years, was a gross exaggeration on the part of his informants, because we know from contemporary authors that the siege of Alindsha lasted eight years only.

BRUUN.

(13.) " There is a city called Scheckhy; it is in a fertile country near the White Sea."—It will be generally admitted that this White Sea is no other than the Caspian. Hammer (note, p. 45) says it was so called to distinguish it from the Black Sea; but Wahl (*Allg. Beschr. d. persischen Reichs*, ii, 679) attributes the distinctive name to the petrified shells, white and gray sand, with which the bed of the sea is overspread. It is pretty certain that White Sea is not a name invented by the author, but that he supplies us with the literal translation of the Georgian words—Tetrysea and Sywa, which have a similar signification, and are even now employed to designate the Caspian Sea. Hammer is mistaken in saying that Schiltberger called the eastern shore of the Caspian by the name of Scherky, as the word appears in Penzel, and which is simply a corruption of "Scheckhy", now known as Sheky, on the left bank of the river Kour, between Georgia, the districts of Gandja, Shirwan and Daghestan. It is said that this part of the country was occupied as early as the 10th century by the Shekis or Shekines, a Christian people given to commerce and industrial pursuits (D'Ohsson, *Des Peup. du Cauc.* 18, and note xiv).

BRUUN.

(14.) "the kingdom Horoson, and its capital is called Hore."— As stated by Neumann, these places are intended for Khorasan and Herat. According to Masoudi (Ritter, *Die Erdkunde* etc., x. 65), there existed at the time of the conquest of Hira near the Euphrates, *circa* A.D. 637, the negotiator Abd-el-Mesy, a man greatly revered by the Arabs in consequence of his wisdom and great age. He had attained his 350th year, and enjoyed the distinction of being considered, if not a saint, at least a servant of God, that is to say, an Ibadite or Jacobite Christian.

Ibn Haukal states that the city of Hira, which was still in existence in the time of Edrisi (*Recueil des Voy. et des Mém.*,

M

iii, 366), was distant one farsang from Koufa, which with Basra was called Basraten—dualis of Basra—or the two Basras, the metropolis of the Nestorians at Basra being known as Euphrates Pherat Mesene or Perat Meissan, a name it had borne since A.D. 310. We are informed by Eastern writers, that at Koufa was the tomb of the saint, Adam (Ritter, *Die Erdkunde* etc., x, 179-184), a name that reminds us of " Phiradamschyech", whose age coincided with that of Abd-el-Mesy.

Schiltberger may perhaps have applied to Herat, which he visited, the legend of Hira, a Shyite place of pilgrimage.

BRUUN.

(15.) " Phiradamschyech."—This is one of the few names in Schiltberger's narrative that appears somewhat difficult to determine. Pir, in Persian, signifies an old, a venerable man; also, a chief. Sheykh has a similar meaning in Arabic. Adam is the Persian, Turkish, and Arabic for man; so that " Phiradamschyech" consists of three substantives, and being interpreted, reads thus : A chief—a man—a chief.

A very similar story is related by Ibn Batouta, Schiltberger's predecessor by about fifty years. After passing the Hindu Kush, he got to a mountain called Bashai where he saw in a cell an old man named Ata Evlia—Father of the Saints—said to be 350 years old, but who appeared to be about fifty. Every hundred years he had a new growth of teeth and hair. There is no doubt whatever of Ibn Batouta's own incredulity as to the reputed history of this man, to whom he put several questions, which, being unsatisfactorily answered, caused him to apprehend that there was no truth in the wonderful statements made about him.

ED.

(16.) " Schiras."—" Kerman."—Sheeraz, the birth place of Saadi and Hafiz, two of the most celebrated and popular poets of Persia, was so called, says a rare Persian manuscript, after a word in the old Persick language signifying—Lion's paunch—because all the wealth of every town in the same region was transported thither not to return elsewhere (Ouseley, *Travels*, etc., ii, 23). Edrisi's definition (*Jaubert edition*, 392) is somewhat clearer, for he says that the name was given because the place consumed without producing anything. This city is said to have been founded in the earliest years of Islam; the walls, which measured 12,500 paces in circumference, being constructed in the 10th century. Kazvini (quoted by Ouseley) observed nine gates, and in 1811 Ouseley saw six only. Ibn Haukal (*Ouseley edition*, 101) wrote of Sheeraz as being a modern city.

In 1627, Sir Thomas Herbert (*Travels into Divers Parts*, etc., 127) found some of the old walls of "the pleasantest of Asiatick cities" still standing, but in Chardin's time (*Langlès edition*, viii, 414) they had disappeared. The present fortifications, erected by Kerim Khan in the middle of the 18th century, were ruined by Aga Mohammed Shah after the struggle between the Zund and Kujjar families. They are of the extent of about three and a half miles, and were originally of such massive construction, that it was said three horsemen might have ridden abreast on them. The population in 1850 was estimated at 35,000 to 40,000; but the general want of employment begat amongst the people that disposition for mischief, brawls and insurrections, for which the place was remarkable beyond any other town in Persia (Abbott, *Southern Cities of Persia*, MS.).

Kirman, also visited by Abbott, is encircled by walls of two and a half miles to three miles in circumference, and had a population (1850) not exceeding 25,000. The appearance of this town and the scenery around, are extremely unpromising and dreary, from the scarcity of trees, the little cultivation, and the few villages about. A vastly different condition to the "good country" noted by Schiltberger, and the statement of Marco Polo (Yule, i, 92), that on quitting the city of Kerman "you ride on for seven days, always finding towns, villages, and handsome dwelling-houses, so that it is very pleasant travelling".

Abbott says further, that Kirman was not of much commercial importance, being so far removed from the direct lines of communication between other chief places, and being adjacent to vast and unproductive regions.

It is by no means clear that Schiltberger was ever at Kirman;

but if his account of that town and of the islands in the Persian Gulf is given from personal observation, which is very doubtful, it is possible that he followed the same route as traced by Colonel Yule in Marco Polo's *Itineraries*, No. ii.   ED.

(17.) " Keschon", " Hognus", " Kaff".—Kishm, Hormuz, and Kais, are three islands in the Persian Gulf, which, however, Schiltberger does not particularise as such. Kishm, the largest of the three, is called by the Persians, Draz Jazyra—Long Island—the more familiar name being Harkh. An excellent harbour is formed on the south side by the island of Angar. Kishm was occupied in 1622 by an English force, which destroyed a fort the Portuguese had erected the previous year, one of the few Englishmen killed upon the occasion being William Baffin who in 1616 sailed round Baffin's Bay.

Colonel Yule (Marco Polo, i, 113) has clearly established the site of ancient Hormuz on the main land, a city that was abandoned for the island of Zarun, afterwards Hormuz, in 1315 (Ouseley, *Travels*, etc., i, 157), as a protection, says Aboulfeda, from the repeated incursions of the Tatars. Already, in the days of Ibn Batouta, who mentions both Old and New Hormuz (*Lee edition*, 63), was Harauna, the new city and residence of the king, a large and beautiful place; and Friar Oderic, his contemporary, remarks on the efficient fortifications of Ormes, and its great store of merchandise and treasure; so that its reputation as a great commercial depôt was well established in Schiltberger's time. Of the many travellers who have described the island, Varthema, 1503-1508 (*Hakluyt Soc. Publ.*, 94), reported, that as many as three hundred vessels belonging to different countries were sometimes assembled at the noble city of Ormus, which was extremely beautiful; and some years later, 1563, Cesare Federici (Hakluyt *Voyages*, ii, 342) noticed a great trade there in all sorts of spice, drugs, silk, cloth of silk, brocardo, and other merchandise. Hormuz, like Kishm, was also recovered from the Portuguese by the English for Shah Abbas in 1623, until which period it was a stately and rich place, of which the inhabitants made the boast that " if the world were a ring, Ormus must be considered as the diamond".

The city has now completely disappeared, and over the space of about one square mile of its site may be seen, here and there, the foundations of houses, those near the sea being the most visible. In the neighbourhood are several hundred reservoirs, and many Mussulman tombs, some of which are enclosed within domed buildings that had some pretensions to architecture (*Persian Gulf Pilot*, 1870, 148).

Kais is mentioned by many authors as being a place of considerable importance. It was the ancient Καταία (*Nearchi Paraplus ex Arriano*, 31; *Hudson edition*, i), is called Keis by the Arabs, is named Ken by Kinnear (*Memoirs of the Persian Empire*, 17), and appears in the Admiralty chart as Kais or Gais, inhabited by pearl fishers. Yagout (Barbier de Meynard, *Dict. Géog.*, etc., 499) in the 13th century says of Kisch, that it was the residence of the sovereigns of Oman, whose authority extended over all the sea, on which they were very powerful; it was the place of call for vessels trading between Fars and India, and a celebrated pearl fishery. Kazvini (*Kosmographie*, 235) speaks of Kis as the resort of merchants who went there to trade; and Benjamin of Tudela, a century earlier, describes it as being a port of transit.

The ancient town of Harira is now represented by tottering masses of masonry; a portion of a minaret of well cut stone, and many fallen pillars of the mosque to which the minaret belonged, being the only architectural remains. Great quantities of broken pottery, some of fine quality, lie scattered among the *débris*. At a distance of a quarter of a mile are large reservoirs for water, all faced with masonry, but in a sad state of decay; some measure 120 ft. in length, by 24 ft., and are 24 ft. in depth.

Admitting the authority of a Persian manuscript, says Ouseley (*l. c.*, i, 170), the name of the island may be assigned to the 10th century, when one Keis, the son of a poor widow in Siraf, embarked for India with his sole property, a cat. There he arrived at a fortunate time, for the king's palace was infested with mice. Keis produced his cat, the noxious animals disappeared, and the adventurer of Siraf was magnificently rewarded. He returned to his home, but afterwards settled with his mother and brothers on the island, which was named Keis, or, according to the Persians,

Keish. Modern attempts to rationalise Whittington may surely be given up, observes Colonel Yule with reference to this story related by Wassaf. ED.

(18.) "Walaschoen."—This name, employed also by Orientals, is now Badakshan, called Badashan by Marco Polo, who says that rubies were found in the province. Ibn Haukal was also aware that Badakshan yielded rubies and lapis-lazuli, and Ibn Batouta asserts that the rubies (balas rubies) from the mountains of Badakshan were commonly called Ak Balaksh. A river flowed from these mountains, the water of which was as white as that of the sea. He adds that Jengiz, king of the Tatars, ruined the country, so that it never flourished afterwards. Judging, however, from Schiltberger's account, it is probable that its condition had improved.

The unicorns may have been horses of a good breed, as alluded to by Marco Polo (Yule, i, 166), who states that, "not long ago they possessed in that province a breed of horses from the strain of Alexander's horse, Bucephalus, all of which had from their birth a particular mark on the forehead". If we consider that in the time of Timour, the nationality of the inhabitants, the military administration, and the breed of horses in this country, were the same as in the days of Kublai, the ruler had, no doubt, ever been a "None", Nono, which Marco Polo (*idem*, i, 183) gives as the equivalent for Count. Whatever the origin and primitive significations of this term, I may, perhaps, not be far out in asserting, that in the present instance it designated a noyon or myriarch, such as was Jebe, the vanquisher of the Russians at the battle of the Kalka in 1223 (Berezin, *Nashestvye Mongolov*, 226), and Noë, Duke of Sousdal, who, at about the same period, gave to Julian the missionary, letters of recommendation to Bela IV., King of Hungary (Kunik, *Outch. Zap.*, etc., iii, 739), and Tolak Timour the cruel governor of Soudak (*Zap. Odess. Obstschest.*, v, 507).

BRUNN.

(18A.) When Captain Wood was in Badakshan, he was told that the valley of Meshid was extremely populous in former times, and a legend was current to the effect that it used to be greatly infested with scorpions (*Journey to the Source of the River Oxus*, 1872). Colonel Yule thinks, that if the existence of unicorns was not a mere fable, the animal referred to was probably the rhinoceros, at that time common in the country near Peshawur—not very far from Badakshan. ED.

CHAPTER XXXIV.

(1.) "Marburtirudt."—These measurements agree so exactly with the dimensions to be found in Herodotus, who gives the height of the walls of Babylon at 200 cubits and their thickness at 50 cubits, that the extent of the city, 480 stadia, was probably obtained from the same source. But four stadia do not make one Italian mile. The Italian mile is equal to eight stadia, 480 stadia are, therefore, 60 Italian, or 55½ English miles, no great difference from the 75 miles or 25 leagues noted in the text as being the extent of the wall of Babylon.

The Tower of Babel, represented as being 54 stadia from the city, must have been distant 6.75 Italian, or 6.21 English miles, precisely the position of Birs Nimroud—Prison of Nimrod—called "Marburtirudt", for Marbout Nimroud. It was to these ruins that Benjamin of Tudela (Ritter, *Die Erdkunde* etc., x, 263) referred when describing the tower constructed before the dispersion of the people, situated on the right bank of the Euphrates, and one and a half hour's journey from Hillah; it measured 240 yards in diameter, and was about 100 canna in height; a gallery conducted to the summit, whence the view around extended over the plain to a distance of eight leagues. Schiltberger expresses himself to the same effect when he says, "in several places it is x leagues in length and in breadth". In adding that the tower stood on the Chaldæan side of the Arabian desert, he has no intention of directing us to Arabia proper, but to Irak Araby, the country of the ancient Chaldæans. BRUUN.

(2.) "And one inch is the first member of the thumb."—Schiltberger fails to distinguish the Italian from the Lombard mile; we are therefore at liberty to conclude that he here alludes to the ancient Roman mile, .75 of a degree, which consists of 59,800 untz or zoll, the zoll being equal to the English inch. In saying that the Italian or Lombard mile consists of 45,000 inches only, Schiltberger gives us to understand that the "schuch" was one-fourth shorter than the foot; in other words, he refers to the palma, an Italian measure of his day. It follows, therefore, that the pace of five palmas must have measured 3 ft. 9 in.   BRUUN.

(3.) "Schatt."—The Tigris is still known as the Schat (Ritter, *Die Erdkunde* etc., xi, 4), not only from its junction with the Euphrates, but also along the whole of its upper course (Rachid-Eddin by Quatremère, xxix), which justified Barbaro in having said that Hassanchiph was near the Set.   BRUUN.

(3A.) This is confirmed by Colonel Chesney (*Exped. to the Euphr. and Tigris*, i, 60), who writes that Shatt, or more correctly Shatt-el-Arab, is the name given to the rivers Euphrates and Tigris after their junction at the walled town of Kournah; but that the designation belongs properly to the Tigris. This river is clearly called Schot by Olearius.   ED.

(4.) "Kinna."—This fruit, called "kurnia" in Penzel's edition, is probably the khourmà, date-plum—Diospyros lotus—an ebanaceous tree growing plentifully in Persia and Transcaucasia, and perhaps the kheilan of Ibn Batouta. The berry is largely imported into Russia, and a favourite spirit distilled from it. It is totally distinct from the date-palm—Phœnix dactylifera—called in the East, taltal. Marco Polo (Yule, i, 110) speaks of a very good wine made from dates, mixed with spices.   ED.

(5.) "In this kingdom the people are not warlike."—It is not surprising that Schiltberger should have been struck by the pacific disposition of the people of Baghdad, a city that owed its opulence to industry and commerce. Baghdad was reconstructed by Ahmen ben Oweis after its destruction by Timour (Weil, *Gesch. der Chal.*, v, 98). The inhabitants were Arabs and Persians, as they are now. That a large park and menagerie should have existed is in the highest degree probable, for we read in Zosimus (*Hist. Rom.*, iii, 23), that the troops of the emperor Julian discovered a royal garden in Mesopotamia, in which wild beasts were kept: εἰς περίβολον ὃν Βασιλέως θήραν ἐκάλον. The Greeks of Heraclius's expedition, A.D. 627, found a large park close to the residence of Chosroes (Ritter, *Die Erdkunde* etc., ix, 503), in which were many ostriches, wild boar, peacocks, pheasants, lions, tigers, etc. Another instance was the residence, near Baghdad, of the caliph El-Harim, which stood within grounds wherein were wild beasts of every description (*ibid.*, x, 258).

BRUUN.

(6.) "It has long fore-legs, and the hinder are short."—Soon after the battle of Angora, the sultan Faradj sent two ambassadors with rich presents to Timour, one being a giraffe (Weil, *Gesch. der Chal.*, v, 97), which Clavijo, who met the Egyptian envoys at Khoi, designated a gornufa. Schiltberger must have originally written surnofa, rather than "surnasa". The giraffe he saw in Timour's possession was probably one of the finest of its species, so that allowance should be made for his ascribing to its neck a length of four fathoms; indeed, we learn from Clavijo that this very animal was able to extend its neck so as to reach herbage at a height of 30 feet to 36 feet.

Schiltberger was under the impression, as was his contemporary De Lannoy (*Voy. et Ambass.*, 88), that the Nile traversed India before entering Egypt,* which accounts for his supposition that the giraffe was indigenous to the former country.

BRUUN.

(6A.) Zerypha— yellow-coloured — is the Persian for giraffe, from zerd—yellow—and fam—colour; a name corrupted by the Turks and Arabs to zerafè, whence "surnasa". The giraffe at the British Museum could have reached food at a height of at least twenty feet, as Dr. Günther, Keeper of Zoology, has been good enough to inform me. The finest specimen at the Museum d'Histoire Naturelle, at Paris, is even inferior in size, according to the

---

* That Ethiopia was called India, and thus confounded with real India, is fully set forth by Colonel Yule in a note to Marco Polo, ii, 426.

ED.

measurements kindly supplied by Professor Milne-Edward of that institution. Schiltberger must have greatly miscalculated the proportions of the animal he saw, allowing even for probable degeneration; large giraffes having now become very scarce. ED.

(7.) "Zekatay."—Jagatai owes its name to the second son of Jengiz Khan, who received in appanage the countries to the east and south-east of the Oulons of Jujy, that is to say, from the limits of Khorasan (until taken from the Jujy by Timour) on both sides of the Amu-Darya, to Turkestan. All those territories were included under the name of Jagatai, as were also the dialects of the inhabitants. The last princes of the house, and in whose name Timour ruled, were Suurgatmysh and Mahmoud; their coinage was struck at Bokhara, Samarkand, Termed, Kesh, Badakshan, and Otrar; but their residence was at Besh balyk—Five Cities— until transferred by Timour to Samarkand, which the despot sought to place at the head of all cities in Asia, by means of the vigorous measures to which Clavijo bears witness. BRUUN.

CHAPTER XXXV.

(1.) "Great Tartaria."—The details entered into by Schiltberger in this chapter, demonstrate that he includes in Great Tatary the possessions of the three branches of the Jujy. First, the Ordou Itchen or the White Horde, who were the successors of the eldest son of Jujy. Secondly, those of the Golden Horde, the successors of Batou, the second son; and, Thirdly, those of Shaïban, the fifth son, who, in recompense for his brilliant services during Batou's campaign in Russia, received from the Ordou Itchen some territories near the Ural for his summer encampment; and for his winter use, those near the Syr Darya, that is to say, the actual steppe of the Kirghis, so that the domains of the Shaïbani separated the Golden Horde from the White Horde. Their dominions afterwards extended northwards, when they nominated khans to Siberia. BRUUN.

(1A.) "Tartaria" and "Tartaren", as the names are spelled throughout the text, are substituted in these Notes by Tatary and Tatars, it is hoped on fair grounds. Professor Nève asserts (*Exposé des Guerres de Tamerlan*, etc. : *d'après la Chronique Arménienne inédite de* Thomas de Medzoph, 24) that Tatar is the term employed by Armenian chroniclers, and he names no exceptions ; and is not her ancient literature one of the several excellencies of which Armenia may be justly proud ? A note by Dr. Smith in Gibbon (*Rise and Fall*, etc., iii, 294) shows how the Tatars became accidentally named Tartars, through an exclamation of St. Louis of France, although it must be admitted that according to other authors, the use of the word Tartar, in Western Europe, is of earlier date ; and Genebrard states (*Lib. Heb. Chro. Bib.*, i, 158) that Tatar, which in the Hebrew and Syriac signifies abandoned, deserted, should more correctly be written without an r. The Russians, whose pronunciation of these words is, for obvious reasons, entitled to every consideration, speak of Tatáry'ya—Tatary — and Tatáry — Tatars—unquestionably the sound uttered by the various people themselves, claiming the distinctive appellation, whether on the banks of the Volga, in South Russia, the Crimea, or in the steppes and lowlands of Transcaucasia, as the writer of this note is prepared to testify. The Russian word Tatarui, or Tatars, says Ralston (*Early Russian History*, 198, wherein is cited F. Porter Smith's *Vocab.*, etc., 52), modified in Western Europe by a reference to Tartarus into Tartars, is now generally applied by Russian writers to what used to be the Turkish subjects of the Mongol Empire. It is said to be a corruption of Tah-tan, the name under which the Mongols were anciently known to the Chinese. Morrison writes Tătă as Chinese for Tartars.

Colonel Yule (Marco Polo, i, 12) calls attention to an article in the *Journal Asiatique*, ser. v, tom. xi, 203, to show that the name Tartar is of Armenian rather than of European origin, whilst admitting that Tatar was used by Oriental writers of Polo's age, exactly as Tartar was then, and is still, used in Western Europe as a generic title for the Turanian hosts who followed Chingis and his successors ; but he believes that the name in this sense was not known in Western Europe before the time of Chingis.

In Howorth's *History of the Mongols*, 1877 (the one volume as yet published), a ponderous book of 743 pages, replete with the most erudite information, but unhappily unprovided with any guide to its contents, will be found at page 700, a long note, in which admission is made that the word Tartar has given rise to much discussion; and whilst the Russian and Byzantine authors, the Bohemian chronicler Dalemil, Ivo of Narbonne, and Thomas of Spalatro, are cited in favour of the use of Tatar, other authorities are quoted to establish a respectable pedigree for Tartar. ED.

(2.) "Seat him on white felt, and raise him in it three times." —The raising to the White Felt is similarly described by Giovanni dal Piano di Carpino (*Recueil de Voy. et de Mém.*, etc.). Vambery (*Trav. in Central Asia*, 356) says that the being raised to the White Felt is still the exclusive privilege of the gray-beards of the tribe of Jagatai, and that the custom is kept up at the investiture of the khans of Khokand. ED.

CHAPTER XXXVI.

(1.) "Edil, which is a great river."— The large river here called "Edil", the Turkish for river, could have been no other than the Oxus or Amu-Darya. Orden cannot in any manner be identified with "Origens", mentioned in chapter 25, where the author stayed when on his journey from Derbent to Joulad. That city of "Origens", however, was also at an "Edil", so that Schiltberger may possibly have confounded its name of Ornas, Arnatch, or Andjaz, with Ourjenj, equally situated on an "Edil" (in this instance not the Terek but the Oxus); the possessions of his iron lord extending from the neighbourhood of one river to that of the other. BRUUN.

(2.) "A city called Haitzicherchen, which is a large city."— Hadjy-tarkhan was situated on the right bank of the Volga, a few miles above the modern Astrahan, and near Itil, capital of the kingdom of the Khozars, an ancient city that had already disappeared in the time of Rubruquis, 1253, when Hadjy-tarkhan itself, it would appear, had scarcely begun to exist. Ibn Batouta (1331) notes having sojourned at the last-named place upon the occasion of his journey from Soudagh to Saraï; and Pegolotti says that travellers tarried there when on their way to China. The name appears as Azitarcan in the Catalan atlas, 1375, in which work, and in the splendid map of the brothers Pizzigani, we also find "Civitat de ssara", or "Civitas Regio d'Sara", the city of New Sarai, destroyed by Timour, and mentioned by Schiltberger. Its ruins are still to be seen near the town of Tzaref on the Akhtouba, an arm of the Volga. There was, however, the other Saraï, spoken of by Aboulfeda, Ibn Batouta, and Pegolotti, the remains of which are visible, also on the Akhtouba, but at a distance of two hundred miles to the south of Tzaref, and near Seliterny-gorodok, where numerous coins of the khan Uzbek have lately been found by a professor of the University of Kazan. No such coins have ever been picked up at Tzaref, which is not surprising, seeing that it was Janibek, the son of Uzbek, who transferred his residence from Saraï to the new city of that name, as Colonel Yule has already shown in one of his notes to Marco Polo (i, 6), and as I have since sought to prove in an article that was published at Kieff in 1876 (*Troudy 3go. Archeo. Syezda*).

Although old Saraï was depopulated by the plague in 1347-48, and new Saraï was destroyed by Timour, both cities recovered from those calamities, and in the later map of the world, by Fra Mauro, they appear near a tributary on the left bank of the Volga, but at a considerable distance from each other. The northernmost is known to the Russians as Great Saraï.

Previously to selecting old Saraï for his residence, the khan Barka was at Bolgar, the ancient capital of the kingdom of the Bolgars on the Volga, which had been subdued in 1236 by his brother and predecessor Batou, the "terrible Batou" of the Russians, surnamed by the Tatars, Saïn—The Good. An indigent Russian village stands on the site of the city, in the midst of ruins which impress the traveller by their extent; an impression I received when engaged in the Fourth Archæological Congress

(1877), the members of which started upon their excursion from Kazan, and descending the river to Spassky-zaton, visited the locality distant seven miles in a direct line from the river. Considering the importance of these ruins, the large extent of ground they cover, the prodigious quantity of ancient oriental coins and other antiquities that are being continually recovered; considering, also, the testimony of Arabian authors and travellers on the commercial relations of the ancient Bolgars of the Volga, the question has frequently arisen—Why should that people have preferred to establish themselves at so great a distance from the river, after the manner of the inhabitants of the "city of the blind", instead of selecting a more advantageous site? The enigma has been solved by Professor Golovkinsky (*Sur la formation permienne du bassin Kama-Volgien*, etc., in the *Mém. de la Soc. Minér. de St. Pétersbourg*, tom. i; and *Anciens débris de l'homme au Gouv*^{t}. *de Cazan*, in the *Travaux de la réunion des Natur. de Russie*, St. Pétersbourg, 1868), formerly of the University of Kazan, now Rector of that at Odessa. The distinguished geologist shows, that the Volga and the Kama have been subjected to great changes in their course above their junction; that to a comparatively recent period, the eastern bank of the bed where the two rivers united, was close to the height upon which is the village of Bolgar, and that this ancient bed is to be traced to an arm of the Kazanka called the Boulak, and to the lake Kaban, both of which flow through the city of Kazan, and through a partly dried up marsh near the said village. BRUUN.

(3.) "a city called Bolar, in which are different kinds of beasts."—These were probably furred animals, furs having been from all time the staple of commerce at Bolgar (whose locality is now established), at Saraï and Astrahan. Schiltberger leads us to the supposition that those cities had recovered from the state of desolation in which they were left by Timour. BRUUN.

(4.) "Ibissibur."— In chapter 25, Schiltberger describes a country called "Ibissibur". That there was a city of the name is clearly established by the Catalan atlas and Pizzigani map, in

which we find Sebur, near a chain of mountains called "los montes
de Sebur", evidently the South Ural, styled Sibirsky kamian in a
Russian work on ancient hydrography (*Knyga bolshem. Tchertejou*,
151, St. P., 1838).

The Sibir of the Russians, known also as Isker, was situated on
the Irtysh, ten miles from Tobolsk; it was the residence of the
Shaïbani khans, and was taken in 1581 by a handful of Cossacks
under their ataman Yermak, who, in his turn, was besieged by
the Tatars, and lost his life in the river during a sortie (1584).
His countrymen have erected a monument at Tobolsk in honour
of this Russian Cortez.   BRUUN.

(5.) "Alathena."—Alla Tana for Tana, which stood where
is now Azoff, was a place of great importance in the 14th and
15th centuries. It was completely destroyed by Timour in
1395, but the Venetians returned soon afterwards, as would
appear by the statement of Clavijo, that " six Venetian galleys
arrived at the great city of Constantinople to meet the ships which
were coming from Tana". They maintained commercial intercourse with Tana even after its destruction by the Tatars in 1410,
by the Turks in 1415, and later again by the Tatars; and there
is the evidence of De Lannoy (*Voy. et Ambass.*, 43) that in 1421,
four Venetian vessels arrived at Caffa from that port. Schiltberger, who visited Tana at this period or shortly afterwards,
proves that it had recovered its commercial prosperity, at all
events so far as regards the fisheries, a fact supported by Barbaro.   BRUUN.

(6.) "Vulchat."—In saying that "Vulchat", intended for
Solkhat, was the capital of "Ephepstzach" or Kiptchak, Schiltberger may not have been aware that this latter name included
the whole of South Russia and the Crimea, of which, Solkhat,
afterwards Esky Crim, actually became the chief town. Neumann
believes the author to have made a mistake, which may have
arisen from the fact that in his time there were many princes, as
has already been shown, who disputed the sovereignty; and a
large portion of Kiptchak may have recognised the authority of
one or the other of those princes who had taken up his residence

at Solkhat, as for instance, the "viel empereur" to whom De Lannoy (*Voy. et Ambass.*, 42) was accredited as the ambassador of Vithold in 1421, and who died at an unfortunate moment, because the knight leaves us in ignorance of his name. I believe that ruler to have been Ydegou, in the absence of any proof of Hammer's statement (*Gesch. d. G. H.*, 352), that Vithold's old ally was the chief of an independent state on the shores of the Black Sea so late as the year 1423.   BRUUN.

(7). "Four thousand houses are in the suburbs."—The importance attached to Caffa and the description of that city, is confirmed from other sources, except with regard to the estimated number of houses within the walls, and in the suburbs. That there were "two kinds of Jews" (the Talmudists and the Karaïms) is a well-authenticated fact. The four towns at the sea-side, dependant on Caffa, must have been Lusce, Gorzuni, Partenice, and Ialita, now known as Aloushta, Gourzouff, Partenite, and Yalta, all on the south coast of the peninsula, and the only places, besides Caffa, at which Genoese consuls were stationed.   BRUUN.

(8.) "Karckeri." — Kyrkyer, now Tchyfout Kaleh — Jew's Fortress—at one time the residence of the Crimean khans, is at present occupied by three or four Karaïm families only. It is situated in the hilly part of the Crimea, which was called Gothia in the 15th century, a name carelessly transcribed in the text as "Sudi", where the people were derisively called by the Tatars "That" or "Tatt", a Turkish designation for a conquered race.

BRUUN.

(9.) "That."—Mourtadd is the Turkish for renegade. Pallas (*Voy. d. les gouv. méridionaux de l'emp. de Russie*, ii, 150) found that the Crimean Tatars applied the contemptuous term of Tadd to the Tatars on the south coast, because they did not consider them of pure descent, in consequence of the intercourse of their ancestors with the Greeks and Genoese during the occupation by those Christian people of that part of the peninsula.   ED.

(10.) "Serucherman." — The author was well informed in

saying that the martyrdom of St. Clement took place here, the Saroukerman of Aboulfeda who had never been in those parts; the "Kersona civitas Clementis" of Rubruquis (*Recueil de Voy. et de Mém.*, etc., iv) and which had been constituted a bishop's see in 1333. BRUUN.

(10A.) Sary kerman—Yellow Castle—was the name by which Cherson, near modern Sevastópol, was known to Eastern writers. Pope Clement I. was exiled by the Emperor Trajan to that part of the Tauric Chersonesus, and suffered martyrdom by being thrown into the sea. According to the legend, the sea receded upon every anniversary of the saint's death, leaving the body exposed on the shore during the space of seven days, until in the 9th century, Cyril and Methodius the Apostles of the Slaves (the originators of the Slave alphabet), caused it to be interred at Cherson, whence the remains were subsequently removed to Kieff by the grand-prince Vladimir upon his conversion to Christianity.

The Church of Rome gives a different version of this legend, and maintains that the relics of the pontiff are preserved in the church of St. Clement on the Esquiline (*The Crimea and Transc.*, i, 22, 98). ED.

(11.) "they suppose that a man struck by lightning is a saint."—The "Starchas" or Tcherkess—Circassians—were known to Giovanni dal Piano di Carpine, Aboulfeda, Barbaro and others, and were more generally called Zikhes and Cossacks, two branches of that people. The proof of the identity of the Zikhes with the Cossacks or Tcherkess is to be found in Interiano (*Ramusio edition*, 196), who visited the country in 1502: "Zychi in lingua vulgare, greca et latina cosi chiamati, et da Tartari et Turchi dimandati Ciarcassi". Their identity, however, is established in the present work, and therefore before the Italian's travels; it being stated in chapter 56 that the Turks designate the "Sygun"—Zikhes—by the name of "Ischerkas"—Tcherkess. In the days of Constantine Porphyrogenitus (*De Adm. Imp.*, c. 42), their territory extended along the Black Sea shore over a distance of three hundred miles, from the river Oukroukh (Kouban), which separated them from Tamatarcha (Taman), to the river Nicopsis at the frontier of Abhase, a country that reached to Soteriopolis situated in all probability where is now Pytzounda the ancient Pityus, to the north west of Soukhoum Kalch, for it is stated by Codinus (*Hieroclis Synecdemus*, etc., 315) that Pityus was at one time called Soteropolis.

The Abhases and the Tcherkess speak different dialects of the same tongue (Güldenstädt, *Reisen durch Russl.*, i, 463). The former were converted to Christianity through the exertions of the emperor Justinian, about A.D. 550; but Christianity was spread among the Zikhes previously to this, and if many adopted the Mahomedan faith, proofs are not wanting that they did so from political motives and to please the Turks (Marigny, *Voy. dans le pays des Tcherkesses*, in Potocki, ii, 308). Their conversion to Christianity has never kept them from a love of pillage and the sale of their own children, as is reported of them by Schiltberger and confirmed by Marigny, who is unable to conceive how a people to whom freedom is the greatest boon could think of thus disposing of their own offspring.

Marigny also confirms the statement that thunder was held in great veneration by the Tcherkess. "They have no god of lightning", says this author, "but we should deceive ourselves in supposing that they never had one. They hold thunder in great veneration, for they say it is an angel who strikes the elect of God. The remains of one killed by lightning are buried with the greatest solemnity, and whilst mourning his loss, relatives congratulate each other upon the distinction by which their family has been visited. When the angel is on his aerial flight, these people hurry out of their dwellings at the noise he makes; and should he not be heard for any length of time, they pray aloud entreating him to come to them." BRUUN.

(11A. The Tcherkess, which include the Natouhaïtz, Shapsoughy, Abadzehy, Abhase and other tribes, were known to Strabo and Procopius as persistent slave dealers and pirates, occupations which, according to the records of every age, they pursued unceasingly until the complete subjugation and annexation of their country by Russia in 1863. Dubois de Montpéreux (*Voy. autour du Caucase*, etc., i, 258) says, writing in 1839, that even under the suzerainty of Russia the Abhases would not give up the nefarious traffic which embraced, under certain circumstances, the sale of a son or daughter or sister; and so lately as 1856, Oliphant (*Trans.-Cauc. Campaign*, 125) found that the Abhases indulged chiefly in the plunder of human beings. "Seizing the handsomest boys and the prettiest girls, they would tear them shrieking from their agonised parents, and swinging them on their saddle-bow, gallop away with them through the forest, followed by the cries and execrations of the whole population."

The custom of placing the dead upon trees is practised at the present time in Abhase, where they are suspended in coffins to the branches, which creak as they are swayed by the wind, and produce melancholy noises (*The Crimea and Transc.*, ii, 136).

Ed.

(12.) "One is called Kayat, the other Inbu, the third Mugal." —Considering the little care taken by Schiltberger and his transcribers to hand down to us proper and geographical names with sufficient exactness to enable us to prove their identity, it is no easy task to determine what were the "Kayat" and "Inbu" who, with the Mongols, formed the population of Great Tatary. Whatever the correct names, they were probably communicated to Schiltberger by the natives or their Mongol chiefs. The latter were able to distinguish from their own people, those who had retained for a longer period than others their hereditary chiefs under the suzerainty of the descendants of Jengiz Khan. The principal tribes were undoubtedly the Keraït and Uïgour, whose rulers, named Edekout, a name reminding us of the celebrated "Edigi" whom Schiltberger accompanied to Siberia, preserved their independence until the year 1328 (Erdmann, *Temud. d. U. R.*, 245). Neumann asserts that two of the tribes named were the Kajat or Kerait, and the Uighur, a statement he leaves unsupported; we are therefore justified in assuming that reference is made rather to the Kaïtak and Jambolouk, two tribes the author must have had frequent opportunities of meeting.

In Masoudi's time, the Kaïtak or Kaïdak inhabited the northern slopes of the Caucasus towards the Caspian Sea. There, also,

Aboulfeda placed them, and there they are to this day. We have seen how futile were their endeavours to oppose Timour upon his last expedition against Toktamish, and that Romanists and Christians of other denominations soon afterwards introduced themselves amongst them; but that they had not discontinued their evil practices is proved by the bitter experience of the Russian merchant Nikitin, who was plundered when shipwrecked on their coast in 1468. It was in vain that he sought to recover his property, even though he appealed to Shirvan Shah, brother-in-law to Ali Bek their prince (Dorn, *Versuch einer Gesch. der Schirwan-Sch.*, 582). The Kaïtak were a people of sufficient importance to have attracted the notice of Schiltberger, when he passed through their territory on his way from Persia to Great Tatary.

Whilst in those parts, the author must have spent some time amongst the Nogaï of the tribes of Jambolouk or Yembolouk, as they are designated by Thunmann (Büsching, *Gr. Erdbeschr.*, iv, 387), and who were so named because their earliest settlements were near the Jem or Yemba which flows into the Caspian. It was only towards the close of the 18th century that they moved to the western shores of the Sea of Azoff, where they met with other Nogaï, at a time that the territory was being annexed to the Russian empire. The wandering life of these Tatars, and their frequent internecine divisions, justify us in assuming that in Schiltberger's time the greater number, if not the whole of the Jambolouks, had moved their encampments in a westerly direction, and this explains why the Tatar duke met by De Lannoy (*Voy. et Ambass.*, 40) in 1421, who lived on the ground with all his people, was named Jambo. It was in the power of the descendants of that duke to remove to any other more convenient site; it is, therefore, very possible, that the fortress and town of Yabou, ceded in 1517 by the Crimean Khan to Sigismund of Poland, together with other places on the Dnieper, may have belonged to him (*Sbornyk* by Prince Obolensky, i, 88). I feel that we are at liberty to infer from these several facts that the "Inbu" were Tatars of the Jambolouk Horde.   BRUUN.

(13.) "and has daily twenty thousand men at his court."—In writing after his own fashion the native name of Fostat as "Missir", erroneously called Old Cairo by Europeans (Abd-Allalif, *S. de Sacy edition*, 424), Schiltberger imagined that the name was equally applicable to Cairo, because at that period the two towns had largely extended towards each other, so as to form one city. De Lannoy (*Voy. et Ambass.*, 80) distinguishes Cairo from Fostat or Misr, which he calls Babylon, a name it had received in consequence of the settlement there of a Babylonian colony in the reign of Cambyses (Noroff, *Pout. po Yeghyptou*, i, 154). Even now the Copts include a part of Cairo and of Fostat under the name of Boblien—Little Babylon—the new Babylon of the writers of the middle ages, who took it upon themselves to bestow on the sovereigns of Egypt the title of Sultan of Babylon, and some of whom, Arnold of Lubeck for instance (*Geschichtschr. der Deutsch. Vorzeit.*, etc., xiii *Jahrhund.* iii, 283), have even confounded the Euphrates with the Nile. De Lannoy assists us in a measure to discern the error into which Schiltberger has fallen . . . . " est à-sçavoir que le Kaire, Babillonne et Boulacq furent jadis chascune ville à par lui, mais à présent s'est tellement édifiée, que ce n'est que une mesme chose, et y a aucune manière de fossez entre deux plas sans eaue, combien qu'il y a moult de maisons et chemins entre deux, et peut avoir du Kaire à Babillonne trois milles et de Boulacq au Kaire trois mille." Noroff considered Boulak to be the Egyptian Manchester, because of the manufactories established there by Mehemet Ali. The population of the three towns was quite in proportion to their extent, and certainly so continued until about twenty years before De Lannoy's arrival, when it decreased; indeed it is stated by Aboul-Mahazin, that Egypt and Syria had fallen preys to every sort of calamity during the reign of Faradj, 1399-1412. Apart from the Mongol invasion and incessant civil war, those countries were assailed by the European maritime powers, and visited by plague and famine, so that the population was reduced by one-third.

There was a time when it was generally believed that the people in Cairo could not be numbered, because it was considered the most populous city in the world, with more inhabitants than all Italy contained, the vagabonds it sheltered sufficing to fill Venice ! In saying this, Breidenbach (Webb, *A Survey of Egypt and Syria*, etc.) does not fail to observe : " Audita refero—neque enim ipse numeravi." Schiltberger may have thought the same, when he computed the streets in " Missir" to be as numerous as were the houses in Caffa ; and this he did that his readers might be the better able to judge of the difference between the two cities.

That the sultan's suite consisted of twenty thousand men is most probable, allusion being made to the dwellers in the citadel. Thus, De Lannoy :—" est ledit chastel moult grant comme une ville fermée, et y habite dedens avecq le soudan grant quantité de gens, en espécial bien le nombre de deux mille esclaves de cheval qu'il paye à ses souldées comme ses meilleurs gens d'armes à garder son corps, femmes et enffans, et autres gens grant nombre."

In 1778, thirty thousand people lived in the citadel, one half of that number being troops (Parsons, *Travels in Asia and Africa*, etc., 382). BRUUN.

(14.) " no person can be made king-sultan unless he has been sold."—The Mamelouk militia, formed, as the name indicates, of old slaves, arrogated to themselves the right of elevating to the throne one of their own number, upon the death of the sultan. See De Lannoy (83). BRUUN.

CHAPTER XXXVII.

(1.) " and on the spike he must rot."—Among those who had reigned or assumed the supreme power in Egypt, appear the names of " Marochloch" and " Jusuphda", intended for Barkok and Faradj ; also " Mathas", whose reign intervened between that of " Marochloch" and " Jusuphda". The successors of the latter were " Zechem", " Schyachin", and " Malleckchafcharff" also known as " Balmander", who was no other than Boursbaï, 1422-1438 ; he assumed upon his accession, according to custom, the title of Ak Melyk, and the distinctive prefix of Alashraf Seif uddin Aboul-Nazr—The most Noble Sword of the Faith, and Father of Victory (Weil, *Gesch. der Chal.*, v, 167). "Mathas" was Mintash or Mantash, governor of Malatia, who, after having for a time replaced Barkok, perished in 1393 by being broken on the wheel. It is possible, however, that Arabian authors have otherwise described the mode of Mantash's execution, through misapprehension, because the sawing in two parts was a punishment of antiquity, practised in eastern countries other than Egypt. Dion Cassius (lxviii, 32) relates that the Jews in Cyrene and Egypt, under Trajan, having revolted, sawed in two the Romans and Greeks who fell into their hands, staining their faces with the blood of their victims, and adorning themselves with the skin. In one of the admirable notes to his translation of Makrizi, Quatremère (i, 72, note 103) cites numerous instances of this kind of punishment in Schiltberger's day, not in Egypt only, but also in Persia and among the Mongols. The Russian princes captured after the battle of the Kalka, in 1223, were thus tortured (Karamsin, *Hist. de Russie*, iii, 291).

"Zechem" is to be identified with Jakam, governor of Syria, who revolted against Faradj. He was acknowledged as sultan in Syria, but succumbed in a war with Kara Yclek in 1405-06.

"Schyachin" is a name that slightly recals to mind Sheykh Mahmoud, sultan in 1421 ; he was successor to the caliph Abbas al-mustein Billahy who reigned for a few months after the death of Faradj in 1412 ; but Sheykh Mahmoud died a natural death at an advanced age, and could not therefore have been the ruler whose execution Schiltberger describes so minutely, that he must have been a witness to his torments. None of Boursbaï's predecessors—Ahmed, the eldest son of Mahmoud—Tater, an old Mamelouk—or Mohammed, the youngest son of Mahmoud, deposed by Boursbaï, met with the fate of "Schyachin", a name intended perhaps for Azahiri, governor of Safad, who raised the standard of revolt at the very commencement of Boursbaï's reign. He was deserted by his followers, and having surrendered was put to torture, 1422, perhaps enduring the sufferings to which "Schyachin" was subjected. BRUUN.

(2.) "his title and superscription."—Neumann believes that this letter, with the titles it confers on the sultan, was the invention of the Armenians who communicated it to the author; but there is nothing very extraordinary or improbable in the statement, that Boursbaï had sent letters to various Christian potentates upon the occasion of his daughter's marriage, because that sovereign entertained diplomatic and commercial relations with the maritime republics of Italy, with the kings of Aragon and Cyprus, and the emperor of Byzantium, to each of whom, and not to the Pope, was addressed the letter to "Rom", a word allowably substituted for Roum, a name which included Greece and the Turkish possessions in Europe. BRUUN.

(3.) "the all-powerful of Carthago."—Boursbaï certainly committed an anachronism in styling himself the autocrat of Carthage, for he could only have possessed the ruins of that city. As the successor of the Fatimites, or protector of the Abbasside caliphate, the sultan may have claimed Tunis, built partly at his own expense, near the remains of Rome's ancient rival, whose renown in Africa must have survived, and whose name may therefore have been preferred to that of Tunis. But I am more inclined to substitute for Carthage that noted sanctuary of Islam, Kairvan, called by Aboulfeda, Cayroan, and which was considered the most beautiful city in Magreb. BRUUN.

(4.) "Lord of Zuspillen, Lord of the highest God in Jherusalem."—"Zuspillen" is applicable either to Sicily, which at one time belonged to the Aghlabites, or still more so to Seville, called Ishbilia by the Persians.

In a letter to Shah Rokh the son of Timour, in 833 of the Hegira, the sultan Boursbaï styles himself Lord of Jerusalem; possibly the sense of the passage turned by Schiltberger into "ain herr des obristen gots," which, being an imitation of the Hebrew, was Hebrew to him. BRUUN.

(5.) "Capadocie."—It is doubtful whether Boursbaï, or the inventor of his titles, would have mentioned any one place for the second time, yet the name "Capadocie" appears twice. In his letter to Shah Rokh, Boursbaï entitles Jerusalem, the Venerable; so that this "Capadocie" may have been similarly intended for an appellation, since the region of that name would be quite out of place between Jerusalem and the Jordan. It is possible, however, that for "Capadocie" we should read Capernaum, now known as Tell-Hum, where are many ruins which comprise those of an edifice surpassing in grandeur and magnificence anything Robinson (*Biblical Researches*, etc.) saw in Palestine. BRUUN.

(6.) "her son our nephew of Nazareth."—It may fairly be doubted whether this passage was really included amongst the sultan's titles, its appearance in the MS. being due to some misconception on the part of the author, from his being but indifferently initiated in the mysteries of Mahomedanism; how, otherwise, could he have supposed that his protector had entitled Jesus his "neff"—nephew. With regard to Bethlehem and Nazareth, names conceivably included in the list, Schiltberger may have been informed that Mahomedans revere our Saviour as being one of their own Neby or chief prophets; or he may have been told that Christ was designated Neffs, Neps—spirit, soul. Jesus is also called Rouh—the Spirit of God.

Through some similar misconception, Boursbaï is made to boast of his relationship to the Virgin Mary, which could not have been the case either, seeing that she, in like manner, is venerated by Mussulmans. BRUUN.

(7.) "seventy-two towers all embellished with marble."—That the number seventy-two was employed by Asiatics to designate a large number, is demonstrated by numerous examples, other than the following. Seventy-two was the number of tribes in Syria; of the Mahomedan sects; of the disciples of our Saviour; of the Persian Mushids; of the towers of Jeziret-ibn-Omer, etc., etc. As to the seventy-two towers of "Germoni", Robinson (*Biblical Researches*, etc.) has noted that Hermon is surrounded as if by a belt of temples.

"Talapharum" is the well-known Tell-el-Faras at the termination of Jabal-el-Heis, a spur of Jabal-el-Sheykh or Hermon.

BRUUN.

(8.) "inhabited by seventy-two languages."—This "great forest" is the Caucasus, the extent of the great mountain range in a direct line from sea to sea, agreeing exactly with the length given. The seventy-two languages are the seventy-two nationalities (Dorn, *Geog. Cauc.*, 221), each of which spoke a different tongue; they were the seventy-two nations confined by Alexander beyond the Caspian Gates.

There exists a tradition, that when upon his death-bed Mahomet recommended to the faithful the conquest of the Caucasus, a country he had ever held in special veneration, so that several Shyite sects place it, in point of sanctity, above the cities of Arabia (D'Ohsson, *Des Peup. du Cauc.*, ii, 182). It is therefore not at all strange that the sovereignty over a region so specially blessed and in which the sultan himself was born, should have been included amongst his dignities, since he was entitled, in a measure, to consider the power of the founder of Alexandria to be his heritage.

Claiming the monarchy, as he did, over the forests of the Caucasus, the sultan naturally added thereunto his possession of Cappadocia, a portion of which did indeed belong to him, and wherein he had every right to situate Paradise. Mahomedans believe, as do Christians and Jews, that the Garden was in a beautiful land called Adn, watered by a marvellous river which was the source of the Euphrates, of the Tigris, the Jihoun (Pyramus of the ancients) and the Syhoun (Sarus), all in Cappadocia or in its immediate neighbourhood. Really, Boursbaï was no farther out in his calculations, than were those learned men who recognised the two last-named rivers in the Oxus and Jaxartes (Hammer), in the Araxes and Phasis (Brugsch), and even in the Volga and Indus (Raumer). BRUUN.

(9.) "the guardian of the caves."—The disappearance, A.D. 873, at the age of twelve, of Mohammed the descendant of Ali and the twelfth and last Imam, in a cave near Sermen Rey, distant thirty-two miles from Baghdad, gave rise to numerous conjectures, all of equal absurdity. The Shyites believe that this Mehdy, or celestial judge, is still in the unknown cave, and they await his return as impatiently as do the Jews that of the Messiah. The Sunnites are satisfied that when the world comes to an end, he will make his appearance accompanied by three hundred and sixty celestial spirits, and prevail upon the people of the earth to embrace Islamism (D'Ohsson, *Tableau. général de l'E. O.*, i, 152).

The sultan of Egypt is said to have styled himself "the guardian of the caves" (ein vogt der hellen), perhaps because the cavern was under his protection; but it is also possible that for "hellen" we should read Helle or Halle, the German for Hillah, on the site of ancient Babylon, and celebrated for such holy places in its neighbourhood as Kerbela and Mesjyd Ali, the Campo Santo to which the Shyites perform pilgrimages (Ritter, *Die Erdkunde* etc., ix, 842, 869, 955). BRUUN.

(10.) "Destructor of the Gods."—It is impossible to agree with Penzel, that Schiltberger entertained the strange notion of having seen a protector of hell in that Boursbaï, whom Penzel himself admits had glorified himself as being the friend of all gods (aller Gotter Freund), because the last title on the list is "Destructor of the Gods" (Ain mäg der götter). But here Penzel is again at fault in his interpretation of Schiltberger's meaning, because the monarch who claimed to be the Light of the true Faith (S. de Sacy, *Chrestom. Arabe*, 322), rather than boast of his friendship for the gods, would have declared himself to be, in keeping with the tenets of his religion, the implacable enemy to idolatry, a destructor of gods, a Mahhy, transformed in the text into "mäg".

There is some difficulty in accounting for the sultan's usurpation of the title of "the mighty emperor of Constantinoppel". In his letter to Shah Rokh, alluded to in note 4, page 184, he wrote as follows: "The kings of the earth have come from all parts as the bearers of their homage. The King of Hormuz, the Sultan of Hisn, the son of Karaman; these princes, sovereigns of their countries, the Sultan of the revered city of Mecca, the Sultans of Yemen, of Magreb, and of Tekrour, the King of Cyprus, since dead, all have presented themselves at my Court". This king of Cyprus, who was named John and died in 1432, was captured by the Egyptians on their expedition to the island in 1426, and being forced to acknowledge the suzerainty of the sultan, agreed to pay annual tribute to the amount of twenty thousand dinars, to enable him to obtain his freedom (Weil, *Gesch. der Chal.*, v, 177). John II., emperor of Byzantium, sought, but in vain, to intercede for the king by entering into negociations with the sultan (*ibid.*, 173), upon which occasion he may possibly have stooped to pay homage as others did, for he was not ashamed at another time to prostrate himself and kiss the Pope's slipper. It is likely enough that he presented himself under the name of Tekrour, a country Silvester de Sacy is at a loss to determine. Tekrour, however, need not have been the name of a country at all, but a corruption of Takfour, a designation in the East for the emperor of Constantinople.

The homage of the ruling powers on earth, did not suffice to satisfy the despot Boursbaï, for his ambition wafted him to the skies ("the lord [of the places] where Enoch and Helyas are buried"), the place of sepulture, say the Mahomedans, of their prophets Enoch, and Elias the protector of travellers, and who is believed by the Jews to have been borne away to heaven (D'Ohsson, *l. c.*, i, 51, 111).

Another title, though less bombastic, is still more puzzling, unless "Kaylamer" is to be identified with the fortress of Kalamil visited in 1221 by Willbrand of Oldenburg (Viv. de Saint-Martin, *Desc. de l'A. M.*, i, 488), after leaving Mamistra (Mopsvesta of the ancients, Mimistra of the Byzantines, the actual Missis). When upon this journey, Willbrand left on his right hand a place called the King's Black Castle, an indication that conducts us with Saint-Martin to the defile known to the ancients as the Pylæ Armeniæ or Pylæ Ciliciæ, now called Demyr Kapou by the Turks; evidently the same locality as that noticed by Marino Sanudo (*Liber Secret. Fidel.*, etc., 221—Pauthier, Marco Polo, cxxxii, 1). " Tartari autem sequenti anno (1260) violenter irrumpentes, ceperunt Alapiam, Harem, Hamam, Calamelam et Damascum." The fortress of Calamela being included among the chief cities in Syria, it is to be inferred that its strategical and commercial importance had greatly increased during the half century that transpired after Willbrand's visit. Nor does Calamila seem to have escaped the notice of Italian navigators, for the name, slightly varied, appears in the hydrographic charts of the 14th century. In the Catalan atlas, 1375, for instance, Caramila is evidently the same as the Cramela spoken of by the author of *Liber Secretorum Fidelium*, etc., who observes that it stood on the site of ancient Issus, the gulf of this city being marked on the chart, " golfo de Cramela". At that time, Cramela divided the possessions of the sultan of Egypt from those of the king of Armenia; and considering its importance, the sultan may not have disdained to style himself amir of Calamila, transformed by Schiltberger into "Amorach of Kaylamer".

The next name, "Galgarien", is undoubtedly intended for Khozary or Gazary, described by Marino Sanudo (Kunstmann, *Stud. über M. S.* 105) as Galgaria, a dependancy of the Tatars, inhabited by "Gothi et aliqui Alani". It was a Genoese possession in the Crimea, whence was carried on a large export trade, chiefly in slaves to Alexandria, where many afterwards became men of note; but Khozary was a dependancy of Kiptchak, a name that signifies—hollow tree—the distinctive title immediately following that of " the mighty emperor of Galgarien" as " the Lord of the withered tree". The rulers of Kiptchak, or khans of the Golden Horde, were long bound by the strictest ties of friendship to the sultans of Egypt, and as zealous followers of Mahomet, were not likely to question their right to hold the first place among the monarchs of Islam.

That the high position attained by those sultans did not influence them against according their protection to Christian potentates, is evident from the intimate relations that existed between themselves and the kings or emperors of Abyssinia, among whom should certainly be included " Prester John, in enclosed Rumany".

It is now generally admitted that Marco Polo, with his usual good faith, stated the precise truth in affirming that in his time, one George, a descendent of Prester John, became the governor of a province as a vassal of China. This prince professed the Roman Catholic faith, instead of Nestorianism as did his grandfather Ovang Khan, chief of the Keraits, and not, as Oppert has sought to prove (*Der Presb. Johannes in Sage und Gesch.*, etc., Berlin, 1864) of the Gour Khan of the Karakhitaians mentioned by Rubruquis. In either case it is pretty certain that so soon as European intercourse with the interior of Asia decreased, the existence of a Christian state on the Nile, to the south of Egypt, became more generally known; a state to which Haythoun, the Armenian historian, had already directed the Pope's attention (*De Tartaria*, c. 57, apud Webb, *A Survey of Egypt and Syria*, etc., 394), and it thereafter became the custom to metamorphose the Christian monarch of the Nubians and Abyssinians into Prester John. Like Schiltberger, De Lannoy (*Voy. et Ambass.*, 93) knew of no other Prester John, and far from admitting his dependance on the sultan, a condition to be inferred by the title of protector attributed to the latter by Schiltberger, the knight implies that it was rather the sultan who was in a state of dependance on Prester John, in whose power it lay to "destourber le cruschon" of the Nile, which he certainly would have done, but for the fear of victimising the many Christians in Egypt.

In another chapter, De Lannoy terms these Christians "Christians of the girdle", a name that was applied, says his commentator (Webb), in consequence of a law promulgated A.D. 856 by the caliph Motonakek, which prescribed that Jews and Christians should wear a broad leathern girdle. It appears, however, that in course of time the Nestorians and Jacobites also became subject to the same law, and this accounts for the expression, " Prester John, in enclosed Rumany", which, if intended for Abyssinia, a country mistaken by Marco Polo and De Lannoy for that of the Brahmins, would indicate that the former was inhabited by the Christians of the girdle. (De Lannoy styles the primate of the Copts, the primate of India.) That they were believed to be in Abyssinia is proved in the following lines from Juan de la Encina's narrative of his journey to Jerusalem in the year 1500.

> "Hay muchas naciones alli de Christianos,
> De Griegos, Latinos, y de Jacobitas,
> Y de los Armenios, y mas Maronistas
> Y de la cintura, que son Gorgianos :

Y de estos parecen los mas Indianos,
De habito y gesto mas feo, que pulcro :
Mas quanto al gozar del Santo Sepulcro
Son prógimos todos en Christo y hermanos."

This author evidently confounds the Georgians with the Abhases and the latter with the Abyssinians, as had frequently been done before him. In quoting from documents preserved among the archives at Königsberg, a letter from Conrad of Jungingen, Grand-Master of the Teutonic Order, dated January 20, 1407, and addressed to Prester John, " regi Abassiæ", Karamsin (*Hist. de Russie*, iii, 388), observes, that the superscription applies to the king of Abhase in the region of the Caucasus, and not to the king of Abyssinia. We read, likewise, in the chronicle of Alberic (*Rel. de Jean du Plan de Carpin*, 161) that the legate Pelagius "misit nuntios suos in Abyssiniam terram et Georgianorum, qui sunt viri catholici".

The friendship that existed between the "negus christianissimus" and the sultan was certainly but rarely interrupted, probably because they sympathised in each other's apprehensions ; but the sentiments entertained by Boursbaï towards the caliph, must have been of a different nature, so that he may have taken upon himself to borrow the title of "guardian of Wadach", or Baghdad. BRUUN.

(11.) " This is done on all the roads of the king-sultan."—It would appear that during the author's stay in Egypt, the ladies of that country exceeded all bounds in the abuse of the freedom they were permitted to enjoy during the Baïram festivities, judging by the severe measures adopted by the sultan, to their prejudice, in 1432 (Weil, *Gesch. der Chal.*, v, 208). It was forbidden to every woman, and there were no exceptions, to leave her house, so that the unmarried even incurred the risk of dying of starvation. This law was subsequently modified in favour of coloured slaves and old women, and the young were only permitted to leave their home for the bath, on the express understanding that they returned immediately afterwards.

By another decree, promulgated in the early part of his reign, the sultan Boursbaï abolished the ancient custom which required that the ground should be kissed by all who were admitted to his presence; and it was thenceforth ordained, that according to the rank of the person introduced, so his hand or the hem of his garment should be kissed. But he was soon persuaded to resort to the old usage, except that instead of kissing the ground with the mouth, those presented were to touch the ground with the hand, which was then to be kissed. Schiltberger could not have been in Egypt before the abolition of the above ridiculous and barbarous custom, in the first year of Boursbaï's reign; but there were no doubt numerous instances in his day of obsequious courtiers and other parasites who did actually kiss the ground. The ceremonial and etiquette observed at the presentation and reception of ambassadors, was in accordance with the customs of the Turks and Tatars upon such occasions.

The little bell for post-horses was introduced by the Mongols into Russia, and having been in use on post-roads ever since the time of their domination, has substituted the horn of the French and German postillion. BRUUN.

(12.) "and they send it to whosoever it belongs."—Pigeons were employed in Asia as carriers, in very remote times. It was pigeon service of which the daughter of the governor of Atra, Hatra, or al Hadr, availed herself, that enabled Sapor, king of Persia, 240-271, to capture the city which the emperor Severus had failed to take. It is recorded by numerous European and Eastern writers, that the pigeon-post was in general use in Syria and Egypt during the Crusades. In his story of the Crusade under Henry VI., in 1196, Arnold, bishop of Lubeck, describes the training of pigeons, which was similar to what we read in the text, and observes that "the Infidels are more highly gifted than the children of light", the training of pigeons being the invention of the Infidels, whose practice was imitated by their enemies. After the fall of Baïrouth in 1197, Boemund, prince of Antioch, announced the good tidings to his subjects by despatching a pigeon.

Khalil Daheri (Quatremère, i, 55, note 77), an Arabian writer of the 15th century, reports that Belbeis, Salchieh, Katia, and Varradeh or Barideh, were the pigeon-post stations on the road to Syria. According to Makrizi (*ibid.*, 56), Varradeh was distant eighteen miles from Alarih. Query? Fort Arich or el-Arich in Lower Egypt, where the French capitulation was signed in 1800. Aboul-Mahazin declares that Bir al-Kady—The Kady's well—must have marked the limits of Syria and Egypt.

Another Arabian writer (Abd-Allalif, *S. de Sacy edition*, 43) calls Alarich, Alaris—changed by the bishop of Lubeck, as his German editors believe, into Ahir, a name almost to be identified with "Archey", one of the principal pigeon stations.

Bruun.

(13.) "sacka."—Literally, in Turkish, a water-carrier. A pelican is sákà koútchou. Ed.

CHAPTER XXXVIII.

(1.) "The Infidels call the mountain Muntagi."—Hushan dagh, the correct name given by the Arabs, is here handed down to us as "Muntagi", which differs so widely from the native appellation of Sinaï, that it may have been derived from the word Montagna, possibly the generic name by which the mount was known to pilgrims. In such a case, Schiltberger's companions would have been Italians, who, on the supposition that they were mariners, supplied him with the details he gives on the Red Sea—its breadth, which is represented at double its actual extent—and the information that it had to be crossed to attain Sinai; although we know from De Lannoy that the journey from Egypt was performed "en costiant la mer". The knight makes no mention of the wonderful supply of oil at the monastery of St. Catherine, nor of the other miracles performed by the saint; but he explains why the Infidels went to Sinai. At the foot of the mount was a church of St. Catherine, "à manière d'un chastel, forte et quarrée, où les trois lois de Jhésu-Crist, de Moyse et de Mahommet sont en trois églises représentées". Bruun.

(1A.) This somewhat confused description of St. Catherine's mount and of Mount Sinaï, is to be accounted for by Schiltberger's statement that he had not ascended the latter, and that he described the sites from hearsay only. He distinguishes, however, St. Catherine from what he calls "Muntagi, the mountain of the apparition", upon which, as he was informed, God appeared to Moses in a burning bush; where flows the spring from the rock that Moses struck with his staff; the site where our Lord delivered to him the tables with the ten Commandments, etc., etc. "Muntagi" may therefore have been intended for Musa dagh, the Turkish, as Jabal Musa is the Arabic for Mountain of Moses, about which, in the words of Dean Stanley (*Sinai and Palestine*, 39) the traditions of Israel have lingered, certainly since the 6th century, and perhaps from a still earlier date. Mount Sinaï is called Tur Sina by Ibn Haukal, and Jabal Tur and Et Tur by Edrisi and Aboulfeda. ED.

CHAPTER XXXIX.

(1.) "the village of Mambertal."—"Mambertal" for Mamre, by which name Hebron also was known (Gen. xii, 18 ; xxxv, 27), and was probably so called after Mamre the Amorite, the friend of Abraham (Gen. xiv, 13). Sir John Mandevile's tradition of the Dry Tree (*Voyages and Travels*, etc.) as it was related to him, agrees almost word for word with the tale in the text, except that Sir John saw an oak, whereas Schiltberger's tree was called by the Infidels "carpe" (Sir John writes Dirpe), and selvy is the Turkish for cypress. Commentators on the Holy Scriptures have said that plains of Mamre (Gen. xiii, 18 ; xviii, 1) is a mis-translation for oaks of Mamre, but the Turkish for oak is meyshe. The great tree seen by Robinson in 1838 (*Biblical Researches*, etc., ii, 81) was an oak ; it measured 22½ feet in circumference in the lower part, the branches extending over a diameter of 89 feet. It stood solitarily near a well in the midst of a field, and was sound and in a thriving state. A long and comprehensive note on the Arbre Sec or Arbre Sol, will be found in Yule's Marco Polo, i, 132.

ED.

(2.) "it is well taken care of."—The distance from Hebron to Jerusalem, as given in chapter 40, is correct (Raumer, *Palæstina*, etc., 201); so is the statement that Hebron was the chief city of the Philistines, for Josephus (*Wars*, etc., xii, 10) says that it was a royal city of the Canaanites.

"Carpe" may have indicated the caroub or locust tree (*Die charube von Kufin ;* see Rosen, *Die Patriarchengruft zu Hebron*, in *Zeitschrift f. allg. Erdk.*, neue Folge, xiv, 426), or the turpentine tree, which Josephus and others have stated grew in those parts, where a small and sterile valley still bears the significant name of Sallet-el-Boutmeh—Place of the Turpentine tree. In course of time, the turpentine tree of Josephus became confounded with Abraham's oak, mentioned in the Bible, which the Russian pilgrim Daniel (Noroff, *Pèler. en T. S.*, 77) says he found in leaf, and might have been a huge tree of the sort noticed by Robinson. The tree seen by Schiltberger must have been of another kind, because it was withered; he could not otherwise have transmitted to us the prophecy so encouraging to our own desires, and in accordance with the presentiments of the Infidels themselves, that the day will come when they shall be expelled from the holy places.

No person is allowed to enter the mosque wherein the holy patriarchs lie (see page 60), as was the case in the 15th century, unless provided with the sultan's firman. We are told by Novairi and other authors (Makrizi by Quatremère, ii, 249), that when the sultan Bibars, 1260-1264, visited Khalil (Hebron), and learnt that Christians and Jews were permitted to enter upon payment of a fee, he at once put a stop to the practice. Hammer (*Gesch. der Ilchane*, etc., 129) states that Mussulmans have held Hebron in great estimation since the reign of the caliph Mostershid (stabbed to death by an assassin in 1120), when the remains of several bodies found in the caves, were passed off as being those of Abraham, Isaac, and Jacob, although, according to Moses, they were interred at Hebron, where their places of sepulture are pointed out by Christians.

The author of Itinerarium Hierosolymitanum (Parthey et Pinder, *Itiner. Ant. Aug.*, etc., 283) thus writes with reference to the beautiful church constructed by Constantine the Great near the turpentine tree of Abraham : "Inde Terebinth Cebron mil. ii, ubi est memoria per quadrum ex lapidibus miræ pulchritudinis, in qua positi sunt Abraham, Isaac, Jacob, Sarra, Rebecca et Lea."

About the year 600, there was already a cathedral in the quadrum, and twelve months later Bishop Arnulphus found the monolith cenotaphs of the three patriarchs, one being that of Adam ; other smaller ones were assigned to their wives. At that period Hebron belonged to the Arabs, who gloried in their descent from Abraham, which accounts for the erection by them of a mosque over the remains of their ancestor. It was only after the conquest of Jerusalem by the Crusaders that the place was made over to the Christians for religious purposes ; this we learn from Sœwulf (*Recueil de Voy. et de Mém.*, etc., 817-854) who went to Palestine in 1102, and the Russian pilgrim Daniel (Noroff, *Péler. en T. S.*, 95), who in 1115 saw a superb edifice at Hebron, in the crypt of which was the sepulchre of the patriarch within a chapel of circular form. Rosen says that the presence of Jews within this sanctuary was tolerated by the Crusaders, a privilege, however, for which they had to pay, according to the evidence of Benjamin of Tudela, and of his co-religionist Petachy of Ratisbon, who travelled in Palestine twelve years later. Hebron passed into the hands of the Mussulmans long before the fall of Acre, after which event the Christians in their turn were taxed for the liberty of entering.

Among those of Schiltberger's predecessors who have left an account of what they saw and learnt during their sojourn in Palestine, are the German monk, Brocardus, towards the close of the 13th century—Sir John Mandevile, 1372—and the German pilgrim, Ludolph von Suchem, whose work, *Libellus de Itinere ad T. S.*, is considered the best itinerary for the Holy Land in the 14th century.

De Lannoy was in Palestine at about the same time as the author, but does not report having been at Hebron ; he however supplies a list of the holy places, that was compiled, as he states, by Pope Sylvester at the request of the emperor Constantine and of "Sainte Helaine", his mother. Three cities of " Ebron" are included: "La neufve et la moienne, de laquelle est l'esglise où sont ensepvelis Adam, Abraham, Isaac et Jacob et leurs femmes" ..... "*Item*, Ebron, la vielle, eu laquelle David regna sept ans et six mois." It is desirable that these two passages should be quoted, because in the works I have cited, such as Noroff's, Raumer's, Rosen's, and in others which dwell largely on Hebron, one city only of the name is mentioned. BRUUN.

(3.) " but now there is only a pillar."—If tradition is to be relied on, it was the mother of Constantine who built the Church of the Annunciation, which had already ceased to exist in Schiltberger's time. In 1620 a handsome church was erected on the same site (Raumer, *Palæstina*, etc., 136), and a column at the foot of seventeen steps indicated the spot where the angel Gabriel appeared to the Virgin; it was possibly the pillar referred to in the text. The pilgrim Daniel describes the earliest church, situated in the centre of the city, as being large and handsome, and enclosing three altars. It was destroyed by the sultan Bibars in 1263 (Weil, *Gesch. der Chal.*, iv, 46; Makrizi by Quatremère, I, i, 200). BRUUN.

CHAPTER XL.

(1.) "I went twice to Jherusalem with a koldigen."—Schiltberger's commentators have not been able to identify the word "koldigen", to which Koehler (*Germania*, vii, 371-380) puts a mark of interrogation, observing that it is written in precisely the same manner in two early editions. Frescobaldi in 1384 (*Viaggi in Terra Santa*) speaks of the monks at the monastery on Sinaï as Calores, instead of Καλογέροι. If Joseph, Schiltberger's companion, was a Christian, he might very possibly have been a Kalogeros, a title turned into "Koldigen". BRUUN.

(1A.) Another suggestion! Khodja is a corruption of the Persian word Khaja, a term that in the East generally denotes a merchant (Garcin de Tassy, *Les Noms Propres et les Titres Musulm.*, 68). Or an interpretation of "Koldigen" is perhaps to

be found in Koul, the Turkish for a detachment or small body of
men, and jy, a termination significative of office, profession, or
trade, as for instance, arabajy, one who drives; kayikjy, a boat-
man; ghemijy, a sailor, and similarly, Kouljy, one who leads a
body of men. In European Turkey, however, Kouljy means also
a coast-guard-man, and in other parts of that empire the term is
applied to a keeper or custodian. In his Russian edition, Professor Bruun submits the word Koljy derived from Koll, the title
of those of the second class of the Monastic Order of Kalender,
the founder of which Order, singularly enough, was one named
Joseph. With the reader must remain the privilege of deciding
upon Joseph's calling, whether monk, merchant, coast-guard-man,
or custodian! ED.

(2.) "The Infidels call Jherusalem, Kurtzitalil."—Jerusalem is
called by the Turks, Kouds Shereef, with the first part of which
name might be associated the first syllable "Kurtz"; but Shereef
could scarcely have been corrupted to "italil", which reminds
me of Halil, a term pre-eminently applied to Abraham the
friend of God, and given to the gate of the city that leads to
Hebron, known as the Bab-el-Halil (Raumer, *Palæstina*, etc.,
201). BRUUN.

(3.) "the pilgrims can kiss and touch it."—The Russian pilgrim Daniel observed three openings in the marble slab, through
which the sacred stone could be seen and kissed; but the indis-
creet zeal of pilgrims, says Noroff, who contrived to chip off
fragments, necessitated its protection from further mutilation.
BRUUN.

(4.) "a brightness above the holy sepulchre, that is like fire."
—Some people believed that this miracle was performed through
the intervention of a dove, while others attributed it to lightning.
The Russian pilgrim Daniel explains to his readers that it is only
those who have not attended during the celebration in church
that could be sceptic as to the appearance of this light from

heaven, and he trusts that the truly faithful and of good repute will believe in all the miracles that take place within the sanctuary! He concludes his observations by quoting Luke xvi, 10. BRUUN.

(4A.) Of the lamp that burned in front of the Holy Sepulchre, Sir John Mandeville has also recorded that "it went out of itself, on Good Friday, and again lit itself at the hour that our Lord rose from the dead." This lamp Schiltberger may have seen, but it appears doubtful whether he witnessed the performance of the miracle of the Holy Fire, "the brightness above the Holy Sepulchre, that is like fire", or he surely would have described the supernatural occurrence.

This Easter miracle at the Holy Sepulchre has been the theme of most travellers who have witnessed it ever since the days of Charlemagne. Henry Maundrell (*Journey from Aleppo to Jerusalem*, etc., 96) was present at the Easter festival (1697) during the ceremony kept up by the Greeks and Armenians, upon the persuasion that every Easter a miraculous flame descends from heaven into the Holy Sepulchre. He describes the fearful tumult and clamour made by the people in their wild excitement in anticipation of the miraculous appearance of the Holy Fire at the sepulchre, produced, as he exposes, by the two miracle-mongers, the Greek and Armenian bishops, who had entered the sepulchre alone for the purpose. When they issued with two blazing torches in their hands, all the people rushed with candles that they might obtain the purest fire sent down from heaven, which they instantly applied to their beards, faces, and bosoms, pretending that it would not burn like an earthly flame; but Maundrell says he saw plainly that none could endure the experiment long enough to make good that pretension.

Dean Stanley, who was at Jerusalem in 1853 (*Sinaï and Palestine*, 467), states that Maundrell's account is an almost exact transcript of what was still to be seen. Captain Warren also witnessed the strange doings in 1867-70 (*Underground Jerusalem*, 429-437); and in *The Graphic*, Sept. 21, 1878, was published an interesting illustration of the interior of the Church of the Holy Sepulchre during the performance of the miracle, together with a short account of the proceedings. "After a procession of bishops and priests thrice round the building, the Patriarch enters the Sepulchre. Now the noise becomes greater and greater . . . . . making the place more like an Inferno than the Church of Christ. . . . . . . The Holy Fire now issues from the holes in the walls, and hundreds of hands are stretched out as they frantically try to light their candles at the flame. . . . . By this time one candle has ignited the other, and the crowd below is one mass of moving flame." There is no abatement, in this the 19th century, in the huge sham, with its attendant blind superstition and noisy demonstrations. ED.

(5.) "the priests from the country of Prester John."—Upon descending the steps on the east side of Calvary (Raumer, *Palæstina*, etc., 301), another flight of twenty-four steps is reached, at the foot of which is the Chapel of St. Helena, whence another flight of eleven steps conducts to the place where the cross of Christ and those of the two thieves were found. Here is an altar of the Latin church. The chapel of the Jacobites must have been higher up, near the Chapel of St. John which enclosed the tomb of the Baron of the Holy Sepulchre and of his brother, the first king of Jerusalem; interesting monuments that have been destroyed, not by the Turks but by the Greeks (Richter, *Wallfahrten in Morgenlande*, 22). BRUUN.

(6.) "the church of Saint Steffan, where he was stoned."—It is asserted on tradition (Noroff, *Péler. en T. S.*, 19) that St. Stephen was stoned in front of the sepulchre of the Holy Virgin, on the road that leads from the Gate of St. Stephen, called also the Gate of Gethsemane. But there was another gate on the north side of the city, that was named by the Crusaders after the first Christian martyr, because it was believed that he was stoned in front of it; this gate is now the Gate of Damascus.

Noroff states further, that in ancient times there was upon the same side a church of St. Stephen, which was demolished by the Christians in consequence of its proximity to the walls, and because it presented an obstacle to their defence. Daniel the

Russian pilgrim, saw that church intact, and asserts that St. Stephen there met his death and was buried. Schiltberger, no doubt, found it in ruins. De Lannoy, without mentioning the church, was of opinion that the martyr suffered death close to the gate which bore his name, the spot being near Kedron and the sepulchre of the Holy Virgin. The old chronicler Adamnanus (Raumer, *Palæstina*, etc., 312, note 92), in describing the basilica of Zion with its cœnaculum, says: "Hic petra monstratur supra quam Stephanus lapidatus extra civitatem obdormitavit." According to Daniel, Zion was not within the city.   BRUUN.

(7.) "Another hospital that rests on fifty-four marble columns."—The ruins of this, the palace of the Hospitallers or Knights of the Order of St. John of Jerusalem, are still to be seen to the south of, and at no great distance from the Church of the Resurrection. A church and monastery dedicated to the Holy Virgin were erected on this spot in 1048; and shortly afterwards were constructed near these edifices, another church, a monastery, and hospital, dedicated to St. John the Baptist. Gerard, almoner of this hospital, instituted in 1118 the celebrated Order of Hospitallers.   BRUUN.

(7A.) Benjamin of Tudela knew of two hospitals at Jerusalem which supported four hundred knights, and afforded shelter to the sick. The four hundred knights were ever ready to wage war together with those who came from the country of the Franks. One hospital was called that of Salmon, having been originally the palace built by Solomon.   ED.

(8.) "Infidels do not allow either Christians or Jews to enter it."—This must be the place where Omar about the year 640 constructed the great mosque, afterwards converted into a Christian church that was named Τὰ Ἅγια τῶν Ἁγίων. The Crusaders called it Templum Domini, by which designation it was know to Schiltberger, although it was in the hands of the Mahomedans.   BRUUN.

(9.) "called the throne of Salomon."—This has reference to the site of the mosque of Aksa, previously the Church of the Presentation of the Virgin, built by Justinian in 530. The Russian pilgrim, Daniel, saw it in the wrecked state to which it had been reduced at the conquest of Jerusalem by the Franks, who there met with the most determined resistance on the part of the Mussulmans. BRUUN.

(10). "there our Lord healed the bed-ridden man."—It was generally supposed that the pool and the palace of the templars occupied the site of the temple of Solomon, close to the mosque of Aksa (Raumer, *Palæstina*, etc., 297). Daniel knew of the residence of Solomon only, because the palace was not constructed until the Order of Hospitallers was established in 1119, that is to say, four or five years after his stay in the Holy Land. The church, and the dwellings of the templars, were destroyed in 1187 by Saladin, so that there was nothing for Schiltberger to see but their remains. BRUUN.

(11). "the house of Herod."—At no great distance from the pool, stood a house said to have been that of Pilate; the modern edifice on the south side of the Sakhara or mosque constructed by Omar in 637, is the residence of the pasha. It is supposed that the palace of Herod was farther away to the east, and to the right of the Via Dolorosa. BRUUN.

(12.) "A church, called that of Saint Annen," is noticed by De Lannoy, who adds that this was the birth-place of St. Anne, the mother of the Virgin Mary; but he makes no allusion to the head of St. Stephen, or the arm of St. John Chrysostom, relics which, through some mistake of the author, or of a scribe, have usurped the place of those of St. Joachim the spouse of St. Anne. Daniel asserts that a church consecrated to the latter existed in his day; it stood over their dwelling and place of burial. BRUUN.

(13.) "Mount Syon .... stands higher than the city."—The wall constructed by Souleiman, the Magnificent, 1536-1539, traverses the ridge of the hills. Within it, near an Armenian chapel, is pointed out the house of Annas, and at a short distance is the principal church of the Armenians, dedicated to St. James the Elder who was there beheaded. Within the wall stood the house of Caiphas the high priest, now the Church of the Holy Saviour also belonging to the Armenians, and in which is preserved the slab that closed the Saviour's tomb. This is probably the same church as described by Schiltberger; called that of the Holy Saviour by De Lannoy (*Voy. et Ambass.*, 54), who says that it was in the occupation of Catholics, or perhaps of Armenians who recognised the supremacy of the Pope, but not of the Gregorians. This church could not have existed in the time of Daniel, because he simply mentions the house of Caiphas.

Close at hand was the cœnaculum, in which the Last Supper took place—where the Holy Ghost fell on the apostles—where the Holy Virgin expired, and where Jesus Christ washed the apostles' feet. The Church of Zion or of the Virgin Mary, that stood here and is described by Daniel and others, was afterwards occupied by the Franciscan friars, and eventually became a mosque. William of Tyre (Raumer, *Palæstina*, etc., 312), Schiltberger and his contemporaries, Zosimus (*Pout. Rouss. Ioud.*, ii, 50) and De Lannoy, all agree that here was the tomb of St. Stephen; De Lannoy, however, adds that it was the second place of his interment.
BRUUN.

(14). "A beautiful castle which was built by the king-sultan." —This citadel on the western side of the mount was constructed during the Crusades by the Pisans, the tower of David which formed a part of it being of more ancient date. Daniel and others considered it a formidable fortification.
BRUUN.

(15.) "King Soldan."—The tomb of Solomon, described by several pilgrims, adjoined that of David. De Lannoy calls it the burial place of twelve other kings.
BRUUN.

(16.) "A brook in the valley of Josophat."—On the banks of this stream, the Kedron, and at no great distance from the garden of Gethsemane, is a large rectangular edifice that was constructed by the Empress Helena. Tobler (*Die Siloahquelle*, 149), who has taken the trouble to record the number of steps counted by thirty-eight travellers, his predecessors, without however including Schiltberger, places the tomb of the Virgin at the foot of forty-seven steps. Near the above edifice are four sepulchral monuments that have been differently described, as their origin is unknown. Their style is partly Greek and partly Egyptian, and they somewhat resemble the monuments at Petra. They are fully described by Robinson, *Biblical Researches*, etc., and Kraft, *Die Topographie Jerusalems*, Berlin, 1846.   BRUUN.

(17.) "the mount of Galilee."—This is intended to designate the northern summit of the Mount of Olives, on which was the tower Viri Galilei, so called because two men in white stood there at the moment of the Ascension (Raumer, *Palæstina*, etc., 310). De Lannoy refers to this spot when describing pilgrimages to the Mount of Olives: "*Item*, le lieu de Galilée, où Jhésu-Crist s'apparut à ses onze appostres"; only he has confounded the place where the two stood with that of the eleven.   BRUUN.

(18.) " Dead Sea, which is one hundred and fifty stadia wide." —Josephus (*Wars*, etc., iv, 8, 3) wrote that the Dead Sea was 580 stadia in length, and 150 stadia wide. Seetzen (*Reiseberichte in Monatliche Correspondenz*, Berlin, 1854, xviii, 440), gives the width at 13½ English miles, which Robinson reduces to 11¼ miles, at the same time observing that the water level rose from 10 feet to 15 feet; and that when he happened to be there in the month of May, the water had sufficiently risen to inundate, over the space of one mile, a salt lake on its southern shore. The indications of Josephus and of Schiltberger may have reference to the same season of the year.   BRUUN.

(18A.) Captain Warren (*Underground Jerusalem*, 175) gives much new and valuable information on the Jordan and the valley of that river, and explains that the rise and fall in the level of the Dead Sea is caused by the fluctuations in the rush of water, the time of greater evaporations not coinciding with that of the freshets. This rise and fall might possibly be greater, were there no other regulating arrangement than evaporation; but at the southern end there is a vast tract of land, only submerged by a few feet (here is Robinson's salt lake), and when this is covered the evaporation is great; and should the waters be unduly extracted, this becomes dry land. The Jordan overflows its banks at harvest time, which is simply owing to the harvest being early in that semi-tropical district, when the waters of the river are swollen by the waters of Hermon. The disparity in the dimensions of the Dead Sea, as noted by different authors, is here accounted for and explained. See Duc de Luynes' *Voy. d'Exploration à la Mer Morte*, etc., Paris, 1874. ED.

(19.) "Christians usually bathe in the Jordan."—Pilgrims, even in the days of Josephus and of Jerome, looked for salvation through baptism in the Jordan, and still may thousands be seen on Easter Monday, wending their way from Jerusalem to Jericho, performing the distance in five hours; two other hours bring them to the Jordan, and they assemble at the ruins of a church and monastery that were dedicated to St. John the Baptist. The church was equally a ruin in Daniel's time, but the monastery and vaulted chapel near Hermon were in existence. It is clear that this mount could not have been either the great Hermon of the Lebanon, or the lesser Hermon which is situated in the middle of the plain of Jezreel to the south of Mount Tabor.

The monastery of St. John the Baptist (De Lannoy) was perhaps identical with that constructed, according to Adamnanus (Raumer, *Palæstina*, etc., 60), by St. Helena, at the place where Christ was baptised. Pocock (*Desc. of the East*, etc., ii, 49) makes it distant one mile from the Jordan, and says that Greeks and Latins, who are at issue as to the exact locality, are mistaken in seeking it on the western bank of the river, John having baptised at Bethany beyond the Jordan. Noroff (*Péler. en T. S.*, 49) points out that Pocock himself is in error, and that the Greeks and Latins were quite right in keeping to the western bank, in front of Bethabara and not of Bethany. BRUUN.

(20.) "from these it has its name."—Many authors, from Josephus to Burkhardt, have derived the name of the river Jordan from the two springs, Jor and Dan, although the sources are in reality the Banias, Dan, and Hasbeny; so that every allowance should be made if Schiltberger has failed to give the correct etymology of the name, which signifies in Hebrew "that which flows downwards". BRUUN.

(21.) "where the Infidels often have a fair during the year."— This beautiful plain was in all probability the valley of Jericho, watered by the Jordan after it leaves the lake of Tiberias or Gennesareth, and traverses two calcareous hills, described by Justin in words similar to those of Schiltberger,—"Est namque vallis quæ continuis montibus velut muro quodam clauditur."

The valley of Jericho, compared by Josephus to a paradise, Θεῶν χωρίον, tractum divinum, is far from meriting such encomium, even though we cannot but agree with Ritter that, considering the profusion and utility of the vegetation still growing wildly in this fertile valley, and the scattered remains of old aqueducts, it must have been one of the most beautiful gardens in Palestine whilst in a state of cultivation during the Crusades.

That the sepulchre of St. James was in this valley is a very puzzling statement, because it is asserted on tradition that the Apostle of that name, surnamed the Elder, was beheaded on Mount Zion, on the spot where stands the church that bears his name; it is alluded to by Schiltberger and De Lannoy, and is actually in the custody of the Armenians, who state that the head of the saint was carried off to Spain, Quaresimus (*Elucidatio Terræ Sanctæ*, ii, 77) asserting that the body, as well as the head, is at Campostella. According to Daniel and De Lannoy, the tomb of St. James the Less was in the valley of Josaphat, near that of the prophet Zacharias, close to which, says Schiltberger, reposed the remains of the prophet Jacob, a name substituted for that of James, or rather James the Less, who, it is said, concealed himself in a tomb near to that of Zacharias, upon the day that our Lord was betrayed. BRUUN.

(22.) "twelve hundred and eighty years from Christ."—The holy places had been frequently won and lost during the Crusades, but they were never again recovered from the Egyptians, after the expulsion of the Mongols from Syria by the sultan Koutouz and his amir Beïbars in 1260, the year 658 of the Hegira. Schiltberger's error in computation, of twenty years, probably arose from his having added the years of this date, 658 instead of 638 to the 622 years that had elapsed from the birth of Christ to the commencement of the Mahomedan era. These dates amount together to 1280, which he must have thought corresponded to 658 of the Hegira, the period indicated to him as that at which Mussulman rule was established in Syria and Palestine, and Christians lost their influence.   BRUUN.

(23.) "and this they do that they may make more profit."— Many travellers in Egypt, whether previous to, during, or since the Crusades, have noticed that balsam was to be obtained only from the Matarea garden near Cairo. To his translation of Abd-Allatif's description of Egypt, Silvester de Sacy adds several passages on the cultivation of balsam in that country, being extracts from the reports of European and Eastern writers; but he omits Arnold of Lubeck and De Lannoy. Whilst at Cairo, the latter was presented by the patriarch of India with a "fyole de fin balme de la vigne, où il croist, dont il est en partie seigneur"; and he repeats the tradition related by Brocardus (*Terræ Sanctæ Descr.*, 311), that the vine of the balsam had been brought to Babylon, meaning Cairo, by Cleopatra.

Schiltberger was in Syria and Egypt at about the same time as De Lannoy, and may have heard this tradition, also the legend that was related to the Bishop of Lubeck, to the effect that the balsam tree did not put forth in the garden of Matarea until the Virgin, in passing by when on her flight from the persecutions of Herod, had washed her son's clothes in the stream that irrigated the garden. Makrizi associates this very fable with the well at Matarea, adding, that the balm-tree had quite disappeared from the country about the Jordan where it was formerly exclusively obtained. Strabo (XVI, ii, 41) and Pliny (XII, v, 4) both say that this plant was cultivated in the royal gardens at Jericho, of which it was the chief ornament (Josephus, *Wars*, etc., iv, 8); but it is doubtful whether it disappeared entirely from Judæa after the days of Cleopatra and Augustus, because some was purchased at Jerusalem in 705 by St. Guillebaud (cited by S. de Sacy, Abd-Allatif, 91); and Burkhardt learnt that balm-oil was to be obtained at Tiberias, extracted from a fruit that greatly resembled the cucumber, and grew on a stem very like the balsam tree at Mecca.

Now-a-days, a sort of oil, produced from the myrobalsamum and prepared at Jerusalem, is sold to superstitious pilgrims for genuine balsam or extract of opobalsamum, although it does not possess its qualities. Deception was also practised in Schiltberger's time, but he has shewn himself not to have been so great a simpleton as the many who are being continually duped.

That the sale of balsam was a great source of revenue to the sultan (the patriarch of Armenia paid a high price for it, see page 92), is confirmed by others. Makrizi considered it a most useful commodity. Christian sovereigns vied with each other in securing a supply, and it was greatly esteemed by Christians in general, because baptism was not considered efficacious unless oil of balsam was dropped into the water prepared for the purpose.

BRUUN.

(23A.) A plant called the balsam, from which oil was extracted, and not to be found in any other part of the world, grew in the vicinity of Fostat the chief city of Egypt, situated on the river Nile to the north. So wrote Ibn Haukal in the 10th century. It was near Fostat that Cairo was founded in 968. Jacques de Vitry, a bishop in Palestine in the 13th century (afterwards bishop of Tusculum, the modern Frascati) alludes to the produce of balsam in Egypt, which previously was to be obtained in the Holy Land only (*Gesta Dei per Francos*, etc., Hanoviæ, MDCXI, *Bongars edition*). According to De Lannoy, it grew by the shore near the city of Cairo, and De Maillet, Consul for France at that city in the early part of the last century, specially describes the plant, which, however, he could not have seen, as it had disappeared two hundred years before his time.

The last of the plants that grew in the garden of Matarea, says this author, were not more than two or three cubits in height, the stem being about one inch in thickness; the leaves of a beautiful green, on slender branches, resembled those of the rue. The stem had a double bark, the outer of a reddish colour, the inner, the thinnest, being perfectly green. The smell of the two barks was not unlike that of the turpentine tree, but when bruised between the fingers emitted an odour similar to that of cardamom. Like the vine, this plant was pruned annually, and De Maillet supposes that then was extracted the valuable balsam so greatly esteemed by all Christians, especially those of the Coptic church, the efficacy of baptism without its application being generally doubted (*Descr. de l'Egypte*, edited by the Abbé Le Mascrier, à la Haye, 1740). De Maillet distinguishes the balsam of Cairo from that of Mecca, which Ali Bey (*Travels*, etc.) informs us was not made there, but, on the contrary, was very scarce, as it could only be obtained when brought by the Bedouins. Ali Bey was told that it came from Medina. According to some authors, the last of the balsam plants growing in Egypt were destroyed in 1615 by an inundation of the Nile. ED.

CHAPTER XLI.

(1.) "Of these four rivers I have seen three."—Well versed as Schiltberger was in the Holy Scriptures, he could not but have been aware that the Euphrates and Tigris were included among the four rivers that had their source in Paradise; but he substitutes the Nile and Rison for the Gihon and Pison.

It is noticed elsewhere, that in the time of the Crusades the Nile and Euphrates were mistaken for each other, in consequence of the name by which a part of Cairo was known. When, after a time, the error was discovered, the Indus was substituted for the Euphrates, partly, perhaps, because Koush—Ethiopia—was confounded with the country of the Cossæi, peopled, according to the classic authors, by Ethiopians; and also because it had formerly been mistaken for $Κύσσια\ χώρα$ of the ancients, known to the Hebrews as Eriz Koush, situated to the east of Babylon (Fürst,

Gesch. des Karäerth., 102). Thus was it that Giovanni de' Marignolli (*Reis. in das Morgenl.*, 18) who passed through China and India soon after Marco Polo, mistook the Gihon of the Bible for the Indus and the Nile. Even De Lannoy (*Voy. et Ambass.*, 88) does not venture to refute the opinion as to the continuity of these two rivers. Being under the impression that the Nile was a continuation of the Indus, Schiltberger calls the two rivers, which he believed were united, the Nile, imagining that they were identical with the Gihon or Sihon, a name that greatly resembles the Hebrew denomination of the Nile.

" Rison" could scarcely have been other than the Pison of the Bible, spelled Phison in the Nuremberg MS. (*Penzel edition*, 123); this accounts for the statement that gold and precious stones were found in it, produce for which the territory of Khivila, watered by the Phison, was celebrated. Schiltberger adds, that the " Rison" traversed India, whilst he identifies the Indus with the Nile; his fourth river must therefore have been the Ganges, the Phison of Moses of Chorene, who states that the river was at the limits of the two peninsulas of India, although Haythoun, his countryman, believed the Phison to be the Oxus because it divided Persia into two parts: one containing Samarkand and Bokhara; the other, the southern cities of Nishapur, Ispahan, etc. Not satisfied with having reconciled the contradictory opinions of his predecessors, in identifying the Phison with the Ganges, Giovanni de' Marignolli unites to these two rivers the Hoang-Ho and even the Volga (Raumer, *Palæstina*, etc., Appendix, vii), and he represents that, after irrigating Evilach in India, the Phison passes, not only into China, where it is called the Karamora (Kara-mouran—Black River —was the name given by the Mongols to the Yellow River of the Chinese), but after disappearing in the sands behind Caffa, again shews itself and forms the Sea of Bakou—Caspian—behind Chana —Tana, now Azoff. We are bound to admit that Schiltberger is nearer the truth in saying that he had never seen the " Rison" at all, than was the bishop of Bisignano who recognised it in too many rivers at one and the same time.   BRUUN.

CHAPTER XLII.

(1.) "the city of Lambe, in a forest called Lambor."—Pepper was cultivated in Malabar, the country indicated by these two names, long before Schiltberger's time. Kazvini, who died in 1283, Aboulfeda and Ibn Batouta, all mention its produce, and Giovanni de' Marignolli, who visited Malabar in 1348, describes the cultivation of pepper in pretty much the same terms as does our author, equally refuting the story that the black colour was owing to smoke employed to drive away serpents. We are informed by this author of the existence of many Christians of St. Thomas in the country, and that there was a Latin church dedicated to St. George in the town of Columbus, doubtlessly the Kollam of the Arabs (Peschel, *Gesch. d. Erdkunde*, 162, note 3), the Kuilon of the Chinese, called Coilum by Marco Polo, Chulam by Benjamin of Tudela, Kaalan by Haythoun, Palombo, Alembo, Polumbrum by Oderic and Mandevile, and Koulem by the natives. These names have nothing in common with Koulouri, where the Russian merchant Nikitin spent five months, but they somewhat assimilate that of Colanum taken in 1503 by the Portuguese, who stated that this town on the coast of Malabar was reputed to be the most ancient and the richest in India (Maffei, *Hist. Ind.*, i, 52, xii, 289). Colanum may have been one of the places mentioned by Schiltberger, the other being Calicut, touched at by Vasco de Gama in 1498.

The colonisation of the Christian communities soon by the Portuguese at the south-west extremity of the Deccan, dates from the earliest centuries of our era. Neander says (*Allg. Gesch. d. christlichen Relig. und Kirche*, I, i, 114) that the Syriac-Persian community on the coast of Malabar owes its origin to St. Thomas, although its existence, according to Cosmas "Indicopleustes", cannot be traced earlier than the 6th century. Gregory of Nazianzus asserts (*Orat.*, 25) that the Gospel was preached in India by the apostle St. Thomas, who was murdered at a place near Madras called Mailapur, on the Coromandel Coast, the Maabar of Marco Polo, and identical with Mirapolis, where Giovanni de' Marignolli tells us the apostle was buried. We are scarcely encouraged to look for the forest of "Lambor" in the province of Maabar, because there happened to be indications of Christian churches, rather than on the coast of Melibar or Malabar, where the produce of pepper in ancient times is fully established. BRUUN.

(1A.) Friar Jordanus, 1333 (*Hakluyt Soc. Publ.*, 27), indignantly denies that fire was placed under the pepper trees, and is satisfied that the fruit turns black simply upon coming to maturity. Oderic (Hakluyt *Voyages*, ii, 160), also a predecessor of Schiltberger, repeats the statement that in the kingdom of Minibar where pepper grows, fires are made with the object of burning up the serpents, that the people might gather at the harvest without injury to themselves. Oderic estimated the circuit of the forest at an eighteen days' journey, and the two cities in it, not named by our author, he calls Flaudrina and Cyncilim. At the south end of the forest stood a city called Polumbrum, noticed in the foregoing note, and at a distance of ten days' journey was the kingdom of Mobar, where lay interred the body of St. Thomas.

"It is seventeen hundred and forty years ago", said the papa or priest at Cacador to Buchanan in 1800, " since a certain saint named Thomas introduced the Nazareens; he landed at Meliapura, and took up his residence on a hill near Madras, now called after his name" (*Journey from Madras*, London, 1807). There he performed a miracle annually, says another authority, until English heretics came into the neighbourhood. St. Thomas afterwards made a voyage to Cochin, and near that place established a church which became the metropolitan; he returned to Meliapura and there died, or, according to others, was put to death. It appears that a bishop of India was present at the Council of Nice, A.D. 325, and in the following century the Christians on the coast of Malabar received the accession of a bishop of Antioch, who was accompanied by a small party of Syrians. That Christians in Malabar were numerous at the time Schiltberger obtained his information is most probable, because Portuguese historians relate that in the year 1503 they possessed upwards of one hundred churches, those in the interior refusing to conform to Rome

(Assemanus, *Bibliot. Orient.*, iv, 391 et seq.; M. Geddes, *The Hist. of the Church of Malabar*, 1694; Gardner, *Faiths of the World*, etc., ii, 900; see also G. B. Howard, *Christians of St. Thomas and their Liturgies*, 1864; Yule's *Marco Polo*, ii, 341 et seq.). ED.

(2.) "the juice of an apple which they call liuon."—There can scarcely be a doubt that this was the lemon, called nimbouka in Sanscrit; neemon, leemon in Hindostani, and lemonn by the Arabs, a fruit with which Schiltberger could scarcely have been familiar in his own country, or in those parts of Asia Minor, Central Asia, and even Egypt, through which he travelled. The lemon, brought from India by the Arabs about A.D. 912, was first planted at Oman; then at Basra in Irak; afterwards in Syria, where the plant became common, whence it was introduced into Palestine and Egypt. Jacques de Vitry includes the lemon tree with others he saw for the first time when in the Holy Land in the 13th century: "sunt ibi speciales arbores tam fructiferæ quam steriles" (*Gesta Dei per Francos*, etc., lxxxvi); from which it might almost be inferred that the Crusaders, who are supposed to have introduced this plant into Europe, did not do so until after Jacques de Vitry wrote. The genus, however, could not have been entirely unknown in the West, it being recorded in *Chronica Montis Cassiniensis*, Pertz Scr., 7, 652, that when the prince of Salerno in the year 1000 (1016?) was besieged by the Arabs, forty Norman knights who passed that way on their homeward journey from the Holy Land, delivered him. Upon taking their leave, the knights were accompanied by ambassadors from the prince, who were bearers of presents of the "poma cedrina (citrina?), amigdalas quoque et deauratas nuces", and a message to the Norman people, inviting them to come to so beautiful a country and help him to defend it (Abd-Allatif, S. de Sacy edition, 115-117; Makrizi in Quatremère; *Journ. Horticultural Society*, ix, 1855; Risso et Poiteau, *Hist. et Culture des Orangers*, Paris, 1872; Hehn, *Kulturpflanzen und Hausthiere in ihrem Uebergang aus Asien nach Griechenl. und Ital.*, Berlin, 1877).

Lemon-juice was employed at Ceylon as protection against the numberless land-leeches that seized upon the bare legs of the natives in the lowlands (Ibn Batouta, *Lee edition,* 188; Knox, *Hist. of Ceylon,* etc., I, iv, 49), precisely the sort of country where the vine pepper—Piper nigrum—grows to best advantage, viz., on level ground along the banks of rivers and rivulets (Simmonds, *Tropl. Agriculture,* 476). In his notice on "Sylan", Friar Oderic says that the people who dive into a lake infested with horse-leeches, for the purpose of recovering precious stones, "take lemons, which they peel, anointing themselves thoroughly with the juice thereof, that so they may dive naked under the water, the horse-leeches not being able to hurt them" (Hakluyt *Voyages,* ii, 160). Sir Emerson Tennent quotes Oderic, and distinguishes the land-from the cattle-leech. The former, so inimical to man, never visits ponds or streams, but is found in the lower ranges of hill country kept damp by frequent showers; it attains a length of two inches (*Natural History of Ceylon,* Chap. xiii). There is strange confusion, in associating the use to which the lemon is put, in Ceylon, with the pepper-growing country of Malabar by no means famous for leeches. ED.

CHAPTER XLIII.

(1.) "those from Venice likewise."—In his admirable treatise on the establishment of Italian commercial depôts in Egypt, Heyd (*d. Ital. Handelscolon,* etc., in the *Zeitschrift f. d. gesammte Staatswissenschaft,* xx, 54-138) confirms the statement that of the several Italian Powers, the Venetians and Genoese were at that time the most interested in trade with Alexandria. Their predecessors the Pisans, who had taken an active part in the eastern trade, were forced at the commencement of the 15th century to abandon their interests in favour of the Florentines, and in great measure also of the Anconitans, Neapolitans, and citizens of Gaeta; but the Catalans, equally with the Italians, kept up extensive commercial relations with Egypt. BRUUN.

(2.) "the king of Zipern."—Allusion is made to the taking of Alexandria, Oct. 10th, 1365, by Peter of Lusignan, king of Cyprus, and his allies the Genoese, Venetians, and knights of Rhodes.

De Lannoy (*Voy. et Ambass.*, 70) records that the allied forces landed near the old port, the entrance to which was ever afterwards closed against all vessels of Christian nationalities. Upon the approach of the Egyptians on the above occasion, the Franks re-embarked after having pillaged the city and carried off five thousand captives (Weil, *Gesch. der Chal.*, iv, 512). This expedition, in which twenty-four Venetian, two Genoese, ten Rhodian, five French, and several Cyprian vessels took part, was completed in the space of a week, so that allowing the requisite time for landing and re-embarking, the occupation of the city would most probably have lasted three days, the period indicated by Schiltberger.

BRUUN.

(3.) "took Alexandria, and remained in it three days."—This tower must have been either the pharos of Alexandria, or some tower on the islet that had become united to the mainland by the sands of the Nile; otherwise, De Lannoy, to whom we are indebted for a detailed description of the port of Alexandria under a strategic point of view, would not have failed to notice it. He simply mentions a long spit, one mile wide, between the old and new ports which both reached to the walls of the city. This islet is now occupied by one of its finest quarters.

Makrizi describes the pharos at Alexandria (S. de Sacy, *Chrestom. Arabe*, ii, 189) as having at the top a large mirror, around which criers were seated. Upon perceiving the approach of an enemy through the agency of this reflector, they gave warning to those in the immediate neighbourhood by loud cries, and flags were displayed to apprise others at a distance, so that people in all parts of the city were immediately on the alert.

De Sacy (Abd-Allatif, 239) is of opinion that the large circles employed in astronomical observations and which were placed on the highest part of such lofty buildings as the pharos, may have led Arabian writers, who usually delighted in the relation of all that was marvellous, to represent that the mirror at the top of the Alexandria lighthouse was placed there for better observing the departure of Greek vessels from their ports. The tower described in the text was no doubt designed for this purpose, because Ijas an Arabian author (Weil. *l. c.*, v, 358) relates, that in 1472 the sultan Kaïtbaï caused a new lighthouse to be constructed near the old one; it communicated with the city by means of a dyke, and was provided with a chapel, a mill, and a bakehouse; also a platform from which strange vessels could be seen at the distance of a day's sail, so that time was afforded for preparing the guns with which the tower was supplied, to resist their approach. Schiltberger was right in saying that there was a temple in the tower, because Abd-Allatif speaks of a mosque as being at the top of the pharos at Alexandria.

Apart from the possibility of there having been a traitor amongst them who ministered in that temple, the Egyptians may have invented the tale narrated in this chapter, in extenuation of their negligence in suffering themselves to be taken by surprise by the Crusaders. BRUUN.

CHAPTER XLIV.

(1.) "had I not seen it, I would not have spoken or written about it."—I do not think I can be far out in attributing this gigantic bone to Alexander of Macedon, not only because "Allenklaisser" is so like the Arabic name Al Iskender, but also because the remembrance of the rapidity with which the founder of Alexandria had carried his conquests in the East, could not have been obliterated in the city which was indebted to him, for having become the central depôt of the commerce of the world during upwards of one thousand years. There can be no manner of doubt that, in the course of ages, other ancient traditions became mixed up with legends of Alexander, especially as regards the Jews, who were treated by the great conqueror with the urbanity that some rulers of the earth, of our own times, would do well to imitate.

We read in Abd-el-Hakam's history of the conquest of Egypt (Makrizi by Quatremère, I, i, 218), that the body of a giant killed by Moses fell across the Nile and served as a bridge. With this legend may be associated Schiltberger's tale, and his credulity need not be wondered at when we consider, that in the 13th century the story was thought worthy of being related; and some there were even bold enough to tell it to the powerful ruler of the Golden Horde, Bercke Khan, who enquired of the ambassadors sent to him in 1263 by the sultan Bibars, whether it was true that the bone of a giant, laid across the Nile, was being used as a bridge! The ambassadors, who had been probably selected from among the most enlightened of the sultan's ministers, replied that they had never seen it, an answer that may have been elicited by the nature of the question, because the strange bridge seen by Schiltberger must have been in Arabia and not in Egypt. It united two rocks separated by a profound ravine in the depths of which coursed a torrent, and as it afforded the only practicable means for crossing the ravine on the high road, travellers were obliged to pass over it.

I cannot believe that these topographic details were invented by Schiltberger, and am therefore inclined to think that he alludes to the neighbourhood of the fortresses of Kerak and Shaubek, places that acquired considerable importance during the Crusades in consequence of their admirable situations. They are easily identified with "Crach" and "Sebach" mentioned by De Lannoy, after he refers to the "montaignes d'Arrabicq" for the purpose of observing, that in the former was "la pierre du desert", and in the latter the sepulchre of Aaron, and that the road thence conducted through a desert to St. Catherine and to Mecca. Quatremère says (Makrizi, II, i, 249) that Karac was the key to the road across the desert. Caravans to and from Damascus and Mecca, merchants, and troops despatched from the capital of Syria to that of Egypt, were obliged to pass close under its walls or at no great distance from them.

Shaubek, the "Mons regalis" of the Crusaders, thirty-six miles from Kerak, was also a strong place. Burckhardt tells us that a ravine, three hundred feet in depth, encircles the citadel, which is in a better state of preservation than the one at Kerak or Krak, called also Petra deserti from its proximity to the ancient city of that name, and to which a part of Arabia owes the name of Arabia Petræa; its situation is characteristically described by Pliny:

"oppidum circumdatum montibus inaccessis, amne interfluente". The valley in which this ancient city was situated, the "vallis Moysi" of the Crusaders, now Wady Mousa (Raumer, *Palæstina*, etc., 271-277), five hundred feet in depth, is watered by a stream and surrounded by steep rocks (Laborde, *Voy. dans l'Arabie pétrée*, 55).

According to an Arabian author quoted by Quatremère (*l. c.* II, i, 245), the road near these two cities was so peculiar that it could have been held by one man against a hundred horsemen. Another reason for the supposition that the bridge seen by Schiltberger was in one of these passages, lies in the fact that the same writer includes the tomb of Iskender among the holy places of pilgrimage in this ancient country; but he does not determine the individuality of that Iskender.

On the hypothesis that "Allenklaisser's" limb was near the tomb of Iskender, I should be inclined to look in the same locality for the bridge that was constructed, according to the inscription it bore, two hundred years before Schiltberger saw it. Judging from other passages in his work, the author was in Egypt probably about the year 1423, the date of the construction of the bridge being therefore 1223; this, however, can scarcely have been the case, because the feuds between Saladin's successors, which commenced soon after his death in 1193, had not ceased, and the Ayoubites were continually in conflict with the Crusaders. It should be borne in mind that although Schiltberger knew that the year 825 of the Hegira corresponded to A.D. 1423, he may not have been aware that the Mahomedan is shorter than the Christian year, whereby 200 Mahomedan years are equal to 193 solar years only; and thus he calculated that the construction of the bridge took place in 1223 instead of 1230. This was the time when Al-Kamyl the nephew of Saladin, having become reconciled with the emperor Frederick II., was recognised by the princes of his house as their suzerain lord, and he thereafter, until his death in 1238, held Syria and Egypt, with the exception of the fortresses of Kerak and Shaubek which he had to cede in 1229 to his nephew Daud or David. This circumstance, no doubt, induced the "king-sultan" to order the construction of a bridge for keeping up communication between two parts of his kingdom, the new bridge being near the old one that was kept smeared with oil, a condition that had the effect of persuading the guileless Bavarian that it was indeed a gigantic bone. BRUUN.

CHAPTER XLV.

(1.) " Others believe in one who was called Molwa."—If, as Neumann supposes, a Molla or Mussulman priest is here implied, I would venture to suggest that allusion is made to Hassan, founder of the sect of Assassins or Mulahidah. The partisans of "the Old Man of the Mountain" had not been entirely exterminated by the Mongols, for not only were they in Asia after Marco Polo, but they reappeared in India at a later period, where the Bohras, another Ismailis sect, existed, and with whom they have been frequently confounded. "The nature of their doctrine indeed", says Colonel Yule (Marco Polo, i, 154), "seems to be very much alike, and the Bohras like the Ismailis attach a divine character to their *Mullah* or chief pontiff, and make a pilgrimage to his presence once in life". BRUUN.

CHAPTER XLVI.

(1.) "thy descendants will also acquire great power."—It is stated in chapter 56 that Mahomet was born in the year of our Lord 609, so that his journey into Egypt took place in 622, the year of the prophet's flight from Mecca to Medina. Schiltberger evidently confuses that memorable event with a journey undertaken by Mahomet when in his thirteenth year, if not into Egypt, at least into Chaldæa, where his great destiny was foretold to him by a Nestorian priest. It is most probable, however, that the author was not quite familiar with Mahomedan traditions, which assert that it was in the year 609, that is to say, thirteen years before the date of the Hegira, that Mahomet was informed of his lofty calling by an angel, and that the archangel Gabriel quickly taught him to read; it is therefore the existence of the prophet, not the birth of the man, that dates from this year. The error is very pardonable, because several miracles attributed to the prophet by Mussulmans, were supposed to have been performed in his youth. They believe, for instance, that from his infancy he was enclosed within an aureola, and could therefore stand in the light of the sun without casting a shadow, which would also have been the case had a black cloud floated over his head as related by Schiltberger, who remained too firmly attached to Christianity not to attribute the phenomenon to the wiles of the Prince of Darkness, rather than to the effect of celestial light. BRUUN.

(1A.) What appears to be the more generally accepted story of Mahomet's first journey from home, is related by Syer Ameer Ali, in *A Critical examination of the Life and Teachings of Mohammed;* London, 1873. When Abu Taleb (the prophet's uncle, for he was an orphan) determined upon making a journey to Syria, leaving Mohammed with his own children, and was on the point of mounting his camel, the boy clasped his knees and cried : Oh ! my uncle, take me with thee ! The heart of Abu Taleb melted within him, and the little orphan nephew joined the commercial expedition of his uncle. They travelled together into Syria. During one of the halts they met an Arab monk, who, struck by the signs of future greatness, and intellectual and moral qualities of the highest type in the countenance of the orphan child of Abdullah, recognised in him the liberator and saviour of his country and people. ED.

(2.) " The first temple is also called Mesgit, the other Medrassa, the third, Amarat."—The designations of these several edifices and their uses are correct. The jamy, called " Sam", is the largest of mosques; " Mesgit", or rather mesjyd, being an ordinary and smaller mosque. " Medrassa", for medressè, is a college usually attached to a mosque, and to be distinguished from the mehteb or boy's school; and " Amarat", for which we should read imaret, is an imperial place of burial, and a name applied also to a hospital, almshouse, etc. ED.

CHAPTER XLVII.

(1.) " Of the Infidel's Easter-day."—This is the first of the two Baïrams, the only religious festivals of the Mahomedans. The first, called Id Fitr—feast of the termination of the fast—falls on the first day of the month of Chewal, immediately after the feast of Ramadan. The second, called Id Addha, or Kourban Baïram—feast of sacrifice—is celebrated seventy days later, on the tenth day of the month of Zilhidshek. Id indicates the anniversary of these periodical feasts, which take place in their turn every season during the space of thirty-three years, according to the lunar months of the Mahomedan calendar. The first festival is of one day's duration only, but it is usually observed for three days. The second, instituted in remembrance of Abraham's sacrifice, is continued for four days. Mussulmans celebrate it by proceeding on a pilgrimage to Mecca, where is the Kaaba or sanctuary, constructed, it is said, by Abraham and his son Ishmael, in the form of the tent or tabernacle that was placed there by angels the day the world was created.

The ancient custom of covering the Kaaba, at this festival, with a black cloth, is still observed, the old cloth being cut up and sold to pilgrims, who preserve the pieces as the most precious of relics. BRUUN.

CHAPTER LI.

(1.) " Those who are in this fellowship are called They."—To those who are unfamiliar with the name, says Neumann, the title of Ghasi would scarcely be recognised in that of They. Neumann misunderstands Schiltberger, who does not at all allude to the Ghasi, but to those of the Malahidah sect called Day (Missionaries), and whom he designates They, just as his own countrymen at times employ the word Toutsche for Deutsche. There certainly were Malahidahs in Asia Minor, or Turkey, as the author called that territory. BRUUN.

CHAPTER LII.

(1). "Machmet is his true messenger."—This invocation in Arabic, in general use among Mussulmans, reads thus: La Illaha illa Allah!—No Gods, but God!—Illaha being the plural of Allah —God—and La, the simple negative, No, in opposition to Yes.

ED.

(2.) "Machmet his chief messenger."—The correct rendering of this passage would be: T'hary byr dour, Messyh kyoull dour, Meryam kara bash dour, M'hammed ressouly dour—God is one, the Messiah is his slave, Mary is a blackhead, Mahomet is his apostle. Mary is here termed a blackhead to signify a slave, because coloured females were employed as slaves, white women being reserved for other purposes. This formula, though no longer obligatory, would still be employed in the Mahomedan provinces of the Caucasus and in Persia, were a Christian to embrace Mahomedanism. The words imply a renunciation of Christianity, as also a recognition that God is One and Mahomet is his apostle.

ED.

CHAPTER LVI.

(1.) "the Winden tongue, which they call Arnaw."—Schiltberger was not wrong in saying that the Venede tongue was known to the Turks as the Arnaut; at least it appears in Pianzola (*Grammatica, Dizionario*, etc.) that the country called by the Italians, Illirice, was identical with the Slavonia of the Greeks and the Arnaut of the Turks. This is no place for solving the question, why the Turks should have designated two people of different origin by the same name; but the circumstance serves to support the opinion of several authors (Köppen, *Krymsky Sbornyk*, 1837, 226) that the Turks were not in the habit of calling people of any distinct nationality by the name of Arnaut, but rather all those who, being the subjects or brothers-in-arms of the Arianite family, had distinguished themselves in their struggles with them; such, for instance, as the Slaves and Albanians or Skipetars, among whom was George Castriota of Slave descent (Jirecek, *Gesch. d. Bulgaren*, 268). His biographer (Barletius, *Vita Scanderbegi*, etc., apud Zinkeisen, *Gesch. d. O. R.*, i, 776) thus expresses himself in allusion to Topia, the compatriot of the Scanderbeg of the Turks. " Hic est ille Arianites qui apud Macedones (Slaves) et Epirotas (Albanians) cognomento Magnus et dictus et habitus est", ... etc. BRUUN.

(2.) " the Yassen tongue, which the Infidels call Afs."—The As, Yasses—the Alains, Alans of antiquity, are the Ossets of to-day, a people inhabiting a strip of territory in the middle of the great mountain range of the Caucasus, and who are believed to be the only connecting link between the Indo-Persian branch and the European branch of the great Indo-Germanic race. The population in 1873 was estimated at 65,000, of which number, it was supposed, 50,000 were Christians; the remainder being Mahomedans and Pagans, or a mingling of the three (*The Crimea and Transc.*, i, 296, ii, 2).

An unpretending sketch of this interesting people, twice alluded to by the author (in chapter 61 he speaks of them as the Jassen and Affs), is here submitted.

The earliest mention of the Alans is made by Josephus (*Wars*, VII, vii, 4), and again by Procopius (*De Bell. Goth.*, iv, 3, 4), from whom we learn that they dwelt on the shores of the Lake Mæotis and to the North of the Caucasus, whence they overran the country of the Medes and of Armenia, until defeated by Artaces who forced them to withdraw beyond the Cyrus; similar predatory incursions into Tauric-Scythia and the West, being arrested by the Goths, who in their turn were overpowered by the Huns. The invasion of Asia Minor by the Alans gave cause of uneasiness to the Roman Empire, but it was successfully resisted by Arrian, prefect of Cappadocia (Forbiger, *Handbuch der Alt. Geogr.*, i, 424), and they were also defeated by Vakhtang " Gourgasal"—Wolf Lion—the sovereign of Georgia, 466-499, upon their venturing to invade that kingdom (Brosset, *Hist. de la Géorgie*, I, 153). In 966, the Yasses were subdued by the Russians

(*Niceph. Greg.*, ii, 842). This "State within a State", no doubt excited the cupidity of the Turks after their assumption of power in Europe, and the removal of the sultan's residence to Adrianople; but the Genoese succeeded for a time in averting the threatening danger by making numerous concessions, as appears by the treaty of commerce concluded by them in 1387 with Murad I., whose successor, Bajazet, lay siege to Constantinople. This monarch, however, was constrained to turn his arms against Timour, and the capital was spared the horrors of a longer siege. The battle of Angora, so fatal to the Ottoman power, delayed for a few decades only the fall of the Greek Empire and the disappearance of the Genoese.   BRUUN.

(2.) "caused two seas to flow into each other."—"La formation et l'origine du Bosphore de Thrace," says Vivien de Saint-Martin (*Desc. de l'A. M.*, ii, 469), "ont donné lieu, chez les anciens comme chez les modernes, aux hypothèses les plus aventureuses, jeux hardis de l'imagination basés sur de vieilles traditions de convulsions et de cataclysmes; les observations de la géologie moderne sont venues anéantir ces systèmes d'époques moins rigoureuses, en démontrant que les terrains de nature différente qui constituent les deux côtés du détroit, n'ont jamais pu être produit par un déchirement, et qu'il existe de toute nécessité depuis l'origine même des choses." Other authors, including some philologists (Menn, in *Jahresbericht über d. Gymn. u. d. Realschule zu Neuss*, 1854, 18), think otherwise, so that we need not be surprised if the sages at Constantinople also differed in opinion, or that the people there should have included the cutting of the strait among the exploits of Alexander.   BRUUN.

(3.) "Troya, on a fine plain, and one can still see where the city stood."—The ruins of the city of Priam did not exist in Schiltberger's time any more than they do now; but in the absence of the material vestiges that Lechevalier and other travellers, his successors, believed they found beneath the surface of the earth, there is Homer's admirable description, precise as that of the most accurate geographer, and which restores to us the primitive map of the Trojan plain. I am here under the necessity of quoting at some length, a passage from Vivien de Saint-Martin's *Description de l'Asie Mineur*, 489 :—" Dès que l'on accepte le plateau de Bounar-Bachi" (a name, says this author, derived from two sources of the Scamander) "comme l'emplacement de la Troie homérique, les indications circonstanciées et si nombreuses que fournit le Poëte sur les localités environnantes, viennent s'adapter d'elles-mêmes au terrain actuel."

" Une ville de fondation éolienne qui usurpe le nom d'Ilion, et qui par la suite des temps et d'obscurité des traditions, prétendit occuper l'emplacement même de la cité de Priam, s'était élevée sur une autre éminence éloignée d'une lieue vers le Nord, et située non plus sur la gauche, mais sur la rive droite du Simoïs. Cette ville est l'Ilium des siècles postérieurs, l'Ilium Recens ; et lorsque les poètes ou les historiens de l'époque romaine parlent du berceau de leur race, c'est toujours à cette Ilium éolienne qu'il faut rapporter leurs allusions et leurs descriptions, car le site réel de l'Ilium primitive était dès lors oublié. La nouvelle Ilium est maintenant ruinée, comme l'Ilium homérique ; près de l'éminence isolée qu'elle occupa, on trouve aujourd'hui le village Turc de Tchiblak."

The ruins near the sea and at no great distance from Constantinople, believed by Schiltberger to have been those of the royal city, must have been the remains of Alexandria Troas opposite the island of Tenedos. It was there that the Russian pilgrim Daniel, and the author's contemporaries, the archdeacon Zosimus and Clavijo, thought they saw the ruins of Troy, as was the case one hundred years later, 1547, with the French traveller Belon, who landed that he might examine them with the greater facility. At the base of a small hillock, but within the circuit of the walls of the city, were some ancient arches and the remains of two palaces in marble (*Obs. de plusieurs singularités trouvées en Grèce, en Asie*, etc. ; in Saint-Martin, ii, 8). Belon passes lightly over the difficulty he experienced in not finding near this, the supposed site of the Homeric city, the two rivers Simoïs and Xanthus.

The honorary president of the Geographical Society at Paris has lately sought to prove, that the city of Priam should be looked for

where Lechevalier conceived it to be, that is to say, at Bunarbashi, whence Dr. Schliemann believes he is justified in removing it to the neighbourhood of Ilium Recens or Hissarlik, as the result of the successful explorations conducted by himself with the assistance of his wife. Although some English and most German authorities applaud the zeal with which his work was performed, and the great importance of his discoveries to students of archæology, all are not so readily persuaded that the question of the position of Ilium is solved, seeing that the topographical details, as we receive them from Homer, are drawn from the imagination of the poet, rather than after the reality. BRUUN.

(4). "for all [kinds of] pastime that might be desired in front of the palace."—The games, chiefly of Eastern origin, that were held in the open space in front of the imperial residence, are mentioned by various authors. It will here suffice to quote from the writings of a predecessor of Schiltberger, and of one who followed after him.

When Edrisi visited Constantinople, circa 1161, sports were held in the hippodrome, which he considered the most marvellous in the universe. It had to be passed before reaching the palace, an edifice unequalled in its proportions and in the beauty of its construction (*Jaubert edition*, 297). Bertrandon de la Brocquière, 1432 (*Early Travels in Palestine*, Bohn edition, 1848), thus describes one of the sports he witnessed in the large and handsome square in front of St. Sophia: "I saw the brother of the emperor, the despot of the Morea, exercise himself with a score of other horsemen. Each had a bow, and they gallopped along the enclosure throwing their hats before them, which, when they had passed, they shot at; and he who with his arrow pierced the hat or was nearest to it, was esteemed the most expert." ED.

(5.) "he has no longer that power, so the apple has disappeared."—Stephen of Novgorod (*Pout. Rouss. loud.*, ii, 14), a pilgrim passing through Constantinople about the year 1350, certifies that the emperor held in his hand a kind of golden apple surmounted by a cross. Clavijo says the "pella redonda dorada" was in its place, and so, we may conclude, was the cross; because in 1420, Zosimus (*Pout. Rouss. loud.*, ii, 38) saw the cross on the apple that was in the emperor's hand; it is probable, therefore, that these insignias were removed between the years 1420-1427, at which latter date Schiltberger spent some months at Constantinople after his escape from bondage.

A short time before the author's arrival in the city of the Cæsars, the aged Manuel died (1425), and John, his son and successor, was forced to sign a treaty of peace with the Turks, the conditions being of the most onerous nature; for he was deprived of all his possessions with the exception of the capital, the appanages in the Morea of the Greek princes, and a few fortresses on the shores of the Black Sea (Zinkeisen, *Gesch. d. O. R.*, i, 533); he also covenanted to pay the sultan an annual tribute of 300,000 aspres, and to make him numerous presents of great value as a mark of personal regard. In such circumstances the unfortunate monarch must have been under the necessity of laying hands upon all the gold he could come across, and Schiltberger's *bon mot* on the disappearance of the apple together with the emperor's power, might be taken literally.

Zosimus relates that the statue which held the apple was distant an arrow's flight from the hippodrome, doubtlessly the "fine square for tilting", now known as the Meïdan. The magnificent palace wherein receptions were held, and that excited the admiration of Schiltberger, must have been the Boukoleon and Daphna which adjoined the hippodrome (Dethier, *Der Bosphor und Constantinopel*, Wien, 1873, 22). This edifice was greatly neglected during the reigns of the last of the Palæologi, and after his conquest of Constantinople, Mahomet II. ordered its complete destruction.

The other palace noticed was the Blackernes, in which Clavijo (*Hakluyt Soc. Publ.* 29) was received by the emperor Manuel. Near it, Bertrandon de la Brocquière found a "fausse braie d'un bon et haut mur en avant du fossé, qui était en glacis excepté dans un espace de deux cents pas à l'une de ses extrémités près du palais". This must have been the place where Schiltberger saw a "getüll."*　　　　　　　　　　　　　　　　　　　　　　BRUUN.

* See page 84.

(5a.) The statement that the statue was placed on a pillar is corroborated by Cedrenus in his Chronicles, and in the Annals of Zonaras, in which works we find it stated that the great pillar Augusteon was erected in the fifteenth year of the reign of Justinian, the statue being placed on it two years later. When Bertrandon de la Brocquière saw the equestrian statue, which he inadvertently calls that of Constantine, it grasped a sceptre in the left hand. Pierre Gilles, the naturalist and author, sent to the Levant by Francis I. of France, found portions of this statue in the melting house where ordnance were cast, it having been overturned and destroyed in 1523 (*Antiquities of Constantinople*, London, 1729); or in 1525, according to the anonymous author of the Constantiniade. The proportions were colossal, for the leg exceeded the height of a man, and the nose was nine inches in length, as were also the hoofs of the horse. Gilles represents that the statue, which was made of brass, faced the East, as if the emperor was marching against the Persians; the right arm was stretched out, and in the left hand was a globe to signify universal power over the whole world, all success in war being attributed to the cross fixed on the top. He was dressed like Achilles, in a coat of mail and shining helmet.

It is certain that the globe and cross disappeared fully one hundred years before the arrival at Constantinople of Gilles, whose detailed description of the statue must have reference to its original condition. ED.

CHAPTER LVIII.

(1.) " Lemprie; in it is a mountain that is so high, it reaches to the clouds."—French and Italian names commencing with a vowel, commonly became transformed by the addition of the article which preceded them, and in this way, Imbro was altered during the Latin empire to Lembro, the name ordinarily given to the island, whence " Lemprie", and Nembro of Clavijo. During a part of the 15th century, Imbros belonged to the Gattilusio, a Genoese family, and in 1450 became subject to the Greek emperor. The island is overspread with the ruins of many castles, the walls of which are covered with inscriptions and armorial bearings (Heyd, *Le Colonie Commer.*, i, 416). BRUUN.

(1A.) The author's statement may be taken as being the reverse of the fact, and that the clouds had descended to the mountain, for the highest point of land on the island of Imbros is only 1959 feet, an altitude altogether insignificant when compared to the mountains he must have seen in his journeys; they include the great range of the Caucasus, shewing summits at upwards of 18,000 feet, and the noble Ararat, rising nearly 15,000 feet above the plains of the Araxes. Had his course lay further to the west, Samothraky, at 5248 feet above the sea, would have excited his imagination still more. ED.

(2.) "wide, large, and thick as a mill-stone."—The "golden discs" may have been simply of golden glass or mosion, with which the interior of the dome of St. Sophia was covered, as we are informed by Theophanes and Cedrenus, whose description refers to the present dome constructed soon after 559, the thirty-second year of the reign of Justinian. ED.

(3.) "I myself was at that same time with the king in Turkey." After the battle of Nicopolis, Bajazet renewed the siege of Constantinople, the city being succoured by a force of 1200 men sent by Charles VI. of France, and bodies of troops from Genoa, Venice, Rhodes, and Lesbos. Marshal Boucicault withstood the siege with his little army, and on quitting the capital in 1399, the command devolved upon Chateaumorant, the emperor Manuel being absent in France, whither he had gone to ask for assistance. It was fortunate for the Greeks that Bajazet was obliged to muster the whole of his forces to enable him to encounter Timour's legions. BRUUN.

CHAPTER LIX.

(1.) "Christus is risen."—The ordinances of the Greek Church have undergone but little change since Schiltberger wrote.

Warm water, τὸ ζέον (ὕδωρ being understood), is always mixed with wine.

Leavened bread for the celebration of the Eucharist, is now ordinarily made and sold by bakers. It is called προσφορά, "prossura" in the text, and is administered to the people in turn by the priest, who stands at the altar. It is also administered to young children after baptism.

Wednesday and Friday continue to be the ordinary fast days.

Women are required to stand apart from the men, so that all churches are built with a γυναικέτης, or place for women; but this rule is not enforced.

The so-called "coleba", more correctly κολάβα, are still given to the priests at the μνημόσυνον, or service for the dead. This custom is very strictly observed.

Fasts are kept at all the periods indicated, except on the day of the Assumption, when there is no fast. The fast for the Apostles commences on the fifty-ninth day after Easter Day.

Χριστὸς ἀνέστη—Christ is risen—is sung daily from Easter Day to the Day of the Assumption.   ED.

CHAPTER LX.

(1.) " because in the same place there is a breakwater."—"Wann es an der selben stat ein getüll hat." The identical word "getüll" appears in the editions of 1475 (?) and 1549, but is altogether omitted by Penzel, and remains unexplained by Neumann. Professor Bruun (Russian edition) interprets it as palisade; I prefer, however, to translate it as breakwater, believing that I recognise in the locality described by Schiltberger that part of the city on the Sea of Marmora, between the Eptapyrgyon—Seven Towers—and the Acropolis, abreast of which huge stones were placed to resist the force of the waves (Cantacuzene, *Hist. de l'Empire d'Orient*). An earlier author (Glycas, *Annales*) states that they were conveyed thither for the construction of the fortifications. At any rate it is a fact, that the Admiralty chart shows what appears to be a submerged reef close inshore in one fathom and a half of water, about one half mile to the westward of Seraglio point, and not quite two miles from the Seven Towers. ED.

(2.) "Many priests wear white garments at Mass."—Every member of the Greek clergy is buried in complete ecclesiastical attire, but the ancient custom of interring in a sitting posture, was and is still observed in the case of a bishop only.

In a recent account of the obsequies at Constantinople of a bishop of the Greek Church (*The Times*, August 29, 1878), the Correspondent writes: "I was ushered into a small densely crowded church, and on walking forward a few steps, found myself confronted by an aged and venerable prelate, seated on a throne in full canonicals, richly decorated with gold and jewels. He sat perfectly motionless, with his eyes closed, and holding in his right hand a jewelled rod resembling a sceptre. Two or three people advanced and devoutly kissed his hand, but he did not return the customary benediction, and gave no sign of consciousness. 'Is he asleep?' I whispered inquiringly to my friend. 'No, he is dead; that is the late patriarch'."

Ἄγιος ὁ Θεὸς is called the Τρισάγιον, as being emblematic of the Holy Trinity. It is not sung in the Greek Church. Κύριε ἐλέησον is the response of the people to a prayer repeated by the priest during the service; and it is quite true that Χριστὲ ἐλέησον is never said in Greek churches.

It is still the custom to kiss the priest's right hand, at the same time saying, Εὐλόγησον, Δέσποτα! — Thy blessing, Your reverence. The priest places his left hand on the person's head and replies, 'Εὐλογία!—A blessing on thee.

A man must certainly be married before he enters the priesthood, and even before he can obtain the degree of deacon; but it is quite immaterial whether he be a father previous to or after ordination. ED.

CHAPTER LXI.

(1.) "after which, he can take another wife, and she another husband."—The obscene and demoralising customs attributed to the Jassen or Yasses are fully and minutely described by the Abbé Chappe d'Auteroche, who witnessed precisely like ceremonies at Tobolsk, where marriages amongst the natives were thus celebrated (*Voyage en Sibérie en* 1761, etc., Paris, 1768, i, 163, *et seq.*). Olearius notices somewhat similar, but certainly milder, doings at Moscow in his time (*Voyages*, etc., 243); and Pitt (*A True and Faithful Account of the Religion and Manners of the Mahommetans*, etc., Exon., 1704) recounts something of the sort as occurring among the Algerines.

It would appear, from a report recently made by the Ethnological Section of the Imperial Geographical Society of St. Petersburg, that similar practices, but in a greatly modified form, are in vogue amongst the peasantry in some parts of Little Russia. ED.

CHAPTER LXII.

(1.) "Karawag."—This must have been the plain of Karabagh, between the rivers Kour and Araxes, where Shah Rokh spent the winter of 1420, being accompanied by his vassals; Khalyl Oullah, the shah of Shirwan, and Minutcher, his own valorous brother, being among his guests (Dorn, *Versuch einer Gesch. d. Schirwan-Sch.*, vi, 4, 549). Like Schiltberger, Barbaro and Contarini have called the Kour, Tigris, and the Tigris, Shat or Set. BRUUN.

(2.) "they call the Germans, Nymitsch."—This term is borrowed from the Slaves, who have applied it to the Germans from the earliest times, either because the latter spoke an incomprehensible, a dumb language, or, as Schafarik explains (*Slawische Alterthümer*, i, 442), because they followed the example of the Celts, who called certain German tribes settled in Gaul, Nemetes.*   BRUUN.

(3.) "then did the sultan of Alkenier conquer it."—Sis became finally subject to the Egyptians in 1374-75, having fallen into their hands upon several previous occasions, to wit, in 1266, 1275, and 1298 (Weil, *Gesch. der Chal.*, iv, 55, 78, 213, 233). They had frequently appeared in force in its neighbourhood, notably in 1278 (Makrizi by Quatremère, I, i, 166), a date which nearly corresponds with the year in which the city was taken; a statement that would have been communicated to the author by his friends the Armenians, the most interested in the fate of their capital. It need not in this case be supposed that Schiltberger confounded the Mahomedan with the Christian year, and that he conceived 655 of the Hegira to correspond to 1277. In 655 or A.D. 1257, Egypt was in too disturbed a state for the sultan to trouble himself about the conquest of Sis.   BRUUN.

CHAPTER LXIII.

(1.) "when Saint Silvester was Pope at Rome."—The Armenian Church teaches that St. Thaddeus, one of the seventy-two disciples of our Lord, and St. Bartholomew, one of the twelve apostles, were the first to preach the gospel in Armenia; but the actual conversion of the Armenians to Christianity was not effected until the reign of Tiridates in the 4th century, by St. Gregory, thenceforth named Lousarovitch—the Enlightener. He was the son of a prince of Parthia, the assassin of Chosroes, king of Armenia, who, though not a kinsman of Gregory, belonged to the race of the Arsacidæ of Parthian origin; St. Gregory's own ancestors, the Surenians, being also a branch of the same royal race. St. Gregory was, therefore, indeed a kinsman of Tiridates, who was the son of Chosroes.

* Nyemoi is the Russian adjective for dumb.   ED.

(2.) "this same king who built the large church at Bethleem, as has been already stated."—It is singular that Bethlehem is not mentioned at all in the chapter devoted to a description of the holy places, so that it is just possible the Nuremberg MS. is a copy of the MS. at Heidelberg, in which that city is not named. Opinions are greatly divided upon this statement of Schiltberger. In a communication from Bishop Aïvazoffsky, I am assured that no church whatever was constructed prior to the king's conversion; but it is stated in an apocryphal writing, that Tiridates caused a church to be built at Jerusalem after his conversion. On the other hand, Vaillant de Florival (*Dictionnaire Historique*, sub vocem, Dertad) inserts that, after his conversion, the king ordered the construction of many churches, one being at Bethlehem, and dedicated to the nativity of Christ.   BRUUN.

(3.) "The king again became a man, and was, with all his people, again a Christian."—This tradition in regard to Tiridates and St. Gregory is told with considerable accuracy. Armenian chroniclers relate that Gregory, having refused to worship the idol set up by the king, was by his orders taken to the fortress in the town of Ardashat, and there thrown into a stinking pit, to be consumed, as we read in the text, by serpents and other reptiles, but where he nevertheless remained miraculously preserved from all harm during the space of fourteen, or, according to others, fifteen years. The place situated in the valley of the Araxes, is now called Khorvyrab—Dry well—the site of a monastery in which is shown the saint's dungeon.

Rhipsime, not Susanna, was the name of the beautiful maiden the king sought to corrupt. She was a devout woman who had fled the importunities of Diocletian, and with Guiane and many other saintly persons of her sex, was put to a cruel death by Tiridates. The story goes on to say that, for these persecutions of Christians, Tiridates was smitten by the Lord, thereby losing his reason and becoming like a wild beast; but his favourite sister, Khosroivitouhdt, having had a vision, caused Gregory to be summoned out of the pit. That holy man restored reason to the king, who thereupon, with all his subjects, became converted to Christianity (*The Crimea and Transc.*, i, 236, 243).   ED.

(4.) "the King Derthat and the man Gregory."—Tiridates was never at Babylon, nor was any Infidel people ever converted by him to Christianity (Bishop Aïvazoffsky); but it should be borne in mind that although the Chaldæans and Nestorians of Kourdistan have nothing in common with the Armenians, they hold St. Gregory in great veneration, as he was sent by Tiridates to Cæsarea in Cappadocia to receive consecration at the hands of St. Leontius, the metropolitan of that country. Schiltberger would have done better to express himself to this effect, instead of saying that St. Gregory was placed at the head of the church by the king.   BRUUN.

CHAPTER LXIV.

(1.) "Saint Silvester."—Agathange, secretary to Tiridates, and Zenobius, a disciple of Gregory, speak of a journey to Rome that was undertaken by those two personages circa 318-19, for the purpose of seeing the Emperor Constantine and Pope Silvester, and concluding with them a treaty of peace and friendship. They remained at Rome one month, and returned to Armenia charged with honours. Moses of Chorene, the catholicos John, Stephen Assolic, and other Armenian historians prior to the 11th century, are united in support of this record of Agathange and Zenobius. Later, during the First and Second Crusades, exaggerated and absurd details, such as those related by Schiltberger, were fabricated; and a monstrous document purporting to be the treaty of peace between Constantine and Tiridates—Sylvester and Gregory, called Tought-tashantz—The Convention—was invented and published after the manner of the false Decretales.

It is in consequence of this controverted document that Armeno-Catholics and other Armenians have enunciated principles and details, such as we read in part in the text (Bishop Aïvazoffsky).

Whilst admitting the fairness of the bishop's observation, I would point out that Schiltberger was simply a ready listener to what the natives, who did not even belong to the Church of Rome, believed to be true; and to what were maintained as incontrovertible facts by the Armeno-Catholics, who in his time were by far the more numerous. BRUUN.

(2.) "a king they call Takchauer."—Cantemir believes that Tekiour is a corruption of τοῦ Κυρίου, and he adds that previous to the conquest of Constantinople, the emperors were called by the Turks, Stamboul Tekioury or Takfoury—Masters of the City. Takavor is the Armenian for king. BRUUN.

CHAPTER LXV.

(1.) "Gregory taught the Christian faith . . . as is above stated."—The Armenians believe, and are prepared to prove, that none of the dogmas of their faith, as they were received from St. Gregory, have undergone any change, and this is why they distinguish themselves as being Gregorians in opposition to Armeno-Catholics. BRUUN.

(2.) "then he must say it himself, right through."—The priest prepares several small loaves, but consecrates one only, and alone recites the prayers and psalms during the preparation. He celebrates the Mass unassisted, other priests performing the functions of deacons in their absence. The practice of Low Mass among the Armenians serves to prove, that the greater number of that people met by Schiltberger were Armeno-Catholics. BRUUN.

(3). "They place much confidence in our religion."—This passage in Neumann's edition stands thus: "Sie machent vil geuartiezi unsers geloubes." The word "geuartiezi" does not appear in the editions of 1475 (?), 1549 and 1814; Neumann does not explain it; Koehler (*Germania*, etc., *herausgegeben von* F. Pfeifer; Wien, vii, 1862), who undertook to correct the errors of Neumann, asks "Was ist geuartiezi?" and Professor Bruun

(Russian edition) believes it to be untranslatable, although he thinks the author meant to imply that the Armenian had borrowed largely from the Roman Catholic Church, or at all events that the one assimilated the other in its types and ceremonies.

The word "gcuärd" occurs in chapter 20, and is possibly intended for gewähr; I have rendered it as "right", or justification from a sense of confidence. Timour's youngest wife (see page 29) was anxious to satisfy her lord, that the letter and ring had been sent to her by one of his vassals without any assurance, any confidence on her part, to warrant him in so doing. It appears to me, considering the careless manner in which the transcriber has performed his work in other places, that a similar interpretation is to be applied to "gcuarticzi" as to "gcuärd"; the words that immediately follow implying prepossession on the part of the Armenians in favour of the Church of Rome—"they also willingly go to Mass in our churches, which the Greeks do not"; apparently because "They place much confidence (have much faith) in our religion". Ed.

(4.) "a saint named Aurencius."—St. Auxentius, priest-martyr, is fêted in the Armeno-Catholic Church on December 25th, and in the Greek Church on December 13th, N. S. Bruun.

(5.) "Saint James the Great."—St. James the Apostle is confounded with St. James bishop of Nisibis, a near relative and contemporary of St. Gregory "the Enlightener". Bruun.

(6.) "his name is Zerlichis."—Sarghis, St. Sergius, was a martyr. The Armenians celebrate his festival fifteen days before Lent. The Armeno-Catholics keep the day on February 24th, and the Greek Church on January 2nd (Bishop Aïvazoffsky). Bruun.

(7.) "our Lady's day in Lent, which they do not hold as we do."—The Armenians do not fast in the name of the Twelve Apostles, and the Ave Maria occurs only in the services of the Armeno-Catholics. On the day of the Annunciation of the Virgin Mary, a hymn is chanted, in which are introduced the words that were spoken to Mary by the Angel. Bruun.

(8.) "then they bury him altogether."—It is quite true that prayers are daily repeated over a grave for the space of a week, and each person attending throws a handful of earth on it as prescribed by the rubric; but the gradual interment is an invention. BRUUN.

(9.) "God forgive thee thy sins."—Asstwadz toghoukhyoùn ta mckhytt, is here intended for the words of absolution pronounced by the priest; but it would be more correct to say—Asstwadz toghoukhuyoùn schnorhestzò—May God grant you absolution. For "Ogornicka" we should read Ogormya or Ogormyha, the modern phrase being: Ter voghormyà yndz—Lord have mercy upon us; but Meghà Asdoutzò— I have sinned before God—is more commonly said by the people. ED.

(10.) "counts, and knights, who are subject to him."—The Armeno-Catholics adopted Low Mass at the commencement of the 14th century. In ancient times prayers were offered for the sovereign and all Christian kings and princes; but never specially for the Roman emperor. BRUUN.

(11.) "if a priest teaches the Word of God, but does not understand and attend to it, he commits a sin."—There is more to confirm than to reject in the information contained in this chapter.

The patriarch must be elected by the unanimous voice of the dignitaries of the Church, who assemble at the patriarchal seat from all parts for the purpose. This has ever been the custom; but since the annexation of Etchmiadzin to Russia, the choice is subject to the emperor's approval.

The preparation of the wafer by women is quite out of the question, and it is also forbidden to laymen by the 22nd Canon of the pontiff Leon; this duty is performed by deacons as well as priests, who first communicate and then administer to the people. In reading the Gospel, the priest faces the congregation, thereby turning his back to the altar, so that the people necessarily look towards the East.

That a priest should separate himself from his wife for three days before and one day after he celebrates the Mass, is strictly in accordance with the Canons of St. Thaddeus; but the observance has become even more stringent in modern times, the priest being required to leave his home and retire to his church during the space of eight days before officiating.

A Canon addressed by Macarius, bishop of Jerusalem, to the pontiff Vertanes, circa 340, requires that the altar shall be furnished with a curtain; a curtain shall likewise fall in front of the sanctuary, within which only the minister celebrating the Mass may enter, other ministers present taking their seats outside according to precedence. This rule has become relaxed in modern times, for deacons as well as priests may now stand at the altar.

As in the Greek Church, no female quæ sit menstrua, may enter a sacred edifice.

It is always the godfather who carries an infant into church for baptism. If the child to be baptised is out of its infancy, it is conducted by a servant of the Church.

Divorce is not to be obtained in the Armenian Church, except in cases of adultery, impotence, and a permanently foul breath.

There is no ykonostass or altar screen as in the Russo-Greek church; but an image, that is to say a painting on canvas or panel, graven images not being tolerated, is always over the altar in the middle of the pem, a raised course in the centre aisle, that is kept covered with carpets, silk, cloth of silver or gold, on which are laid candlesticks, the censer, and a Bible resting on a piece of silk, for the priest does not touch the book with his hands.

The clergy do not pretend to having the power of absolving the penitent; absolution is pronounced in the name of the Almighty.

"Very gorgeous and majestic", says Dr. Issaverdens, "are the garments which the Armenians make use of in their religious ceremonies."

Whatever the restriction in Schiltberger's time, it is certain that all are now free to read the Gospel. That the contrary was ever the case is denied.

The "varthabiet"—Vartabied—is a doctor of divinity possessing knowledge of all holy science, and of all that concerns the study of the Holy Scriptures, of the Fathers, the Councils, and of dog-

R

matical, moral, and disputed theology. The Vartabieds are the first to be consulted in all controversies on religion, its rites, and all ecclesiastical discipline (Issaverdens, *Armenia and the Armenians*, ii, 413, 486; Bishop Meyerditch Kherimian, communicated; *The Crimea and Transc.*, i, 207). ED.

CHAPTER LXVI.

(1.) "that it might be said that thirty Greeks were given for an onion."—This battle between the Armenians and Greeks has reference in all probability to the triumph of Thoros II., or Theodore of the Roupenian dynasty, over Andronicus, who entered Cilicia at the head of an invading army, with instructions from the emperor to seize the king and bind him in chains. Finlay (*Hist. of the Byzantine and Greek Empires*, ii, 242) characterises the two reverses met with by that general in Cilicia, as shameful defeats. Armenian historiographers (Chamich, *Hist. of Armenia*, ii, 195; Issaverdens, *Armenia and the Armenians*, i, 300) enter more largely into details, and describe the great slaughter of Greeks and the multitude of prisoners made, among whom were many chiefs, Andronicus himself effecting his escape with the greatest difficulty.

The emperor being greatly concerned upon learning that a large number of his men remained in the victor's hands, sent ambassadors to treat for their ransom. "If these people were of any use to me," said Thoros, "I would not part with them, but as they are not, take them for what you choose." The reply to this taunt was the dispatch of a large sum of money to the king, for the emperor wished to shew that his men were indeed of great value; but upon seeing the treasure, the king exclaimed with affected astonishment: "What! are my captives truly worth so much?" and ordered that the whole of the money should be distributed among his troops. The ambassadors stood amazed at this munificence, and Thoros merely observed to them: "I reward my soldiers that they may again take your chiefs;" which they did do upon the second invasion by Andronicus, again receiving large sums of money in exchange for the prisoners they made. Chamich sets these events as occurring in the year 1146, and Issaverdens in 1144; but, according to Dr. Leo Alishan of the Mechitaristic Society at Venice, author of *Nerses the Graceful, and his Times*, and other historical works, Thoros II. fought and won about the year 1152. This appears to be the only episode in the history of the Byzantine Empire and of the kingdom of Armenia, that in any degree assimilates the absurdly exaggerated tale of victory invented by those Armenian friends to whom Schiltberger, upon more occasions than this, was too ready to listen.

A curious incident at the close of the late Russo-Turkish war is worth relating, with reference to Schiltberger's version of the value set upon the Greek prisoners. The Porte having entertained the idea of raising the taxation, the Armenians determined upon opposing the measure with vigour, and they accordingly destroyed the house of the Turkish Mudjir; after which, the Armenian women planted onions and garlic over the ruins—an act that is looked upon as a sign of the greatest contempt.—(*The Times*, September 26th, 1878.)

CHAPTER LXVII.

(1.) "Sant Masicia."—This is the ancient Amastris, now called Amasserah. The architecture of its walls of defence bears witness to Genoese occupation, the earliest date of which is not known. In 1346, Amastris was included in the empire of the Palæologi, after having belonged to Nicæa, but it is certain that the Genoese were in possession previous to 1398 (Heyd, *d. Ital. Handelscolon*, etc., in the *Zeitschrift f. d. gesammte Staatswissenschaft*, xviii, 712), at which date they had a consul there. Clavijo calls Amastris, visited by him a few years later, a Genoese town, where he saw many remains of ancient splendour.

After being for a long time a dependency of the Central Administration at Caffa, Samastris, by a decree of 1449, became subject to that of Pera to which it had previously belonged, but had been detached "propter inopiam et imbecilitatem loci ipsius Pere" (*Zap. Odess. Obstschest.*, v, 810). Under these circumstances it is very probable that the Genoese were at Samastris at a still earlier period than that indicated by Heyd. According to Hammer (*Hist. de l'E. O.*, iii, 69), this city fell into the hands of the Turks in the campaign of 1461, together with Sinope and Trebizond.

BRUUN.

(2.) "one hundred are quite of brass."—Schiltberger is scarcely to be charged with exaggeration, if we consider what Manuel Chrysoloras has said of these walls. " I cannot conceive the walls of Constantinople, in regard to their extent and circuit, to have been inferior to those of Babylon. The towers are without number ; the proportions and height of any one tower sufficed to astonish the beholder, and their construction and the large flights of steps excited universal admiration."

In stating that there were one thousand churches, the author intended to convey the idea that they were very numerous; indeed Clavijo estimated the number at three thousand. Schiltberger appears to have been too much dazzled by the magnificence of the church of St. Sophia, to think of entering more largely upon a description of it as others have done. BRUUN.

(3). " A city called Asparseri."—This is Ak-kerman, a name which is the equivalent for Byelgorod, the Slave for White-Town, a place mentioned in the Russian and Polish chronicles of the middle ages— called Tchetate Alba by the Moldavians, and by the Maghyars, Feierwar, not Feriena as it appears through a printer's error in Dlugocz (*Hist. Poloniæ* etc., xi, 324).

The Greeks of the Lower Empire changed the name from White-Town to Mavrocastron, turned by the Italians into Mocastro and Moncastro, as we find it in De Lannoy, Barbaro, and others.

There are good grounds for the supposition that the name White was given originally by the Greeks, because the Aspron mentioned by Constantine Porphyrogenitus (*De Adm. Imp.*, 167) should be looked for in this locality, notwithstanding that the emperor situates it on the Dnieper, a scribe's error for Dniester. I know of no author who speaks of a White-Town on the Lower Dnieper, and the emperor himself describes the place to which he alludes, as being situated on the bank of the river nearest to Bulgaria.

It would appear that the ancient name was not forgotten by the Greeks after they had changed it to Mavrocastron, because some authors of the latter part of the middle ages have alluded to the place as Leucopolichnion or Asprocastron; in all probability identical with "Asparseri", and certainly to be distinguished from White-Town, but a distinction that is to be attributed to a mistake on the part of the transcriber. How otherwise are we to account for the appearance in the Heidelberg MS., of the native name Asparsaraï—White-Town—and for the statement in the Nuremberg MS. (Penzel's edition) that Schiltberger took his departure, not from Asparsaraï but from White-Town, direct for Soutchava* at that time the chief city of Little Walachia or Mavrovlachia as Moldavia was then called.

Grecian colonists were attracted to the neighbourhood of modern Ak-kerman in very remote times. The Tyrites of Herodotus lived there, probably at Ophiussa, a city known to Strabo. There, also, flourished Tyras, to be identified perhaps with Turis, ceded by the emperor Justinian, A.D. 547, to the Antes, a Slave tribe which may have been the first to give the name of Byelgorod to the place which Edrisi certainly had in his mind, when he wrote about the Coman city distant one day's journey from the mouth of the Danube, called Akliba; a name composed of two Turkish words, Ak and liva—White District—and therefore possibly the Coman designation for the "White City" of Schiltberger, the Akkerman of Aboulfeda. BRUUN.

(4.) "Linburgch, the chief city in White Reissen the Lesser."—This White Russia was the eastern part of Galicia, alluded to by Marino Sanudo in his letter to the king of France. "Russia minor quæ confinat ab occidente cum Polonia. . . . ." (Kunstmann, *Stud. über* M. S., 105).

* ... ich zu einer Wallachischen Stadt kam, die unter dem Nahmen der weissen Stadt bekannt ist. Von da kam ich nach Sedhof; welches die Hauptstadt der kleinen Wallachey ist.—Page 205.

In distinguishing White Russia from the kingdom of Russia (see page 50), Schiltberger refers to the grand-duchy of Lithuania, and not only to the White Russia of our own times, which then formed part of the grand-duchy.　　　　　　　　　　Bruun.

(5.) "gemandan."—I am indebted to Mr. Mnatzakan Hakhoumoff of Shousha, for the Lord's Prayer in modern Armenia, and in the tongue spoken by the Tatars west of the Caspian Sea.
　　　　　　　　　　　　　　　　　　　　　　　Ed.

The Lord's Prayer in Modern Armenian.

Haïr mer vor hersince es sourp egwitzy anoun kho egwesouè arkhaïouthyoum kho egwitzy kamkh kho vorpess bergwince ev hergry zhatz mer hanapazort tour mez aïsor, evthogmez zpardys mer vorpess, ev mekh thogoumkh meroz pardabanatz, ev my tanyr zmez y tcharè, zy kho è arkhaïouthyoum zorouthyoun ev pharkh havidians. Ammen.

The Lord's Prayer in the Tatar tongue.

Byzum athamuz ky ghyogdasan pyr olsun sanun adun ghyalsun sanun padshalygun olsun sanun stadygun nedja ky geogda eïla da dïunyada ver byza gyounluk georagymuz va bagushla byzum tahsurlarumuz nedja ky byz baghishlüruh byzum tahsrulara goïma byzy gedah sheïtan ïoluna amma pakh cla byzy pyslugden tchounky sanunkidr padshalus ihtiar va hiurmat ta diunianun abruna.

TITLES OF WORKS NOT FULLY CITED IN THE FOREGOING NOTES.

Abbott, K. E.—*Southern Cities of Persia*, and *Persian Azerbaijan;* in MS.

Abd-Allatif—*Relation de l'Egypte;* trad. et enrichi de Notes par M. Silvestre de Sacy. Paris, 1810.

Abd el Hakam. See Makrizi.

Aboulfeda—*Géographie d';* trad. par Reinaud et De Slane. 3 tom. Paris, 1848.

Aivazoffsky, Bishop, of Theodosia. MS. Communications.

Ali Bey—*Travels of*, 2 vols. London, 1816.

Arabshah—*L'Histoire du Grand Tamerlan;* trad. par Vattier. Paris, 1658.

Arnold von Lübeck—in *Die Geschichtschreiber der Deutschen Vorzeit, herausgegeben* von Pertz, Grimm, etc. Berlin, 1847-67.

Aschbach, J.—*Geschichte Kaiser Sigmund's*, iv. Hamburg, 1833-45.

Assemanus—*Bibliotheca Orientalis Clemento-Vaticana*, etc., iii. Romæ, 1719-1728.

Baier—*De numo Amideo*, in his *Opuscula*. Halæ, 1770.

Benjamin of Tudela—*The Itinerary of;* Asher edition. 2 vols. Berlin, 1840.

Berezin—in Prince Obolensky's *Yárlyk Toktámysha k' Yagáilou*. Kazan, 1850.

Berezin —*Nashestvye Mongolov* in the *Journal du Ministère de l'Instruction publique*.

Blau, O.—*Ueber Volksthum und Sprache der Kumanen* in the *Zeitschrift der Deutschen morgenländischen Gesellschaft*. Leipzig, Band xxix.

Bonfinii, Antonii — *Rerum Ungaricarum Decades quatuor, cum dimidia.* Basileæ, 1568.
Bruun, Prof. P. — *Geographische Bemerkungen zu Schiltberger's Reisen,* in the *Sitzungsberichte der König. Bayer. Akademie.*
München, 1869, 1870.
Büsching—*Grosse Erdbeschreibung,* xii. Troppau, 1784.

Chardin, Le Chev. J.—*Voyages en Perse et autres lieux de l'Orient,* etc. Langlès edition. Paris, 1811.
Clavijo—*Narrative of the Embassy,* trans. by C. R. Markham.
Hakluyt Society's publication, 1859.
Codinus. See Parthey.
Cosmography. Basel, 1874.

De Guignes, J.—*Histoire générale des Huns, des Turcs, des Mongols,* etc. 4 tom. Paris, 1756-58.
De La Croze, M. V.—*Histoire du Christianisme des Indes.*
La Haye, 1724.
De Lannoy, Le Chev. G.—*Voyages et Ambassades,* 1399-1450.
Mons, 1840.
Dlugosz, J.—*Historiæ Poloniæ* etc., etc. 2 vol. Lipsiæ, 1711-12.
D'Ohsson, Mouradja—*Tableau général de l'Empire Othoman,* etc. 3 tom. Paris, 1787-1820.
D'Ohsson, C. Mouradja—*Des Peuples du Caucase,* etc. Paris, 1828.
D'Ohsson, C. Mouradga—*Histoire des Mongols,* etc. 4 tom.
La Haye et Amsterdam, 1834-1835.
Dorn, B.—*Versuch einer Geschichte der Schirwanshache,* in the *Mémoires de l'Académie de St. Pétersbourg.*
Dorn, B.—*Geographica Caucasia,* in the *Mémoires de l'Académie de St. Pétersbourg,* VI ser., vii, 527.

Edrisi—Trad. par Amédée Jaubert, in *Recueil des Voyages et des Mémoires,* tom. v, vi. Paris, 1836-40.
Engel, J. Chr. von—*Geschichte des Ungrischen Reichs,* v.
Wien, 1805.
Erdmann, Dr. F. von—*Temudschin der Unerschütterliche,* etc.
Leipzig, 1862.

Evliya Effendi—*Travels in Europe, Asia, and Africa, in the 17th Century;* trans. from the Turkish, by J. v. Hammer. 2 vols.
London, 1846.

Fallmerayer, J. P.—*Geschichte des Kaiserthums von Trapezunt.*
München, 1827.
Forbiger, A.—*Handbuch der alten Geographie*, etc., ii.
Leipzig, 1842.
Frachn, C. M.—*Ibn Foszlan. und anderer Araber Berichte.*
St. Petersburg, 1823.
Froissart, *Les Chroniques de Sire Jean*—in the Panthéon Littéraire.
Fürst—*Geschichte des Karäerthums*, ii. Leipzig, 1862.

Garcin de Tassy—*Mémoire sur les Noms propres et des Titres mussulmans.* Paris, 1854.
Gardner, Rev. J.—*The Faiths of the World, a Dictionary of all Religions and Religious Sects*, etc., 2 vols.
London and Edinburgh.
Genebrardi, Gilberti—*Libri Hebræorum Chronologici eodem Genebrarde interpreta.* Lugdini, 1609.
Gihan Numa. See Mustafa.
Gilles, Pierre—*Antiquities of Constantinople.* London, 1729.
Grégoire de Nazianze—*Œuvres*, etc., 2 tom. Paris, 1609-11.
Gregoræ, Nicephori—*Byzantinæ Historiæ*, lib. xxiv. 3 vol.
Schopen edition, 1855.
Güldenstädt, J. A.—*Reisen durch Russland*, ii.
St. Petersburg, 1787-1791.

Hadjy Khalpha. See Mustafa.
Hammer, J. von—*Berichtigung der orientalischen Namen Schiltberger's* in *Denkschriften der Königlichen Akademie der Wissenschaften zu München, für die Jahre* 1823 *und* 1824. Band ix.
Hammer-Purgstall—*Histoire de l'Empire Ottoman*, etc., trad. de l'Allemand par Hellert, 3 tom. Paris, 1835-43.

Hammer-Purgstall—*Geschichte der Goldenen Horde in Kiptschak, das ist, der Mongolen in Russland.* Pesth, 1840.
Hammer-Purgstall—*Geschichte der Ilchane, das ist, der Mongolen in Persien,* ii. Darmstadt, 1842-43.
Heyd, Prof. W.—*Die Colonien der Römischen Kirche in den von den Tartaren beherrschten Ländern Asiens und Europe,* ii.
Tübingen, 1858.
Heyd, Prof. W.—*Die Italienischen Handelscolonien,* etc., in the *Zeitschrift für die gesammte Staatswissenschaft,* xviii, xix.
Heyd, Prof. W.—*Le Colonie Commerciali degli Italiani in Oriente, nel Medio Evo;* Dissertazioni rifatte dall' Autore e recate in Italiano dal Professore G. Müller, 2 vols.
Venezia e Torino, 1866.
Hurmuzaky, E. von—*Fragmente zur Geschichte der Rumanen.*
Bukarest, 1878.

Ibn Batouta—*Voyages,* par Defrémery et Sanguinetti.
Paris, 1853-58.
Ibn Batuta—*The Travels of,* trans. by Samuel Lee, D.D.
London, 1829.
Ibn Haukal—*The Oriental Geography of,* trans. by Sir W. Ouseley.
London, 1800.
Issaverdens, Dr.—*Armenia and the Armenians.* Venice, 1875.
Jean du Plan de Carpin—*Relation de,* in *Recueil des Voyages et des Mémoires,* etc.
Jirecek, K. J.—*Geschichte der Bulgaren.* Prag, 1876.
Jordanus Catalani—*Wonders of the East,* trans. by Col. H. Yule.
Hakluyt Society's Publication, 1863.

Kanitz, F.—*Donau-Bulgarien und der Balkan,* etc.
Leipzig, 1875-77.
Kazvini—*Kosmographie,* etc.; trans. by H. Ethè. Leipzig, 1868.
Khanikoff—*Mémoire sur Khacani,* in the *Journal Asiatique,* vi, série, v.
Khanikoff—*O nyekotóryh' Arábskyh' nadpýseh,* in the *Zapýssky Imperátorskavo Geographýtcheskavo Obstschestvà.*

Klaproth, H. J.—*Voyage au Caucase et en Géorgie.*   Paris, 1823.
Köppen, J.—*Krýmsky Sbórnyk, O drévnostyah yoújnavo béreya Krýma y gor Tavrytcheskyh'.*   St. Petersbourg, 1837.
Kraft—*Die Topographie Jerusalems.*   Berlin, 1846.
Kunstmann—*Studien über Marino Sanudo.*   München, 1855.

Lamansky—*O Slavyánah v' Máloy Asii.*   St. Petersburg, 1859.
Leontief—*O Myestopolojény'ye Orny,* in the *Propilei,* iv.
   Moskva, 1874.

Makrizi—*Histoire des Sultans Mamlouks de l'Egypte,* trad. par Quatremère.   Paris, 1837.
Mandevile, Sir John—*Voyages and Travels,* etc.   London, 1670.
Marigny. See Taibout de Marigny.
Maundrell, H.—*A Journey from Aleppo to Jerusalem, at Easter,* 1697.   Oxford, 1749.
Marignolli, Giov. de'—*Reise in das Morgenland, von Jahr* 1339-1353, Meinert edition.   Prag, 1820.
Mosheimii, J. L.—*Historia Tartarorum Ecclesiastica,* etc.
   Helmstadii, 1741.
Mustafa ibn Abd Allah, called Hadjy Khalpha—*Jihan Numa Geographia Orientalis,* etc.   Londini Gothorum, 1818.

Neander, J. A. W.—*Allgemeine Geschichte der christlichen Religion und Kirche.*   Hamburg, 1825-52.
Neshry—*Geschichte des Osmanischen Hauses,* trans. by Noeldecke in the *Morgenländische Zeitschrift,* xv.
Noroff, A. S.—*Pélerinage en Terre Sainte de l'Igoumène Russe Daniel,* etc.   St. Pétersbourg, 1864.
Nikitin. See Sreznevsky.
Notices et Extraits des MSS. de la Bibliothèque du Roy.   Paris.

Olearius—*Voyages faits en Moscovie, Tartarie et Perse,* 2 tom.
   Amsterdam, 1727.
Ouseley, Sir Wm.—*Travels in Various Countries of the East, more particularly Persia,* 2 vols.   London, 1821.

Parthey, G. F. C.—*Hieroclis Synecdemus et notitiæ Græcæ episcopatuum*, etc. Berolini, 1866.
Peschel, O.—*Geschichte der Erdkunde*. München, 1865.
Petis de la Croix, F.—*Histoire de Timur Bec*. Paris, 1722.
Petitot, C. B.—*Collection complète des Mémoires relatifs à l'Histoire de France*, 56 tom. Paris, 1819-24.
Pólnoye Sobrány'ye Roússkyh' Lyétopyssey. Complete Collection of Russian MSS.
Polo, Marco—*The Book of Ser*, newly translated and edited, with Notes, Maps, and other Illustrations, by Col. Henry Yule, C.B., 2 vols., 2nd Ed. London, 1875.
Potocki, Comte J.—*Voyages dans les Steps d'Astrakhan et du Caucase*, etc., 2 tom. Paris, 1829.
Pouteshéstvy'ye Roússkyh' loudyéy. Travels of Russians.
St. Petersburg, 1837.

Rashid-eddin—*Histoire des Mongols de la Perse*, trad. etc., par M. Quatremère. Paris, 1836.
Raumer, K. G. von—*Palästina*, 4th Ed. Leipzig, 1864.
Recueil de Voyages et de Mémoires, etc., publié par la Société de Géographie. Paris, 1839.
Rehm, F.—*Handbuch der Geschichte des Mittelalters seit den Kreuzzügen*, iv. Cassel, 1831-39.
Rehm, F.—*Tableau Générale des Timouriades*, in vol. iii of Rehm's *Handbuch der Geschichte des Mittelalters*.
Richter, E.—*Wallfahrten im Morgenlande*. Berlin, 1823.
Ritter, K.—*Die Erdkunde im Verhältniss zur Natur und zur Geschichte des Menschen; oder, allgemeine vergleichende Geographie*, etc. Berlin, 1822.
Robinson, Dr. E.—*Biblical Researches in Palestine and adjacent Regions*, etc., 3 vols. London, 1866.

Saad-eddin. Saidino—*Chronica dell' Origine, e Progressi della Casa Ottomana*, by V. Bratutti, 1649.
Saint Martin, M. J.—*Mémoires Historiques et Géographiques sur l'Arménie*, etc., 2 tom. Paris, 1818-19.

Saint-Martin, Vivien de—*Description de l'Asie Mineure*, 2 tom.
Paris, 1852.
Sanutus, Marinus—*Liber secretorum fidelium crucis super Terræ Sanctæ recuperatione et conservatione*, etc.; *Gesta Dei per Francos.* Hanoviæ, 1611.
Savelieff—*Monety Joudjydov*, etc. St. Petersburg, 1857.
Schafarik, P. J.—*Slawische Alterthümer.* Deutsch von Moriz Aehrenfeld; Wuttke edition, ii. Leipzig, 1843-1844.
Schwandtnerus, J. G.—*Scriptores Rerum Hungaricarum veteres*, etc., 3 vol. Vindoboni, 1746-48.
Seetzen—*Reiseberichte in monatlicher Correspondenz.*
Berlin, 1854.
Silvestre de Sacy, A. J.—*Chrestomathie Arabe*, 3 tom.
Paris, 1806.
Spratt, Capt. T. A. B., R.N.—*Travels and Researches in Crete*, 2 vols., 2nd Ed. London, 1865.
Sprengel, M. C.—*Geschichte der wichtichsten geographiesch Entdeckungen*, 2nd Ed. Halle, 1792.
Sreznevsky—*Hojdénye za try Móry'ya Afanásia Nikitina*, in Notes of the Academy of Sciences, St. Petersburg, ii, 3.
Stephen of Novgorod. See *Pouteshéstvy'ye Roússkyh' loudyéy.*

Taitbout de Marigny—*Voyage dans le pays des Tcherkesses.* See Potocki.
Taitbout de Marigny—*Hydrographie de la Mer Noire.*
Trieste, 1856.
Telfer, Comm\ufeffr. J. Buchan, R.N.—*The Crimea and Transcaucasia*, 2 vols., 2nd Ed. London, 1877.
Theiner—*Vetera Monumenta Historiam Hungariæ Sacram Illustrantia.* Romæ, 1859.
Thunmann. See Schwandtnerus.
Tobler, T.—*Die Siloahquelle und der Oelberg*, etc.
St. Gallen, 1852.

Wahl, S. F. G.—*Allgemeine Beschreibung des persischen Reiches*, ii.
Leipzig.
Webb.—*A Survey of Egypt and Syria, undertaken in the Year*

1422 *by Sir Gilbert de Lannoy;* in *Archæologia*, vol. 21, 1827, p. 281 *et seq.*

Weil, Dr. G.—*Geschichte der Chalifen, nach handschriftlichen, grösstentheils noch unbenützten Quellen bearbeitet*, iv.
Mannheim, 1846-60.

Weil, Dr. G.—*Geschichte der islamitischen Völker.* Stuttgart, 1866.

Yakout—(Modjem el-Bouldan) in *Dictionnaire Géographique, Historique et Littéraire de la Perse;* par C. Barbier de Meynard.
Paris, 1861.

Ysvestye Imperátorskavo Geographýtcheskavo Obstschestva, or, Reports of the Imperial Geographical Society; St. Petersburg.

Yule, Col. H., C.B.—*Cathay and the Way Thither*, 2 vols.
Hakluyt Society's Publication, 1866.

Zapyssky Odesskavo Obsshtschestvà Ystórii Drévnostey.

Zinkeisen, J. W.—*Geschichte des osmanischen Reiches in Europa,*
vi. Gotha, 1840-43.

Zosimus, see *Pouteshêstvy'ye Rousskyk loudyéy.*

INDEX.

The Names in parenthesis are those employed by Schiltberger.

Abel's offering, 65
Abhase (Abkas), an unhealthy country, 43, 178
Abhases, the, are of the Greek Church, 78 ; dress and customs, 43, 178
Aboubekr (Abubach), the caliph, 67
———— (Aububachir), son of Miran Shah, 33, 134, 135
Abraham, 56, 60, 71, 76, 194, 195
Adam's grave, 60, 65 ; created in God's image, 71
Adana (Adalia) taken by Bajazet, 19, 123
Adrianople (Adranopoli), a city in Greece, 6, 39
Ahmed (Mirachamat), the amir, 10
———— ben Oweis (king of Babylon), 7, 113 ; quits Babylon, 24, 130 ; is beheaded, 32, 135, 160
Aidin (Edein), 40
Aintab (Anthap), 22 ; pillaged by Timour, 127-128
Akhlat, 126
Ak-kerman (Asparseri), 101, 244-245
Akshcher, 21, 118
Aktam (Achtum), 32, 134
Aleppo (Hallapp), taken by Timour, 22, 127, 128
Alexander the Great, legends of, 79, 226, 216
Alexandria, described, 62 ; Italians at, 62 ; mirror of, 63, 215 ; taken by king of Cyprus and his allies, 62, 64, 214
(Allenklaisser), a great giant, 64, 216
Ali (Aly), the caliph, a persecutor of Christians, 44 ; and giant, 65 ; chief over all Mahomedans, 67
Ali Koutchava's revolt at Ispahan, 27, 133
Alindsha (Aluitze), 24, 130, 44, 160, 136
Amasserah, Amastris (Sant Masicia), 100, 243
Anconitans, in Egypt, 214

Angora (Angarus, Augury), besieged by White Tatars, 18 ; battle of, 21, 117 ; a city of Turkey, 40
Ani, the ancient capital of Armenia, 126
Anjak (Origens), 34, 136-138
Ann's, St., well, 58
Annas the high priest, house of, 59, 203
(Antioch) Nisibis, 44, 160
Arabia, gold of, 26, 46, 64, 67
Ararat, 44, 231
Arjish (Agrich), 38
Armenia (Ermenia), 26, 86,
———— Greater, 7, 117, 61, 89
———— Lesser, 20, 31, 43, 61, 86, 117
Armenian Church, 87, 90, 91-96, 238, 242
Armenians, at Angora, 40 ; at Caffa, 49 ; are favoured by Mahomedans, 73 ; friendly to Germans, 86, 234 ; their conversion to Christianity, 87, 235 ; in Cyprus, 88 ; enemies of the Greeks, 96 ; are brave and clever, 98 ; in Cilicia and Syria, 117
Arnauts (Arnaw), are of the Greek church, 78, 222
Astara (Strana), 34, 136
Astrabad (Strawba), 44, 160
Astrahan, Hadjy-tarkhan (Haitzicherchen), 49, 172, 136, 139, 141, 142, 154

Babel, tower of (Marburtirudt), 46, 167
Babylon, 24, 33, 46, 52, 86, 88, 89, 187
———— New, 47
Badakshan (Walaschoen), 46, 166-167
Baghdad (Wadach, Waydat), 46, 167, 52, 191, 157, 168 ; *see* Babylon
Baïram, the, 70, 221
Bajazet (Weyasat, Weyasit), at Nicopolis, 2, 3, 108, 109 ; slaughter and distribution of prisoners, 4, 7, 112,

113, 115, 146; invades duchy of Pettau, 6; besieges Konieh, 8; occupies Karamau, 10; takes Samsoun, 12, 14; occupies Sebaste, 18; takes Malatia, 18; Adana, 19; succours Faradj, 19, 124; conquers Lesser Armenia, 20, 125; capture at Angora, and death, 21, 126; besieges Constantinople, 80, 231
Balsam in Egypt, 60, 61, 207-208, 92
Baptism in Greek Church, 82, 83; in Armenian Church, 92; in river Jordan, 205; place of the Saviour's, 205
Barkok (Warchloch, Marochloch), 19, 124, 51, 182, 113
Barley planted over Babylon, 24
Batou, 137, 173
Batoum, 153
Battle, of Nicopolis, 2, 4, 107-112; Konieh, 7, 8; Angora, 21; Delhi, 25, 130, 132; Karabagh, 31, 134; Aktam, 32, 134
Bavaria (Payren), 1, 38
Beard, never cut by Walachians, 38; forbidden to Mahomedans to cut the, 71; not shaven by Greek priests, 83; not shaven by Armenian priests, 92
Beasts, wild, in Siberia, 35; Badakshan, 46; Babylon, 47, 168; Bolgar, 49, 174
Behesna (Wehessum), 22, 127-128, 123
Beshtamak (Bestan), 49, 138-139
Bethlehem (Bethlaem, Bethlahen), 35, 51, 185, 87, 236
Bishop's see, et Joulad, 34, 139; Makou, 44, 159; Caffa, 49; Sary Kerman or Cherson, 177
Bistan (Bestan, capital of Kourdistan), 43, 152
Blood of horses, as food, 48
Bolgar (Bolar), a city, 49, 174, 139, 141, 142, 173
Bolgara (Walher), a country, 36
Borrak (Waroch), 37, 142
Bosphorus, the, 79, 226
Boucicault, Marshal (Hanns Putzokardo), 4, 107, 111, 112, 231
Bourhan uddin (Wurthanadin) defeated by a son of Bajazet, 10; is executed by Kara Yelek, 16, 121, 114, 120
Boursbai (Malleckchafcharff, Balmander), 51, 182-191; his letter to Shah Rokh, 184, 187
Bread, not eaten in Siberia, 36; made of millet, 41; not eaten in Jagatai, 47; nor in Great Tatary, 48

Breslau (Bressla), 102
Broussa (Wursa, Wurssa), 6, 10, 34, 40
Buddhism, 140
Bulgaria (Pulgrey), 2, 39, 78, 89
——— Eastern, 107, 120
——— Western, 107
——— Central, 13
Bulgarians, are of the Greek Church, 78
Burgundy (Burguny), Duke of; see Comte de Nevers.
Burial or disposal of the dead, in Siberia, 36; Circassia, 50; by Mahomedans, 69; Greeks, 83; Greek priests, 84, 233; Armenians, 94, 95; Armenian priests, 94, 240
Burzelland (Zwürtzenland), 38, 144

Caffa, 49, 176, 79, 99
Caiphas, house of, 203
Cairo (Miser, Alkenier, Kayr), 23, 50, 181-182, 60, 64, 87
Caliph (Calypha), the, 98
Calvary, Mount (Calvarie), 57
Camels, at Adana, 19, 123; India, 25, 132; milk and flesh as food, 48 (Capadocie), 51, 52, 184, 186
Capernaum, 185
(Carthago) Kairvan?, 51, 184
Caspian Sea (White Sea), 45; sea of Ghel, 160
Castle of the Sparrow-hawk, 41-43, 149
Catalans, in Egypt, 214
Caucasus, forest of the, 52, 186
Chaldæa (Kalda), 46, 167
Chateaumorant (Centumaranto), a prisoner at Nicopolis, 4, 111; defends Constantinople, 231
(Chebakh) Kepek?, a vassal of Timour, 26
China (Chetey, Cetey), 28, 133
Christians, at Samsoun, 13; Joulad, 34, 138; Caffa, 49, 176, 99; on the Jordan, 60; in Malabar, 61, 211-212; conversion of, to Mahomedanism, 74, 222; on the Nile, 190; in Egypt, 190; of St. Thomas, 211-212
"Christians of the girdle", 190
Christmas in the Armenian Church, 93
Church, of the Holy Sepulchre, 57, 198, 60; of St. Sophia, 80, 231, 101
Churches at Jerusalem, 58-60, 196, 197-203
Churches in Armenia, building of, 94
Circassia (Starchas, Zerckchas), 50, 99
Circassians (Ischerkas), slave dealers,

INDEX.   257

50, 178, 179 ; are of the Greek Church, 78 ; Tcherkess and Zikhes, 177
Citadel on Mount Sion, 59, 203
Coins, of the Golden Horde, 139, 141, 142 ; of Jagataï, 170 ; of the khan Uzbek, 173 ; of the Bolgars, 174
Constantine, the emperor, 80, 83, 84, 89
Constantine, ancient city of, 151
Constantinople (Stampol, Istimboli), 4, 39, 52, 79, 80, 83, 84, 96, 100, 101, 119, 231
Conversion of Christians to Mahomedanism, 74, 222
Corn in Kiptchak (Ephepstznch), 49
Cotton grown in Ghilan, 44
Couriers in Egypt, 52-53 ; in Russia, 192
Court ceremonials in Egypt, 52, 54, 192
Cracow (Krackow), 101
Croatia (Windischy land), 6, 113
Cross, shining, at Angora, 40
Cyprus I. (Zypern, Zyperen), 19, 62, 64, 88 ; John, king of, captured by the Egyptians, 187

Damascus (Damaschk, Tamaschcn), siege of, 22 ; destruction of the great mosque, 23, 128-129
Daniel the prophet, where buried, 59
Danube R. (Tunaw), 2, 4, 38, 39, 79, 101
Dardanelles (Hellespant and Poges for Boghaz), 79
Darial pass, the, 89
D'Artois, Philippe, Comte d'Eu, 109
Date-plum, the, 47, 168
David, King, where buried, 59
Day (They), the, 74, 221
Dead, prayers for the, in Armenian Church, 94
Death, by cutting in two parts, 19 ; burial alive, 20, 125, 22 ; hanging, 24 ; trampling under the hoofs of horses, 28, 133 ; strangulation, 33 ; sawing in two parts, 51, 183 ; impalement, 51 ; poisoning, 154 ; breaking on the wheel, 183
Delhi (Dily), besieged by Timour, 26, 131 ; capital of Lesser India, 47
Denisly (Donguslu), 40, 148
De Noillac, Philibert, grand-master of Rhodes, 109, 110
Derbent, 34, 136
Desert, at the end of the earth, 35 ; of Arabia, 46, 54
Despot of Servia, 3, 111
——— of the Morea, 228

Devlett byrdy (Doblabardi), 37, 142
Divorce in Armenia, 94, 241
Dobroudja, the, 110
Dogs, in Siberia, 35 ; where they are eaten, 35
Dokouz Khatoum, protectress of Christians, 157
Don R. (Tena), 49
Dragons, in the desert of Arabia, 46 ; at Rome, 90-91
Dyarbekr (Hamunt, capital of Black Turkey), 43, 152

(Edigi) ; see Ydegou
Eger, 102
Egypt, 50, 61
Elephants, at battle of Angora, 21 ; in India, routed by camels, 25, 132 ; in Lesser India, 47
Elias, his burial-place, 52 ; chapel on Horeb, 55 ; a prophet of the Mahomedans, 188
Emperor, the Greek, 101
——— the Roman, 95, 240
Enoch, his burial-place, 52 ; a prophet of the Mahomedans, 188
Ephesus (Asia), 40, 146
Epiphany, the, in the Armenian Church, 93
Erivan (Erban), 33, 136
Ersingan (Ersinggan), taken by Bajazet, 21 ; capital of Lesser Armenia, 43 ; a kingdom of Armenia, 86
Esaias, the prophet, 59
Ethiopia, 209
Eucharist, the, in Syrian Church, 78 ; in Greek Church, 81, 232 ; in Armenian Church, 91-92, 238, 240
Euphrates R., 43, 151, 46, 61, 209, 117, 168, 186
Eve, the grave of, 60

Faradj (Joseph, Jusuphda), 19, 124, 51, 122
Fasting, among Mahomedans, 70 ; in the Greek Church, 82, 83, 232 ; in the Armenian Church, 93, 239
Felt, raising to the White, 48, 172
Female, warriors in Great Tatary, 37 ; debauchery in Egypt, 52, 191
Fictions, battle of serpents and vipers, 12 ; Timour lies uneasy in his grave, 30 ; castle of the sparrow-hawk, 41-42 ; (Phiradamschyech), a tercentenarian, 45, 162 ; destruction of mirror at Alexandria, 63, 215 ; the giant's shin-bone, 64, 216 ; the Bosphorus, a cutting by Alexander the Great, 79, 226 ; the emperor Constantine, 83 ; Tiridates is turned

into a pig, 88, 236 ; Tiridates, the dragon and unicorn, 90 ; the forty Armenian knights, 96-98
Fire worship, 65
Fish, exported from Tana, 49, 175; in the R. Jordan, 60
Florentines, in Egypt, 214
Fortress, of Alindsha, 24, 44 ; Gallipoli, 39 ; Kilia, 101. See these names
Frioul (Frigaul), 89
Frisingen, 102
Furs, articles of commerce, at Bolgar, 174 ; Saraï, 174 ; Astrahan, 174

Gabriel the archangel, 57
Gaetans, in Egypt, 214
Galata (Kalathan), 79, 225
(Galgarien) ; *see* Khozary
Galilee, Mt., 59, 204
Galleys, in Danube, 4, 38 ; sea of Azoff, 49 ; of Cyprus, 63
Gallipoli (Karipoli, Chalipoli), 6, 112, 39
Ganges, R. (Rison), 61, 210
Genoa, 49, 79
Genoese, at Samsoun, 13, 119 ; Alexandria, 62, 214 ; Galata, 79 ; relations with Persia, 154 ; secure the silk of Ghilan, 160 ; in Crimea, 189 ; at defence of Constantinople, 231
Georgia (Gursey, Kursi), a kingdom, 34, 43
Georgians (Gorchillas, Kurtzi), are Christians and warlike, 43 ; are of the Greek Church, 78
Gharny (Kirna), 44, 158
Ghilan, 44, 160
Giant, story of a, 64, 216-219
Ginger, in Malabar, 62
Giraffe (surnasa), in Lesser India, 47 ; 169
Gold, of India, 26 ; Arabia, 26 ; in river Ganges, 61, 210
Golden Horde ; *see* Great Tatary
Gori, 43, 153
Gospel, the (Evangely), 77 ; not read in Armenia, 96, 241
Gothia (Sudi), 50
Goths (Kuthia) are of the Greek Church, 78
Grass poisoned, 23
Greece, 6, 39, 96
Greek Church, 78, 81-85, 231-232, 233
Greeks, in Lazistan, 43 ; Caffa, 49 ; Gothia, 50
(Greiff, Hannsen), executed after Nicopolis, 5

Hair, never cut by Walachians, 38 ; not cut by Armenian priests, 92
(Hamunt) Kara Amid ; *see* Dyarbekr
(Hanns, burgrave of Nuremberg), 3
Hebron (Ebron), 56, 195-196, 60
Herat (Herren, Hore), 30, 45, 161
Herman (of Cily), 3
Hermanstadt (Hermenstat), 38
Hermon (Germoni), 52, 185
Herod, house of, 58, 202
Hillah, 187
Hippodrome at Constantinople, 79, 228
(Hoder of Hungary), 7
Holy Fire, the, 57, 198-200
Holy Places, the, 57-60, 198-206 ; when possessed by the Mahomedans, 60, 207
Holy Sepulchre, the, 57-60, 198-200
Holy Trinity, the, rejected by the Greeks, 81 ; accepted by the Armenians, 87
Horeb (Oreb), 55
Hormuz I (Hognaas) 45, 164
Hormuzd, worship of, 150
Horse flesh, the food of Tatars, 48
Horses, in Siberia, 35
Hospitals, at Broussa, 40; at Jerusalem, 58, 201
Houlakou's tomb at Meragha, 157
Houses, in Adrianople, 39 ; Broussa, 40 ; Herat, 45 ; Caffa, 49 ; Cairo, 50-182
Hungarians, the, 3
Hungary (Ungern, Ungeren), 1-2, 6, 38, 39, 89

Ibraila (Ubereil), 38
Imbros I (Lempric), 80, 230
Impalement in Egypt, 51
Incense, employed in Armenia, 96 ; of Arabia and India, 96
India, Greater, 45, 46
——— Lesser, 24-26, 130, 47
(Indian Sea), 47
Indus, R., 209
Iron cage, the, 126
Iron gate (Temurtapit), on the Danube, 2, 39 ; Darial pass, 89 ; Derbent, 34, 136 ; Khorasan, 25, 131, 136
Isaac, 60, 195
Ispahan (Hisspahan), occupied by Timour, and Ali Koutchava's revolt, 27, 133 ; 45
Italy, 87, 101
Italians, at Samsoun, 13 ; Caffa, 49 ; Alexandria, 62

Jacob, grave of, 60, 195
Jacobites, in Syria, 78, 190; their chapel at Jerusalem, 200, 225
Jagataï (Zakatay), 47, 170
Jakam (Zechem), 51, 183
Jalal uddin (Segelalladin), 37, 141, 158
Janibek, 154, 173
Janyk (Genyck, Tcyenick, Zegnikch), province of, 12, 41
Jambolouk (Inbu) Tatars, the, 50, 180
Jehangir (Zychanger), 32, 134
Jengiz Khan, 113, 166
Jericho, valley of, 60, 206
Jerusalem (Kurtzitalil), 51, 56, 57-60, 198, 93
Jews, at Caffa, 49, 176; Jerusalem, 60
Jihoun, R., 186
Jordan, R., 51, 57, 59, 60, 205, 206
Josophat, valley of, 52
Joulad (Setzulet, Zulat), 34, 138, 49
Justinian, statue of, at Constantinople, 80, 228-230

Kaffa; see Caffa
Kais or Keis I (Kaff), 46, 165
Kaisarieh (Gaissaria), 16, 41
Kaïtak (Kayat) Tatars, the, 50, 179
Kaliakra (Kallacercka), 39, 145
Karabagh (Scharabach, Karawag), 31, 134, 86, 234
Karaman, at war with Bajazet, 7; his capture and execution, 8, 118
——— conquest of, by Bajazet, 7-10; a country in Great Turkey, 40
——— (Laranda), the capital of Karaman, 7, 118, 40
Karamora, Black River, 210
Kara Yelek (Otman), 14-18, 120, 20, 114, 154
Kara Youssouf (Joseph), 30, 32, 33, 134, 154
Kars (Kray), 33, 136
Kashan (Kaffer), 34
(Kaylamer) Kalamila? 52, 188
Kedron, R., 59, 203
Keghart monastery, 159
Kemakh (Kamach), 43, 150
(Kennan) Kermian? 40
Kepek (Tchebackh), a ruler of the Golden Horde, 37, 141
Kerak, in Arabia, 217
Kerasous (Kureson), 41, 148, 43
Kerym byrdy (Kerumberdin), 37, 142
Khau, the, of White Tatary, 16; of Chetey, 28
Kharput (Kayburt), 43, 150
Khelat (Gelat), 44, 158
Khorasan (Horosscu), a kingdom of Persia, 30, 45, 161

Khozary (Galgarien), 52, 189
Khwarezm (Horosaman), 49, 172
Kiankary (Wegureisari), 40, 148
Kilia (Gily), 101
(King-sultan); see Mamelouk sultan
(Kings of Great Tartaria), 36-37, 140-143
Kiptchak (Distihipschach, Ephepstzach), 37, 49, 189
Kirman (Kerman), 45, 163
Kishm I (Keschon), 45, 164
Knitted shoes, worn in Ghilan, 44
(Kocken), in Danube, 38, 144; at Tana, 49; Black Sea, 100
Kohrasar (Karasser), 43, 151
(Koldigen), 57, 197
Konieh (Konia), 7-9, 40
Koran (Alkoray, Alkoran), the, 67, 76
Kour, R. (Chur, Tygris), 86, 234
Kourdistan (Churten, Churt), 31, 43, 152
Koutahieh (Kachey), 40
Kronstadt or Cronstadt; Brassova (Bassaw), 38, 144
(Kuchler, Ulrich), killed at Nicopolis, 4
Kyrkyer (Karckeri), 49, 176, 224

(Lambe), Quilon? 61, 212
Landshut (Landzhut), 102
Lapis lazuli, in the church of St. Sophia, 80
Lazistan (Lasia), 43, 150
League, a, defined by the author, 46, 167
Leah (Lia), the grave of, 60
Lemburg (Limburgch), 101
Lemon (linon), the, employed in Malabar against serpents, 62; history of, 213; employed in Ceylon against leeches, 213-214
Lezghistan (Lochinschan), 34, 136
Lightning, death by, courted in Circassia, 50, 178
Lions, in Babylon, 47; Lesser India, 47
Lombardy (Lamparten), 89
Lord's prayer, in Armenian, 102; Tatar, 102
Lucca (Lickcha), 34

Magnesia (Maganasa), 40, 147
(Mäg), Mahhy? destructor of gods, a title of Boursbaï, 52, 187
Mahomedans, their sects, 65, 73-74, 221; at prayer, 67-68; neglect of prayer, how punished, 69; places for worship, 69, 220; burial of the dead, 69; fasting, 70; call to prayer, 70; festivals, 70-71, 221; grief for the

dead, 72; wine forbidden and the reason why, 72; good custom in trade, 73; estimate of the Saviour, 75-76; of Christianity, 76-78
Mahomet, 44; his tomb, 54, 71; birth and appearance of, 65, 219-220, 78; becomes Caliph, 67; doctrine and laws, 67-75; held the Caucasus in veneration, 186
Makou (Meya), 44, 159
Malabar (Lambor), where pepper grows, 61, 211
Malahidah sect, the; *see* the Day
Malatia (Malathea), 18, 122-123
Mamelouk sultans, captives sent to, by Bajazet, 7, 113; their succession, 51, 182; court ceremonials, 52, 54, 192; courriers, 52, 192; pigeon service, 53, 192
Mamre (Mambertal), 56, 194
(Manstzusch), 99, 143
(Mansur), a brother of Aboubekr, 33, 135
Mardin (Merdin), 43, 154
Mare's milk drank fasting, 48
Marriage customs, of the Yasses and Georgians, 85, 234; Armenians, 95
Mary Magdalen, 58
—— Cleophas, 58
Massanderan, 26, 29, 44
Meat, raw, eaten by Tatars, 48
Medina (Madina), 71
Mehdy, the, or celestial judge, Shyite belief of him, 186; Sunnite belief, 187
Meisen (Neichsen), 102
Menagerie at Babylon, 47, 168
Meragha (Maragara), 44, 157
Mile, an Italian, defined by the author, 46, 167
Milk of mares and camels for food, 48
Millet, in Siberia, 36; Sinope, 41; Great Tatary, 48
Mingrelia (Magrill, Megrellen), 43, 153, 99
Mingrelians, are of the Greek Church, 43, 78
Mintash or Mantash (Mathas), 51, 183
Miracle, at Samsoun, 12; by St. Demetrius, 39, 146; at Angora, 40; Sinaï, 55, 193; the Withered tree, 56; Holy Sepulchre, 57, 199; St. Ann's well, 58, 202; walls of Constantinople, 84; by St. Gregory, 88-90; St. Silvester, 88; St. John the Evangelist, 147
Miran Shah (Mirenschach), 30, 32, 133, 134, 114
Mirror at Alexandria, 62-63, 215

Mirtcha, John (Werterwaywod), voyevoda of Wallachia, 2, 110, 145
Miszr Khodja (Miseri), 32, 134
Mitrovitz (Mittrotz), 6
Mocenigo, Giovanni, 110
Mohammed, the descendant of Ali, 186
(Molwa), an infidel priest, 65, 219
Mongols, the (Mugal), 50, 179, 114, 126
Moses, 54-56, 76
Mosque at Damascus, described, 22, 128; destroyed, 23, 129
Mouhammed, son of Bajazet, defeats Bourhan uddin, 10; is ruler of Sebaste, 18, 121
Mouravieff, M. Andréy, 147

Nahitchevan (Nachson), 44, 156
Nazareth, 52, 56, 185
Neapolitans, in Egypt, 214
Nestorians, 140, 157, 158, 162, 190
Nevers, Comte de (Duke of Burguny), at Nicopolis, 3, 111; a prisoner, 4, 111, 113; intercedes for several nobles, 5, 112; at Gallipoli and Broussa, 6-7, 112
Nicopolis, siege and battle of, 2-4, 107-112, 100
Nile, R. (Nilus), 61, 62, 169
Nisibis (Antioch), 44, 160
Noah, 44
"None", Nono, ruler in Badakshan, 166

Olives, Mt. of, 59
Oljaïtou, tomb of, 132
Omar, the caliph, 67
(Origens); *see* Anjak
Orsova, 107
Ossets, Alans (Yassen, Aff), are of the Greek Church, 78; marriage customs, 85, 234; history, 223-224
Ostriches, in Lesser India, 47
Othman, the caliph, 67
Oulou Mohammed (Machmet), 37, 142
Ourjenj (Orden), 49, 172, 154
Ormi, the Ur of Jordanus Catalani, 157-158
Ourroum Kaleh (Hrumkula), 22, 127-128
Oxus, R. (Edil), 49, 172

Palaces at Constantinople, 79, 228
Paradise, 43, 61, 209, 186
Parrots, in Lesser India, 47
Pearls, at Kishm I; 45
Pelicans, in Arabia, 54, 193
(Pentznawer, Wernher), killed at Nicopolis, 4

INDEX. 261

Pera, 79, 225
Pergri, 126
Persia, 26, 30, 34, 43, 44, 45, 61, 89
―――― King of, 7, 114
Pepper, cultivation of, at Malabar; 61, 62
Pettau (Petaw); Duchy of, 6
(Phiradamschyech), a tercentenarian; 45, 161-162
Pigeons, carrier, in Egypt, and their training, 53, 192
Pilate, house of, 58, 202
Pirates in Black Sea, 100
Pisans, in Egypt, 214
Poland (Polan), 102
Pope, the, 63, 81
Poti (Kathon, Bothan), 43, 153, 99
Poulad (Polet), 37, 141
Prayers for the dead, in the Armenian Church, 94
Preachers, Order of, 44, 159
Precious stones, at Hormuz, 46; Badakshan, 46, 166; in the Ganges, 61, 210
Prester John, 52, 189, 57, 58, 140, 191

Quilon? (Lambe), 61, 212

Rahova, 2, 108
Raw meat as food, 48
Rebecca's grave, 60
Regensburg, 102
Relics, of St. Catherine, 55; St. John Chrysostom, 58, 202; St. Stephen, 58, 202; St. Nicholas, 147; St. Clement, 177; St. Joachim, 202
Resht (Ress), 44, 160
Rey (Rei), 44, 155
Rhinosceros? in Badakshan, 167
Rhodes, knights of, Smyrna their possession, 147; at taking of Alexandria, 214; at defence of Constantinople, 231
Rice, grown in Ghilan, 44
Richartinger, Leonard (Lienhart), the author's master, 1; unhorsed at Nicopolis, 3; killed in that battle, 4
Rivers that flow out of Paradise, 61, 209-210
Robbers, in Circassia, 50, 178
Roman Catholics, at Makou, 44; Caffa, 49
(Rom) Asia Minor, 51, 52
Rome, 63, 81, 89, 91
(Rumany) Abyssinia? 52, 190
Russia (Rewschen), 50, 89
Russia (Reissen), White, the Lesser, 101, 245
Russians (Rivssen), are of the Greek Church, 78, 137

(Sadurmelickh), 37, 144
St. Ann, 58
St. Auxentius (Aurencius), 93, 239
St. Basil, 41, 148
St. Bartholomew (Bartlome), 87, 235
St. Catherine, 54-56, 193-194
St. Clement, 50, 177
St. Constantine, 83
St. Demetrius (Sanctiniter), 39, 146
St. George (Jörig), patron saint of Georgia, 34
St. Gregory, the "Illuminator"; 87-93, 235-238
St. Helena, 197
St. James the Less, 59, 206
―――― the Greater, 93, 239
St. Joachim, 202
St. John the Baptist, 58, 201, 205
St. John the Evangelist, 40, 147, 58
St. John Chrysostom, 58, 202
St. Nicholas, 40, 147
St. Rhipsime (Susanna), 87, 236
St. Sergius (Zerlichis), 93, 239
St. Silvester, 87-90, 237
St. Stephen (Steffan), 58, 200, 59, 202, 203
St. Thaddeus (Thaten), 87, 235, 160
St. Thomas, 211-212
Salonica (Salonikch), 39, 145
Samarkand (Semerchant), 28, 33, 47, 154
Samsoun (Samson), 12, 119, 14, 41, 79
Saracens, 51, 137
Sarah, the grave of, 60
Saraï (Sarei), 49, 173, 139, 141
Saraï, New, 173
Saraï-Banou, 137
Saros (Seres), 39
Saroukhan (Serochon), 40
Sary Kerman (Serucherman), 50, 176-177
Savages, in Siberia, 35, 139
Save, R. (Saw), 6
Saviour, the, 35, 52, 185, 56, 75-78, 83, 84
Saxony, 102
(Schenisis) Shems uddin? 40
Schiltberger, Johann, addresses the reader, 1; at battle of Nicopolis, is made a prisoner and bound with a cord, 2-4; his life is spared, 5; suffers from wounds, 7; his duty as runner to Bajazet, 7; attempts to escape, 10-12; sent to the relief of Sebaste, 17; sent to Egypt, 19; becomes Timour's prisoner, 21; is subject to Shah Rokh and Miran Shah, 30-31; passes into the hands of Aboubekr, 33; sent into Great Tatary, 33; enumerates the coun-

tries he visited, 38-50; is three months at Gallipoli, 39; at the siege of Constantinople ? 80; spends three months at Constantinople, 81; is in the service of "Manstzusch", 99; effects his escape, 99; voyage to Constantinople, 100; enters that city, and is taken before the Emperor, 101; returns to his home, 101-102
Schliemann, Dr., 228
(Schyackin), 51, 183
Scorpions, in Badakshan, 167
Scutari (Skuter), 79
Sea, the Black, 13, 41, 49, 50, 79, 99, 101
——— the Dead, 59, 204
——— (the Great) or Black, 79
(——— the Indian), 47
——— the Red, 54, 193
(——— the White), or Caspian, 45, 161
(——— the White), 39
Sea monsters, in the Tigris, 47
Sects, Mahomedan, 65, 73-74
Serpents, at Samsoun, 12; Badakshan, 46; Desert of Arabia, 46; near the Tigris, 47; in Malabar, 62
Servia (Iriseh), Stephen, prince of, 3, 111, 109
Shabran, (Samabram), 34, 135
Shabran-tchaï, 135
Shahinshah (Schachister), 27
Shah Rokh (Scharock), 30-31, 86, 234, 126
Shaubek, in Arabia, 217
Sheeraz (Schiras), 45, 162-163
Shekis, the, 161
Sheky (Scheckhy), 44, 161
Shemahà (Schomachy), 45
Schirwan (Schuruan), 34, 45
Shishman (Schuffmanes), 13, 120, 107
Shoeless, Order of the, 34, 139
Shurky (Scherch), 23, 129
Shvishtov (Schiltaw), 2, 108-110
Shyites (Raphak), at Rey, 44, 156; destructors of mosque at Damascus, 129; their place of pilgrimage, 187
Siberia (Ibissibur), a country, described, 34-36, 139
Sibir or Isker (Ibissibur), a city, 49, 174; residence of the Shaïbani Khans, 174
Siege, of Nicopolis, 2, 107-109; Konieh, 8-9; Samsoun, 12; Sebaste, by Kara Yelck, 15; Malatia, 18; Sebaste by Timour, 20, 125; Aleppo, 22; Ain-tab, 22; Behesna, 22; Damascus, 22; Babylon, 24; Delhi, 26; Ispahan, 27; Alindsha, 44, 160, 130, Constantinople, 80, 231, 226

Sigismund, King of Hungary; appeals to Christendom, and invades Bulgaria, 1 2; occupies Widdin, 2; Rahova, 2; besieges Nicopolis, 2; at battle of Nicopolis, 2-4, 107, 109; flight, 3-4, 110, 113; passes the Dardanelles, 6
Silesia (Slesy), 102
Silk, at Astara, 34; Lezghistan, 34; Shirwan, 34, 45; Resht, 44; Sheky, 44
Silvester, Pope, 87-91
Simontornya (Synüher), Stephen, 5, 112
Sinaï (Muntagi), 52, 54-56, 193-194
Sindjar, 154
Sinope (Zepun, Synopp), 41, 100, 120
Sion, Mount, 59, 202-203
Sis (Syos, Siss), a kingdom of Armenia, 86; taken by Egypt, 87, 235, 126
Sivas, or Siwas (Sebast, Tamastk, Damastchk), 10, 118; 15-18; 20, 124-125; 41
Sledges, in Siberia, 35
Smyrna (Ismira), 40, 147
Snakes, in Siberia, 35
Solkhat (Vulchat), capital of Kiptchak, 49, 175
Solomon, temple of, 58, 59
——— tomb of, 59, 203
Soukhoum Kaleh (Zuchtun), 43, 152-153
Souleiman, son of Bajazet; spares the author's life, 5; intercedes for re-captured prisoners, 12; goes to the relief of Sebaste, 17, 121; defeats the (White Tartars), 19
Souleiman Shah (Suleymanschach), a counsellor of Timour, 25
Soultanyà (Soltania), 26, 132, 44
Soutchava (Sedschoff), 101
Spices, at Damascus, 24; Kais I, 46; Malabar, 62
Sracimir, John (Hannsen of Bodem), 5, 112, 107
(Stainer, little), killed at Nicopolis, 4
Storks, near the Tigris, 47
Strength, feats of, by Aboubekr, 33; (Sadurmelickh), 37
(Sygun), or Zikhes; see Circassians
Syhoun, R., 186
Syria, 22, 57
Syrians, at Caffa, 49; are Jacobites, 78, 224

Tabreez (Thaures), a kingdom of Persia, 30, 32; chief city of all Persia, 44, 154
Taharten (Tarathan), 21, 125, 126

INDEX.

Takavor (Takchauer), the Armenian for king, 90, 238
Takfour, title of Greek emperor, 188, 238
Tamerlane; *see* Timour
Tana (Alathena), now Azoff, 49, 175, 79, 138
Tartars or Tatars? 171-172
Tatars, White, besiege Angora, 18; vanquished by Souleiman, 19; desert Bajazet at Angora, 21, 117
Tatary, Great, 33, 48, 170; khans of, 36-37, 140-143; customs in, 48, 172; steppes of, 50
Tatary, White, 7, 114-116
Tchadibek khan (Sedichbechan), 36, 140
Tchekre (Zeggra), 33-37, 139, 99, 142
Tell el-faras (Talapharum), 52, 185
Terek R. (Edil), 34, 137
Ternovo (Ternau), 13, 120, 39, 108 (That) Mourtadd? Crimean Goths so called, 50, 176
Tiflis (Titfliss), a kingdom of Armenia, 86, 126
Tigris R. (Schatt), 47, 168, 61, 209, 186
Timour, at Sebaste, 20, 125; at Angora, 21; Broussa, 21; campaign in Syria, 22, 125, 127; besieges Damascus, 23, 128-129; destroys "Babylon", 24; invades Lesser India, 24-26, 130-131; expedition to Masanderan, 27; besieges Ispahan, and his treachery there, 27, 133; expedition to China, 28, 133; illness and death, 29, 133; lies uneasy in his grave, 30; his sons, 30, 133; his capital, 33; cruelties, at Sebaste, 20, 125; Aleppo, 22, 127; Damascus, 23, 128; Ispahan, 27-28, 133
Timour Tash, 118, 123
Tirgovisht (Türckisch), 38
Tiridates (Derthatt), king of Armenia, 87-91, 236 237, 159
——— throne of, 159
Toktamish, 115, 138, 140. 154
Towers of human heads, at Damascus, 23; Ispahan, 27
Transylvania (Sybenbürgen), 38
Trebizond (Trabessanda), a kingdom, 41, 79, 150
Troy (Troya), its ruins, 79, 226-228
Turkey, Black, 43
Turkey, Great, 40

Turkomans of the White Sheep, 152
Turks, Ottoman, 114
Tuscany (Duschkan), 89
Tzaref, 173

(Ugine), the, Ung Kut? 36, 139-140
Unicorns, in Badakshan, 46, 166-167; at Rome, 90-91

Velvet, made at Venice, 34; Lucca, 34
Venetians, in Egypt, 62, 214; at Gallipoli, 112; at Salonica, 146; relations with Persia, 154; secure the silk of Ghilan, 160; at Tana, 175; Galata, 225; defence of Constantinople, 231
Vineyards, at Trebizond, 41; Lazistan, 43; Kohrasar, 43, 151; Crimea (Gothia), 50
Venice, 34, 49
Vipers, at Samsoun, 12; from the Black Sea, 13
Virgin, in the Castle of the Sparrowhawk, 41-43; 9000 carried away captives by Timour, 20
Virgin's castles or towers, 149
Virgin Mary, 52, 185, 57, 58, 75, 76, 93
Volga R., 136, 173

Walachia (Walachy, Walchi), 2, 38, 89, 101
——— Greater, 38
——— Lesser, 38, 101
Walachians, are Christians, 38; never cut their hair or beard, 38; are of the Greek Church, 78
Walls of Constantinople, 84, 232, 101, 244
Warlike people, in (Black Turkey), 43; Georgia, 43; Jagataï, 47; Great Tatary, 48
Water poisoned, 23
Widdin or Widin (Bodem), 2, 107, 39
Wine, not drunk in Great Tatary, 48; why forbidden to Mahomedans, 72
Withered Tree, Lord of the, 52, 189; virtue of the, 56, 194-195

Ydegou, (Edigi), 34-37, 140-141, 143, 176

Zacharias, 59, 206
(Zuspillen) Sicily? 51, 184

T. RICHARDS, PRINTER, 37, GREAT QUEEN STREET.

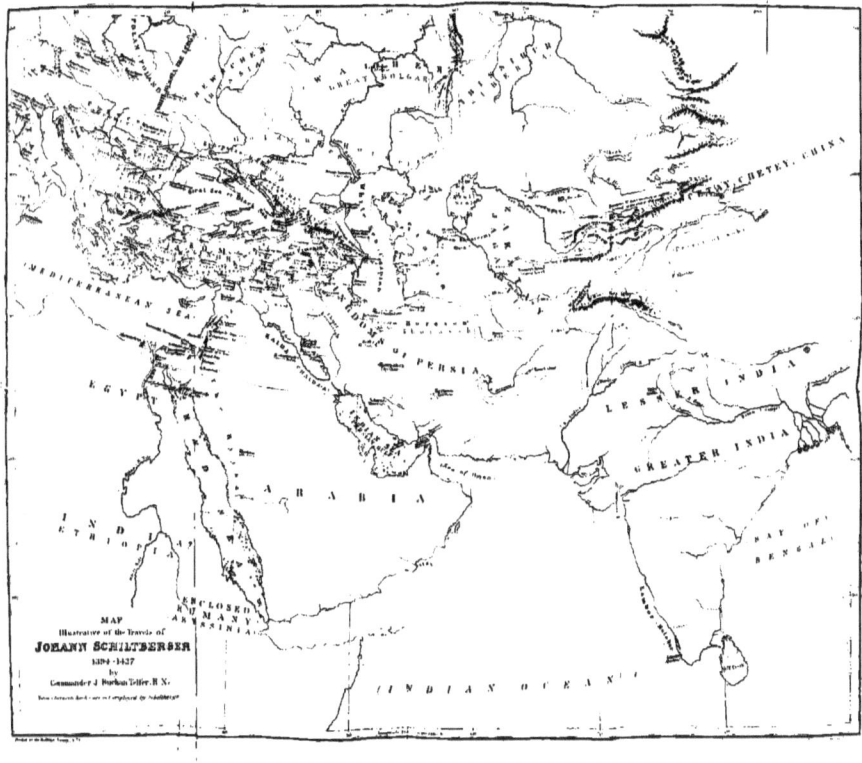

MAP
Illustrative of the Travels of
JOHANN SCHILTBERGER
1394-1427
by
Commander J. Buchan Telfer, R.N.

The Hakluyt Society.

REPORT FOR 1879.

THE Council of the Hakluyt Society have pleasure in being able to report to the Members that their numbers are increasing, and that the funds are in a satisfactory state. The number of effective Members of the Society is now 240.

The attention of the Council has been given to an arrangement which will facilitate the completion of sets of volumes by old Members, and the acquisition of back volumes which they may desire to possess by new Members who may not wish to purchase complete sets. The whole series can now be purchased at the rate of 8s. 6d. a volume; namely, for £24 4s. 6d., the price increasing at the rate of 8s. 6d. as each new volume is added. The same rule applies when a Member requires any portion of the series equal to, or exceeding, a quarter of the whole number of volumes. When a Member requires a single back volume, or any number less than a quarter of the whole series, he may, with the consent of the Council, be supplied at the rate of 10s. each volume.

Since the last Report the following volume has been issued to Members:—

THE HAWKINS' VOYAGES, DURING THE REIGNS OF HENRY VIII, QUEEN ELIZABETH, AND JAMES I. Edited, with an Introduction, by Clements R. Markham, C.B., F.R.S.

And the following volume is nearly ready for issue:—

THE BONDAGE AND TRAVELS OF JOHANN SCHILTBERGER, FROM HIS CAPTURE AT THE BATTLE OF NICOPOLIS IN 1396,

The Hakluyt Society.

REPORT FOR 1879.

THE Council of the Hakluyt Society have pleasure in being able to report to the Members that their numbers are increasing, and that the funds are in a satisfactory state. The number of effective Members of the Society is now 240.

The attention of the Council has been given to an arrangement which will facilitate the completion of sets of volumes by old Members, and the acquisition of back volumes which they may desire to possess by new Members who may not wish to purchase complete sets. The whole series can now be purchased at the rate of 8s. 6d. a volume; namely, for £24 4s. 6d., the price increasing at the rate of 8s. 6d. as each new volume is added. The same rule applies when a Member requires any portion of the series equal to, or exceeding, a quarter of the whole number of volumes. When a Member requires a single back volume, or any number less than a quarter of the whole series, he may, with the consent of the Council, be supplied at the rate of 10s. each volume.

Since the last Report the following volume has been issued to Members:—

THE HAWKINS' VOYAGES, DURING THE REIGNS OF HENRY VIII, QUEEN ELIZABETH, AND JAMES I. Edited, with an Introduction, by Clements R. Markham, C.B., F.R.S.

And the following volume is nearly ready for issue:—

THE BONDAGE AND TRAVELS OF JOHANN SCHILTBERGER, FROM HIS CAPTURE AT THE BATTLE OF NICOPOLIS IN 1396,

TO HIS ESCAPE AND RETURN TO EUROPE IN 1427. Translated and edited by Commander Buchan Telfer, R.N.

Three volumes are in the hands of the printer, namely :—

THE THIRD VOLUME OF THE COMMENTARIES OF AFONSO DALBOQUERQUE. Translated and edited by Walter de Gray Birch, Esq.

THE VOYAGES OF JOHN DAVIS, AND HIS WORKS ON NAVIGATION. Edited by Captain A. H. Markham, R.N.

THE NATURAL HISTORY OF THE WESTERN INDIES, BY FATHER JOACHIM ACOSTA. Edited by Clements R. Markham, C.B., F.R.S.

Besides the above volumes, which will meet the just demands of the Fellows up to the end of the present year, several other works have been undertaken by editors.

These are :—

ROSMITAL'S EMBASSY TO ENGLAND, SPAIN, ETC., IN 1466. Edited by R. E. Graves, Esq.

THE JOURNAL OF THE PILOT GALLEGO, AND OTHER DOCUMENTS RELATING TO THE VOYAGES OF MENDAÑA. Translated and edited by W. A. Tyssen Amherst, Esq.

NARRATIVE OF THE PORTUGUESE EMBASSY TO ABYSSINIA IN 1520, BY FATHER FRANCISCO ALVAREZ. Translated and edited by Lord Stanley of Alderley.

A MANUSCRIPT HISTORY OF BERMUDA IN THE BRITISH MUSEUM (Sloane, 750). Edited by Lieutenant-General Sir J. Henry Lefroy, K.C.M.G., C.B.

VOYAGES OF JAN HUIGEN VAN LINSCHOTEN TO THE EAST INDIES. Edited by Arthur Burnell, Esq., Phil.D.

THE JOURNAL OF THE JESUIT DESIDERI, DURING HIS MISSION TO TIBET; from the original Manuscript. To be translated and edited by C. E. D. Black, Esq.

The following six Members retire from the Council :—

E. A. BOND, ESQ.
ADMIRAL SIR RICHARD COLLINSON, K.C.B.
AUGUSTUS W. FRANKS, ESQ.

W. E. FRERE, ESQ., C.M.G.
J. WINTER JONES, ESQ.
SIR CHARLES NICHOLSON, BART.

Of these the three first are recommended for re-election, and the names of the following are proposed for election:—

THE EARL OF DUCIE, F.R.S.
E. H. BUNBURY, ESQ.
MAJOR-GENERAL SIR H. THUILLIER, C.S.I., F.R.S.

Statement of the Accounts of the Society from May 1877, *to June* 1879.

	£ s. d.		£ s. d.
Balance left at the Bankers (May 1877)	654 15 0	Mr. Richards for printing	337 10 6
Received by Bankers, May 1877, to June 1879	620 2 6	Messrs. Wyman	15 19 0
		Mr. Quaritch for a copy of Acosta	5 0 0
		Signor de Gubernatis for the manuscript of Desideri	40 0 0
		Mr. Coote for transcriptions	10 4 7
		Mr. Muller for the Barents map	10 0 0
		Petty cash	10 0 0
		Cheque books	0 4 6
			428 18 7
		Balance at the Bankers	851 18 11
	£1280 17 6		£1280 17 6

www.ingramcontent.com/pod-product-compliance
Lightning Source LLC
Chambersburg PA
CBHW021623250426
43672CB00037B/1224